Render Me My Song

Sandi Russell grew up in Harlem and is currently living in Britain. As a professional jazz singer, she has performed throughout the United States and in Britain. Her interviews with African–American women writers first appeared in *Women's Review*. She is co-editor of the forthcoming *Virago Book of Love Poetry*, and is currently working on a book of short stories.

Render Me My Song:
African-American Women Writers from Slavery to the Present

Sandi Russell

St. Martin's Press
New York

RENDER ME MY SONG: AFRICAN-AMERICAN WOMEN WRITERS
FROM SLAVERY TO PRESENT.

For information, address St. Martin's Press, 175 Fifth Avenue, New York, N.Y.
10010.

ISBN 0-312-05288-x

Printed and bound in Great Britain by Billing & Sons, Worcester.

For my parents
Gazetta and James Russell
who gave me song

Not to know is bad; not to ask is worse

(African Proverb)

Contents

Foreword

It was Negro History Week in Harlem. In a totally black community, in a totally black school (with mostly white teachers) we had five whole days to consider all the contributions African-Americans had made to their country. We did not study these at all during the other forty-four weeks of the year. So by 1959, when I was thirteen, I had heard of George Washington Carver, Harriet Tubman, Langston Hughes and possibly Phillis Wheatley. But I knew nothing of the history of slavery or the conditions of their lives.

In the early 1960s, my new school did not honour Negro History Week, nor did I read any black writers. But in my last year of High School, something unexpected and extraordinary occurred. I took an evening job at the Schomburg Library. This, it turned out, was the largest repository of African-American literature in the world. I was taught to file books and organize cards, but no one guided me towards this vast collection of black thought. Squeezed between massive shelves, I read like a person gasping for air. But where to begin? Glancing quickly through unfamiliar names, I picked those authors whom I had heard of: James Baldwin and Gwendolyn Brooks. Ms. Brooks, as a black woman writer, looked like an anomaly. Standing alone, in this mass of black male writers, she seemed too brave and brilliant to contemplate. Black women could become singers, dancers, teachers and maybe even doctors, but writers? No.

I began to realize that I had been cheated. Why was I, along with hundreds of other black children, unaware of the prodigious gifts of my people? Here were books upon books, written by Africans and African-Americans, and yet I knew of only a few authors. The Schomburg had opened the door and posed the question; but the answers, for me, were long in coming.

When I entered college the reading-list included one black writer: Ralph Ellison. Yet neither he nor any other African-American was mentioned in the literature courses of a large 'integrated' university, even though the Civil Rights struggle was well under way.

But after the riots of the late 1960s, the Liberation Bookstore was opened on my street-corner in Harlem. The owner, Una Mulzac, was my first guide in discovering my people's past as well as my own. The books I bought there had titles like *Black Rage* and *The Crisis of the Negro Intellectual*.

The Black Power Movement was gaining momentum and more African-American women were expressing themselves in writing. I was excited and felt a kinship with them. I bought the poems of Nikki Giovanni and Sonia Sanchez and began to write my own. Yet I sometimes felt that the whole story wasn't being told. Their work was so immediate, so volatile: I didn't always feel that way.

Not until 1980 did I come across the writer who expressed the ambivalence, the ache, that I felt as a black woman in America. *The Bluest Eye* by Toni Morrison took me into myself. And then came Maya Angelou, Ntozake Shange and Gloria Naylor to tell the 'untold' stories. Alice Walker, in her search for foremothers, rediscovered the great novelist, Zora Neale Hurston. There *was* a history, a line of African-American women who, for over two centuries, had been creating themselves in writing.

So the writers of the present sent me back to a recovery of the past: a past that reached into and through slavery. This personal project involved me in a collective act of 're-membering', which took me back to the Schomburg Library, then to the James Weldon Johnson Collection at Yale University, and eventually to libraries in Britain where I have been living for the past five years.

Seated in these libraries, I touched not only the delicate and worn pages of works by black women writers; I touched their lives, as they did mine. They spoke to me; their songs ran through me and informed my own. This volume is an introduction to their lives and their writings. In it, the many voices of these black women can be heard. They speak to all of us: just listen.

Acknowledgements

This book has been made possible by the help and encouragement of many. Monty Montee and Louis Silverstein provided my 'Yaddo' during the stressful months of its inception. Without the generous sup︵ ︵t of Silvia Dobson and Betty Shoemaker, it could not have been completed. Gwendolyn Brooks graciously gave her constructive comments on Chapter Five and Nellie McKay shared with me her expert knowledge and advice. Rick Devine word-processed parts of the manuscript and was unstinting in his editorial help. Bill Schafer was an astute reader of the first typescript and Lotte and Hugh Shankland gave insightful suggestions in its early stages. Deborah Philips published my first articles in *The Women's Review* and had faith that I could undertake a larger project. Siân Williams has given me her friendship as well as sustained enthusiasm. To Diana Collecott I owe my greatest gratitude. Her patience, guidance and support during the writing of this book is incalculable.

In accordance with Alice Walker's wish that her poems be quoted either in full or not at all, last minute changes had to be made to Chapter 8, which remains nevertheless the first full treatment of her poetry to be published in Britain.

1: Out of Slavery

Say what? Black women were writing in 1746?

> *Eunice Allen see the Indians comeing*
> *And hoped to save herself by running*
> *And had her petticoats stopt her*
> *The awful creatures had not cotched her*
> *And tommyhawked her on the head*
> *And left her on the ground for dead.*[1]

Lucy Terry, a slave, wrote this poem about an Indian raid on Deerfield, Massachusetts in 1746. Known for her skill as an orator and raconteur, she tried her hand at verse and is the first African-American woman writer known to us.

But black women had been in America since 1619, one year before the Mayflower landing. Snatched from their homelands as they spoke and sang in the languages of the Ashanti, Dahomey, Yoruba, Oyo, Benin and Akan, they were packed into ships, living with their own excreta, suffering from disease. Chained to the dead and giving birth, they went through the 'Middle Passage' –

> I saw a pregnant woman give birth to babies while chained to corpses which our drunken overseers had not removed...[2]

– and arrived in an alien land.

Intent on beating their languages and culture out of them, the traders prepared the human cargo for their new status: slavery. But, more often than not, memory and pride persisted:

> Mr. Maverick's Negro woman came to my chamber window, and in her own Countrey language and tune sang her very loud and shrill....

I repaired to my host, to learn of him the cause . . . for that I understood before, that she had been a Queen in her own Countrey. . . . Mr. Maverick was desirous to have a breed of Negroes, and therefore seeing she would not yield by persuasions to company with a Negro young man he had in his use, he commanded him, wil'd she nill'd she, to go to bed with her, which was no sooner done, but she kicked him out again, this she took in high disdain beyond her slavery and this was the cause of her grief.[3]

From the seventeenth century until the end of the Civil War, and the Emancipation Proclamation of 1863, African-Americans for the most part remained in bondage. Because of the crippling conditions of slavery, especially in the nineteenth century, few accounts of this period by black Americans are left to us. Yet, some black men and women managed to escape and tell their stories.

'Belinda', Elizabeth Keckley and Sojourner Truth are among the women who give a harrowing picture of life in slavery. Their narratives were usually written down by white abolitionists. However, it is astounding to learn that some African-American women wrote their own autobiographies and published their essays and speeches: 'Linda Brent', Maria Stewart and Jarena Lee, to name only three.

By the mid-nineteenth century, two black women novelists emerged: Harriet E. Wilson and Francis E.W. Harper. But outstanding, from her own day to ours, is the phenomenal 'slave-poet' of the eighteenth century: Phillis Wheatley. She was, moreover, the only published female poet in the American colonies since Anne Bradstreet a century before.

● ● ●

It was not natural. And she was the first. Come from a country of many tongues tortured by rupture, by theft, by travel like mismatched clothing packed down into the cargo hold of evil ships sailing, irreversible, into slavery. Come to a country to be docile and dumb, to be big and breeding, . . . to be turkey/horse/cow, to be cook/carpenter/ plow, to be 5'6" 140lbs., in good condition and answering to the name of Tom or Mary: to be bed bait: to be legally spread legs for rape by the master/ the master's son/ the master's overseer/ the master's nephew: to be nothing human nothing family nothing from nowhere. . . . How could you, belonging to no one, but property to those despising the smiles of your soul, how could you dare to create yourself: a poet?[4]

She arrived from Africa, in 1761, a frail and sickly seven-year-old, and was sold on the Boston quayside. Purchased by the Wheatleys to be made into a house-servant, Phillis astounded her master and his family by her quick wit and unusual intelligence. Within sixteen months of her arrival in America, she could apparently read the most difficult parts of the Bible, and at the age of twelve, she began to study Latin, translating Ovid. An avid reader of English literature, she took Alexander Pope as her model for writing and published her first poems at the age of thirteen.

It must be noted that, although learning was usually not encouraged for slaves, it was not at this time prohibited by law (as it would later be in the South). Phillis embraced the Christian teachings and way of life of eighteenth century white Bostonians; nowhere in her writing do we find any precise recollection of her African homeland, save for the sunrise ritual she recalls her mother performing each morning.

Bereft of a past, Phillis Wheatley ingested the doctrines and mores of her masters. Mrs. Wheatley referred to her as 'my Phillis', which isolated her from her fellow slaves. An African 'curiosity' to entertain, she could never be accepted by white Bostonian society.

Phillis Wheatley was a slave in status, yet in many respects, she was not treated like a slave. She won fame as a poet, yet she could not enjoy the freedoms of an ordinary white citizen. The strain and strangeness of this situation shows in her writings and in her life. Two incidents illustrate the extreme ambivalence of this woman poet's position in society.

Once, when Phillis sat beside the Wheatleys' black coachman instead of inside the carriage, *he* was reprimanded for treating her merely as a fellow slave. Yet, when Phillis was invited to the white homes of Boston, a problem arose if meals were served. Her biographer writes: 'She developed the habit of always declining the seat offered her at their board, and, requesting that a side-table might be laid for her, dined mostly apart from the rest of the company.'[5]

Alice Walker, in *In Search of Our Mothers' Gardens*, aptly sums up the problem when she says that Phillis was plagued by 'contrary instincts': 'Her loyalties were completely divided, as without question, her mind'.[6]

Considering this confused self-image, it is no wonder that Wheatley's work takes on the colouring of her adopted culture. Only in a few instances does she allude to her own conditions, and even then with a demeaning glance backward to her homeland:

> 'Twas not long since I left my native shore
> The land of errors, and Egyptian gloom:
> Father of mercy, 'twas thy gracious hand
> Brought me in safety from these dark abodes . . .[7]

It is clear from these lines that Wheatley has been led to believe that her own enslavement was a way to salvation. In this reading of her own history, the 'Father of mercy' is almost indistinguishable from the slave master. Even more disturbing is the way Wheatley uses the Biblical story of the Children of Israel; in the imagery of this poem, Africa is equated with the land of Egypt (that is, the place of enslavement for the Jews) and America with the Promised Land (the place of deliverance). We are left to wonder if she recognized the underside of her message or if, in fact, Christianity had all but obliterated such considerations. In the nineteenth century, the same story would be used by African-Americans claiming their own deliverance from slavery:

> When Israel was in Egypt's land
> – Let my people go! . . .

The word 'mercy' occurs again in Wheatley's poem 'On Being Brought from Africa to America':

> 'Twas mercy brought me from my Pagan land
> Taught my benighted soul to understand
> That there's a God, that there's a Saviour too:
> Once I redemption neither sought nor knew.
> Some view our sable race with scornful eye,
> 'Their colour is a diabolic die.'
> Remember, Christians, Negroes, black as Cain
> May be refin'd, and join th' angelic train.[8]

This passage is dominated by the theme of darkness. The key expressions are: *benighted soul, sable race, diabolic die*, and *black as Cain*. All of these literally 'blacken', and all but one are denigrating. The exception is sable, which is a heraldic term and carries noble overtones. Here Phillis Wheatley is using the language of black pride in contrast to those who say 'Their colour is a diabolic die' (i.e. dye) and associate Negroes with the devil. The most however, that Wheatley can claim for her race, is equality with whites in the afterlife when colour is 'refin'd' away with other worldly impurities. It is evident from this poem alone, that whatever her intentions, Wheatley was defeated by the racism inscribed in the English language and natural to eighteenth century Christians. Here the rhetoric of Christian salvation goes hand in glove with that of white supremacy.

Only once does Phillis Wheatley give us an indication of what she might have felt as a slave in America. This is also the one time when Wheatley takes a personal position in her poetry. Ironically, this comes in a plea for the freedom of white American colonists from the English yoke:

> Should you, my lord, while you peruse my song,
> Wonder from whence my love of Freedom sprung,
> Whence flow these wishes for the common good,
> By feeling hearts alone best understood, –

I, young in life, by seeming cruel fate
Was snatched from Afric's fancied happy seat:
What pangs excruciating must molest,
What sorrows labour in my parents breast!
Steeled was that soul, and by no misery moved,
That from a father seized his babe beloved:
Such, such my case. And can I then but pray
Others may never feel tyrannic sway?[9]

This poem has incensed modern black critics. J. Saunders Redding argues that '"seeming cruel" and "fancied happy" give her away as believing neither in the cruelty of the fate that had dragged thousands of her race into bondage in America nor in the happiness of their former freedom in Africa.'[10]

Although this assessment of Phillis Wheatley may be well-founded, Redding does not take into account either her 'separate status' as neither slave nor free, or the early age at which she arrived in America. These considerations enable us to understand how she could be turned into a mouthpiece for white colonists.

Even Wheatley's fame was fraught with contradiction. A poem written in praise of General Washington resulted in an invitation to meet him. There is conjecture as to whether he knew she was a slave when he invited her. Washington's resistance to the enlistment of black soldiers in the Continental Army was at odds with his entertaining a black poet.

Wheatley's reception in England was also double-edged. Her first published poem in 1771 attracted the attention of the Countess of Huntingdon. Two years later, Wheatley sailed to England with the hope of meeting her. The Countess had paved the way for Phillis Wheatley's reception by English society and she was presented with a copy of *Paradise Lost* by the Lord Mayor of London and a translation of *Don Quixote* by the Earl of Dartmouth.

Although the Countess did not meet the black American poet, she was sent Phillis Wheatley's poems and was responsible for their publication. *Poems on Various Subjects, Religious and Moral* appeared in London in 1773, when Ms. Wheatley was nineteen years old, but only after some additions had been included at the insistence of the Countess. It seems that Lady Huntingdon could not believe that such verse could be written by a slave girl. Consequently a drawing was made to authenticate Wheatley's origins; also a testimonial was written by her master, John Wheatley, and signed by eighteen other prestigious residents of Boston, among them John Hancock and the royal governor of Massachusetts. These actions were to set the precedent for most slave publications for the next hundred years. In the eighteenth century, our 'black poet-lady' could not have been published without these affadavits.

As fast as Phillis's rise to fame was her downfall and relegation to oblivion. The refined and tranquil existence known to white middle-class Bostonians was soon to be forgotten. On April 18th, 1775, 'the shot heard round the world' was fired at Lexington, Massachusetts, and the American Revolution had begun.

Families fled as the fighting raged and Phillis was set free to cope on her own. Not equipped for these turbulent times, she began to know the bitter truths of freedom for a female ex-slave during wartime. There was little interest in literary matters among Boston residents, as their immediate concern was whether to flee or to fight. Wheatley's position as a poet had little or no importance and, desperate to sustain life, she had to compete with white workers in a tight job market where she faced insults, threats and mob-violence.[11]

In 1778, Phillis Wheatley married a free black, John Peters, and sank deeper into poverty and pain. Peters had difficulty keeping a job and finally left her. She took work in a common Negro boarding-house, doing menial labour. The hard work broke her frail body and she died at the age of thirty-one. Her third child survived her by only a few hours.

It has been said that Phillis Wheatley travelled 'from an unmarked village in Africa... to an unmarked grave in America.'[12]

Who was she? The constraints and confusions of her existence mean that we shall never really know. What we do know is that she became one of the best known poets of her era: that in itself was a remarkable feat.

●   ●   ●

According to the 'master plan', slaves were to be kept illiterate and uneducated, so that they could not tell of their lives in bondage. Laws were enacted, such as the slave code statutes of the State of North Carolina, which stated that it was a crime 'to teach, or attempt to teach, any slave... to read or write', because, 'the teaching of slaves to read or write has a tendency to excite dissatisfaction in their minds, and to produce insurrection and rebellion.'[13] Yet, despite these laws, the voice of the African-American would not be stifled.

Until recently it was thought that *The Interesting Narrative of Olaudah Equiano, or Gustavas Vassa, the African*, published in 1789, was the first of its genre, but we now know that a woman's narrative, 'Belinda, or the Cruelty of Men Whose Faces Were Like The Moon', was published in the United States in 1787. This narrative was given in the form of a plea to the Legislature of the State of Massachusetts in 1782, asking that they grant her freedom in her old age. 'Belinda' claimed that it was her right, after countless years of toil and servitude. Embodied in this petition is her life story and the first known key to the lives of African-American women under slavery.

In the nineteenth century, some African-American women escaped the overseer's whip and found their way to freedom in the North. The abolitionist movement enabled them to tell their stories in the form of slave narratives dictated to white editors. One of the most famous is Sojourner Truth's *Narrative and Book of Life* (1878). Not content with the publication of her life story, she found her way into many an abolitionist meeting to speak on the horrors of slavery. A great orator and principled woman, she fought to be heard on issues of women's rights as well as racism. At white conventions, she was sometimes an unwelcome visitor. In her narrative she states that at the Women's Rights Convention in Akron, Ohio in 1851, the chairman forbade her to speak. It was felt that she would ruin the movement and have the public believe that their cause was 'mixed with abolition and niggers'.[14]

Even at anti-slavery conventions, Sojourner was not made welcome. At one, to prove that she was not a man, she was asked to submit her breasts to the inspection of the ladies present. She did, and the women still did not come to her defence. Sojourner then turned and bared her breasts to the entire audience. It was a dramatic demonstration of her best-known speech:

> And ain't I a woman? Look at me! ... I have borne thirteen children, and seen them most all sold off to slavery, and when I cried out with my mother's grief, none but Jesus heard me! And ain't I a woman?[15]

Another slave narrative of note is Elizabeth Keckley's *Behind the Scenes, or, Thirty Years a Slave, and Four Years in the White House* (1868). After being beaten and raped in slavery, she bought her freedom with money earned as a seamstress. Elizabeth Keckley secured a position in the White House, under President Abraham Lincoln, and became a close associate of the president's wife.

There were others, many of them, who dared death to tell of a life offering rape, pain and desolation. Their sheer strength and their desire to be heard – to be free – set a precedent for black women then, as well as now.

●   ●   ●

I looked at my hands to see if I was the same person now I was free. There was such glory over everything, the sun came like gold through the trees, and over the fields, and I felt like I was in heaven...

I had crossed the line of which I had so long been dreaming. I was free; but there was no one to welcome me to the land of freedom. I was a stranger in a strange land. . . . But to this solemn resolution I came; I was free, and they should be free also; I would make a home for them in the North, and the Lord helping me, I would bring them all there. Oh how I prayed then, lying all alone on the cold, damp ground; 'Oh dear Lord,' I said, 'I ain't got no friend but you. Come to my help, Lord, for I'm in trouble!'[16]

Although many African-Americans were born into slavery, there were a number, usually living in the North, that were supposedly free from this system of degradation and denial. Yet, even there, opportunities for education were almost non-existent and the roots of racism ran deep. Battling against repression and exclusion, black women, either free-born or escaped slaves, wrote their own speeches, essays and autobiographies. In doing so, they not only revealed the atrocities of life in the South, but challenged the North's claim of 'freedom and justice for all'.

One of the foremost orators of the North was Maria Stewart, born free in Hartford, Connecticut in 1803. She was the first American woman to give a public lecture at Boston's Franklin Hall, on September 21, 1832. Armed with religious fervour and a strong sense of moral duty, Ms. Stewart spoke to whites of black oppression, and to blacks of their need to find inner resources to combat that oppression. She wrote three speeches which were printed in William Lloyd Garrison's *Liberator* in 1831, and a more comprehensive version of her work was published in Boston in 1835 entitled, *Productions of Mrs. Maria W. Stewart.*

In her speeches, Ms. Stewart not only criticized her white audiences for their lack of commitment to the cause of abolition, but at the African-Masonic Hall in 1833, she admonished her black brothers for their frivolous waste of money, which she felt should be used for the cause of black economic advancement. She encountered so much hostility that she left Boston and moved to New York. But before she departed, Maria Stewart acknowledged her right, as a black woman, to speak:

What if I am a woman: is not the God of ancient times the God of these modern days? Did he not raise up Deborah to be a mother and judge in Israel? Did not Queen Esther save the lives of the Jews? And Mary Magdalene first declare the resurrection of Christ from the Dead? . . . What if such women as are here described should rise among our sable race? And it is not impossible; for it is not the color of the skin that makes the man or woman, but the principle formed in the soul.[17]

Meanwhile, in Philadelphia, the history of Jarena Lee was set in print:

THE
LIFE
and
RELIGIOUS EXPERIENCE
of
JARENA LEE,

A Coloured Lady,
Giving An Account Of Her Call To Preach The Gospel.
Revised And Corrected From The Original Manuscript,
Philadelphia:
Printed And Published For The Author.
1836

Jarena Lee was born in 1783, we assume of free parents. Because her family was poor, Jarena was sent away to be a servant at the age of seven. At twenty-one, she experienced Christian conversion. Approximately seven years later, she approached a black minister, the Reverend Richard Allen of the Bethel Church of Philadelphia, expressing her desire to preach. He refused permission, as he had already refused the request of an English-woman. Women could not be ordained and no female, black or white, was acceptable to the church as a preacher.

However, after the death of her husband and other family members, Ms. Lee returned to Rev. Allen, who was now bishop of the African Methodist Church, the first black denomination in America, and he agreed to her holding prayer meetings in her home. Then, while attending a Sunday service, Jarena began to extemporize on one of Rev. Allen's sermons and he was moved to endorse her call. Shortly thereafter, Jarena Lee began her career as an itinerant preacher.

Her fervour led to epic journeys. In 1827, Jarena travelled over two thousand miles and delivered nearly two hundred sermons: an extraordinary accomplishment at this time for a woman over forty. Ms. Lee's auto-biography not only gives us the first account of the role of women in traditional black organized religion, but also challenges the roles prescribed for them, not only in the church, but in society as well.

Outstanding among the slave narratives published before the Civil War was *Incidents in the Life of a Slave Girl: Written by Herself*. The author's real name was Harriet Jacobs, but she used the pseudonym 'Linda Brent' for fear of her life. Although this was published in 1861, it was not until 1981 that African-American male scholars were ready to accept Jacobs's authorship.

Evidence of authenticity exists in a review written in the same year it was published, as well as in statements by many who knew the author.[18]

In her preface Ms. Jacobs states:

> I have not written my experiences in order to attract attention to myself; on the contrary, it would have been more pleasant to me to have been silent about my own history.... But I do earnestly desire to arouse the women of the North to a realizing sense of the condition of two millions of women at the South, still in bondage, suffering what I suffered and most of them far worse.[19]

Like the slave narratives edited by white abolitionists, this work is political and polemical in purpose. Therein lies the only similarity; for it is written by a black woman who, by telling her own story, challenges the popular social conventions of 'true womanhood', embraced by white Southern gentlemen and white Northern abolitionists alike. The basic tenets of this convention were: 'piety, purity, submissiveness and domesticity'. Black women were inevitably excluded from this category since, for many whites, blackness connoted impurity and black women were often stereotyped as 'evil temptresses'.

'Linda Brent''s story is exceptional, in showing how one who is powerless can use intelligence and wit to gain power. She concealed her reading ability to stop her master, Dr. Flint, from sending obscene notes to her. Forced to give up the love of a black man for his own safety, she chooses a white man other than her master, to father her children. By doing so, she takes the power away from Dr. Flint and attempts to control her own sexuality.[20] The father of her children does not uphold his promise to free them. Jacobs cannot endure the thought of her children enslaved, so she secretly makes plans to run away and find her daughter who has been sold into bondage. She flees, dressed as a man, and is hidden in a 'crawl space' in her grandmother's house for seven years. Linda is then taken to New York in disguise. Her freedom is finally purchased by a group of Northern white women, giving Ms. Jacobs control over her own life. But before freedom, she is made acutely aware of her worth: 'Women [slaves] are considered of no value unless they continually increase their owners' stock. They are put on a par with animals.'[21] Noting the complicity of white Southern women in their husbands' sexual licence and the resultant 'mulatto' offspring, Ms. Jacobs says: 'They regard such children as property, as marketable as the pigs on the plantation...'[22]

In this ground-breaking work, Harriet Jacobs takes bold steps to discuss the complex situation of black women in America as a result of their slave status. As Hazel Carby has noted:

> Jacobs's narrative problematized assumptions that dominated Abolitionist literature in general and male slave narratives in particular, assumptions that linked slave women to illicit sexuality. Jacobs's attempt to develop a framework in which to discuss the social, political and economic consequences of black womanhood prefigured the concerns of black women intellectuals after Emancipation.[23]

● ● ●

> – Sometimes I feel like a motherless child (x3)
> A long way from home,
> A long way from home
>
> (Negro Spiritual)

We have concentrated up to now on literate expressions of black women's lives, but there were important oral elements that informed the writing of African-Americans during the nineteenth century and that continue to do so today. In Africa, life and work was accompanied by music. Tasks of every kind were infused with the sonority of song. These various forms of music, along with the oral tradition of story-telling, came with the Africans and merged with Euro-centric music and literature in America.

One example of this is the field-shout or holler, heard on many a Southern plantation:

> I wants a piece of hoecake
> I wants a piece o' bread
> Well, Ise so tired an' hongry
> dat Ise almos' dead.[24]

These hollers were used to communicate messages across long distances and were usually responded to by a chorus, taking the form known as call and response.

The songs sung by the slaves, either secular or sacred, were often coded, using irony and double-entrendre to convey thoughts that they didn't want their masters to comprehend. These oblique references form the basis of the blues as well as providing the distinctiveness of much twentieth century writing. For instance, in a comparatively recent secular song Sarah Martin, better known as 'Signifyin' Mary', announces her presence as the darker-hued woman:

> Now my hair is nappy
> and I don't wear no clothes of silk (*repeat*)
> But the cow that's black and ugly
> has often got the sweetest milk.[25]

Of the many forms of music employed by the slaves in the nineteenth century, it is the Negro Spiritual that has been most closely associated with the period. It is interesting to examine the way in which African-Americans adopted and adapted the concepts of Christianity, as well as white musical forms, to mould a new music and religion that expressed their political as well as spiritual needs.

Although estranged from their homeland, black Americans retained the African belief that the spiritual is in no way separated from the earthly. For instance, God and Jesus were intimate, personal figures who could be addressed directly:

> Gwine to argue wid de Father and chatter wid de son,
> The last trumpet shall sound, I'll be there.
> Gwine talk 'bout de bright world dey 'des come from.
> The last trumpet shall sound, I'll be there.[26]

This merging of the spiritual and material often produced songs of double meaning. For example, 'deliverance' could mean not only relief from worldly care and trouble, but also refer indirectly to emancipation:

> He delivered Daniel from de lion's den,
>   Jonah from de belly ob de whale,
> And de Hebrew children from de fiery furnace,
>   And why not every man?[27]

Often, these songs could have been coded signals for secret meetings or escape to the 'underground railroad'. For example: 'Steal Away', 'Good News, Chariot's Comin'' or:

> De gospel train's a comin'
>   I hear it jus' at hand,
> I hear de car wheels rumblin',
>   And rollin' thru the land.

De fare is cheap an' all can go,
  De rich an' pore are dere,
No second class aboard dis train,
  No difference in de fare.[28]

And this song, clear and compelling, must surely express the exultation of many an ex-slave mother in the South:

Shout Oh chillun
Shout yo' free
Now you has yo' liberty
yo' no mo' slabe
Y'free, free, free

We gwine own de hoe
An' own de plow
We sell de pig, de horse, de cow
But neber mo' chile be sol'[29]

By blending Africa with America, the slaves created a distinct new culture and developed art forms that sustained them through the most harrowing of times, and that continue to do so today in our literature, as well as our lives.

●   ●   ●

Though I've no home to call my own,
My heart shall not repine;
The saint may live on earth unknown,
And yet in glory shine.

When my Redeemer dwelt below,
He chose a lowly lot;
He came unto his own, but lo!
His own received him not.[30]

These words were written around 1852 by the earliest known female African-American novelist, Harriet E. Wilson. Some years later she published her novel, *Our Nig: or Sketches from the Life of a Free Black, In a Two-Story White House, North, Showing That Slavery's Shadows Fall Even There* by 'Our Nig' (1859). This work has recently been rediscovered after almost a century and a half of oblivion. The circumstances surrounding it are quite extraordinary, hence its vital importance in the historical and sociological understanding of the black American woman's struggle to be heard.

Harriet E. Wilson wrote *Our Nig* to her 'colored brethren', rather than to a white abolitionist audience, as a personal plea for survival:

> In offering to the public the following pages, the writer confesses her inability to minister to the refined and cultivated, the pleasure supplied by abler pens. ... Deserted by kindred, disabled by failing health, I am forced to some experiment which shall aid me in maintaining myself and child without extinguishing this feeble life.[31]

Unusual in its form, *Our Nig* progresses from third-person narration to first-person autobiography, as the author draws nearer to the pressing realities of her life. There is no ending, in the sense that readers are accustomed to, for the ending lay in the hands of the purchasing public. If they bought enough copies, the author and child stood a chance for survival; if not, the chances for continuing life were indeed slim.

Our Nig's subsequent fall into obscurity might well have to do with the controversial themes it placed before the public. The North, during the mid-nineteenth century, prided itself on its abolitionist stance. When Ms. Wilson wrote about the racism she encountered in the North as a free black indentured servant in antebellum days, the subject was not welcomed by white abolitionists, nor by free blacks afraid of antagonizing their white benefactors.[32]

Risking the possibility of hostile reactions, Harriet E. Wilson dared to confront the taboo on inter-racial marriage, of which she was an offspring. It has been noted that, before *Our Nig*, 'miscegenation' was never treated 'with any degree of normality' in American literature.[33] The general attitude of the time is expressed in Mrs. Mary Howard Schoolcraft's novel, *The Black Gauntlet* (1860): 'I believe a refined Anglo-Saxon lady would sooner be burned at the stake than married to one of these black descendants of Ham.'

Henry Louis Gates notes that the boldest and most ironical factor of Ms. Wilson's novel is the use of the word 'Nig':

> *Our Nig* makes an ... important statement about the symbolic connotations of blackness in mid-nineteenth century America, and more especially of the epithet, 'nigger'. The book's title derives from the term of abuse that the heroine's antagonists 'rename her,' calling her 'Our Nig' ... Harriet E. Wilson allows these racist characters to name her heroine, only to *invert* such racism by employing the name, in inverted commas, as her pseudonym of authorship ... Its inverted commas underscore the use as an ironic one, one intended to reverse the power relation implicit in renaming-rituals.[34]

The heroine, Frado, was born to a white mother and a black father; her mother married him to escape the shame of being poor and pregnant outside wedlock. After a few years of marriage, Frado's father dies and her mother marries his white business partner. Abandoning her on the doorstep of a white family, Frado's mother and husband flee town. She is left then in the hands of a cruel mistress who overworks her, beats her and has her live in a cramped and stifling room. The master of the house, being kinder than his wife, allows her to be educated for three years, until Mrs. Bellmont feels that she has better things for Frado to do, like work in the fields in the hottest sun to 'darken her'.

After many years of suffering under Mrs. Bellmont's oppressive hand, Frado is on her own to struggle as a free black woman. Sickly for three years, she marries an escaped slave. He is not much of a solace, for his sea-faring ways take him from home and to eventual death by yellow fever. Left with their only son and in failing health, Frado/Harriet E. Wilson writes of her travails as the only means of sustenance left to her.

It has been stated that *Our Nig* can be regarded as 'an allegory of a slave narrative', that is, 'a "slave" narrative set in the free North.'[35] Harriet Wilson used the conventions of the sentimental novel as well as the slave narrative to produce this unique form. *Our Nig* did not conform to the parameters of nineteenth century white fiction, as black women did not conform to the standards of white womanhood.

No contemporary reviews of the novel have yet been found. This is quite unusual, as there was a growing black press anxious to find new material and Boston was then the centre of the abolitionist movement.

Despite Ms. Wilson's fervent plea for support of her book, her only son died six months after *Our Nig's* publication. It is not known when or where Harriet E. Wilson died. We only know of her life from 1850 to 1860. The rest is lost to us, as she herself was until a few years ago.

• • •

While Harriet E. Wilson was the first African-American woman to publish a novel, Frances E. W. Harper was the first black woman to publish a short story. 'The Two Offers' appeared, like *Our Nig*, in 1859. Ms. Harper's life was vastly different from Wilson's painful existence. Born to free parents, Harper enjoyed the fruits of a full education, becoming teacher, orator, champion of abolitionist causes, journalist, novelist, and author of nine volumes of poetry. She fought for the freedom of slaves as well as for women's rights because she was fully aware of the double oppression of racism and sexism. Harper was in the vanguard of those who realised the full implications of white patriarchy, which included the making of a chasm between black and white women. She challenged the estrangement of southern white women from their black sisters:

You can sigh o'er the sad-eyed Armenian
  Who weeps in her desolate home.
You can mourn o'er the exile of Russia
  From kindred and friends doomed to roam.

. . . .

But hark! from our Southland are floating
  Sobs of anguish, murmurs of pain,
And women heart-stricken are weeping
  Over their tortured and their slain.

. . . .

Oh, people sin-laden and guilty,
  So lusty and proud in your prime,
The sharp sickles of God's retribution
  Will gather your harvest of crime.

Weep not, oh my well-sheltered sisters,
  Weep not for the Negro alone,
But weep for your sons who must gather
  The crops which their fathers have sown.[36]

Frances Harper toured through eight states, speaking for the freedom of African-Americans. Although a devout Christian, extolling the virtues of temperance, thrift, industry and initiative, she showed the contradictions of the Christian doctrines with regard to slavery:

And yet within our favored land,
  Where Christian churches rise,
The dark-browed sons of Africa
  Are hated and despised.[37]

Iola Leroy; or, Shadows Uplifted (1895) was Ms. Harper's first novel. It was begun during the Civil War and completed during the Reconstruction that followed, when she was sixty-five years old. Greatly influenced by the success of Harriet Beecher Stowe's abolitionist novel *Uncle Tom's Cabin* (1852), she constructed her story on a sentimental format. Her preface shows that she anticipated an audience of black Sunday School teachers as well as white middle-class women. She clearly aimed to direct their attention to the plight of many blacks in America and to their fortitude in overcoming injustice.

One particular factor that had to be faced was that black women were not considered beautiful by white American society. If Harper was to conform to the novel of the day, then the story had to be based on a 'beautiful' heroine. The only choice open to African-American writers of the nineteenth century, was to make the heroine a mulatta, quadroon or octoroon, as the black author William Wells Brown did in his novel *Clotel; or, The President's Daughter* (1853). To give her some white blood was tantamount to blessing her with 'beauty'. But, as Hazel Carby notes, Harper's choice of a mulatta heroine had deeper implications:

> Iola, as mulatta, allowed Harper to use the literary conventions of women's fiction and to draw on ideologies of womanhood in her heroine's fall from security. But the mulatta also enabled Harper to express the relationship between white privilege and black lack of privilege, for her heroine situated her advantages and social position in direct relation to a system of exploitation.[38]

The forces of good and evil struggle against one another in *Iola Leroy*. The moral theme of this novel is the suffering octoroon guiding the immoral white man to decency. Although her readers' stock expectations left little room for depth of character, Ms. Harper's handling of racial stereotypes is by no means simplistic.

Iola spends the formative years of her idyllic life without the knowledge that she has black blood. Her father, a southern plantation owner, marries the mulatta servant who had nursed him when he was ill. Mr. Leroy tells a friend why he wants to marry her:

> I think that slavery and the lack of outside interests are beginning to tell on the lives of our women. They lean too much on their slaves, have too much irresponsible power in their hands, are narrowly compressed by the routine of plantation life and the lack of intellectual stimulus.[39]

Directing this at her white southern female readers, Ms. Harper confronts one facet of slavery not usually addressed in the literature of the nineteenth century. The same readers are made to sympathize with Iola, who is depicted as a beautiful, refined octoroon. Interestingly, she is seen that way by Tom, a slave:

> But ef you seed dem putty white han's of hern you'd never tink she kept her own house, let 'lone anybody else's... My! but she's putty. Beautiful long hair comes way down her back, putty blue eyes, an' jis' ez white ez anybody's in dis place.[40]

Tom's style of speech contrasts strongly with Mr. Leroy's. While the narrative is written in white dialect, Harper uses black idiom to give the slaves vividness and individuality. For instance, when Iola says to an ex-slave, 'I thought ... that your name was John Andrews', he replies:

All de use I'se got fer dat name is ter git my money wid it; an when dat's done, all's done. Got 'nuff ob my ole Marster in slave times, widout wearin' his name in freedom. When I got done wid him, I got done wid his name.[41]

Harper thus anticipates Zora Neale Hurston's sympathetic use of black dialect to express folk wisdom. This is how the ex-slave's wife sees the way of the world: 'Dere's nuffin goes ober de debil's back dat don't come under his belly.'[42] Harper's use of Black English underlines the moral lesson of the story, that slavery is a horrific institution. The reader learns this lesson as Iola herself does. When sent to a northern school, Iola defends slavery, still unaware of her blood-line. Tragedy strikes the family with the death of her father and it is then that Iola learns of her true heritage. Because of the cruel actions of her father's friend, Iola and family are stripped of their privileged status, to live the life of slaves. At this point, Iola chooses to be known as a black woman. She spurns the love of a white doctor, works to 'uplift' blacks needing education and guidance, lets it be known that women – all women – should work, and has a fruitful and happy life with her mulatto husband, both working for the 'betterment' of the Negro race.

By using stock characters, but having them behave differently than expected, Ms. Harper is able to confront some of the issues of slavery and its immediate aftermath. She inverts the usual history of the 'tragic mulatta' by showing Iola's self-discovery and eventual fulfilment as a black woman. So Frances E. W. Harper, within the confines of the sentimental novel, did her utmost for the cause of abolition and for the rights of women. Her poetry and journalism speak in a much more forthright manner, for there the octoroon was not a necessary factor.

The tradition of using a mulatta heroine was continued by Pauline Hopkins in *Contending Forces*, published in 1900. In this polemical and pedagogical work, she hoped to arouse the kind of sympathy and concern for blacks that had been evidenced during the days of abolitionism. To do this she created 'fictional histories that would explain the present'. One critic notes that,

> Her narratives rewrote contemporary versions of the relationship between the races during slavery in order to challenge contemporary racist ideologies. The social relations of the separation of the races in which Hopkins' fiction was produced – disenfranchisement, lynchings, and the institutionalization of Jim Crow – were displaced by her alternative fictional history of close blood ties through miscegenation.[43]

The overwhelming dominance of the mulatto characters in this novel causes one to wonder if Ms. Hopkins was glorifying the lighter-hued black. Hazel Carby argues against this assumption:

The presence of 'mixed' characters in the text did not represent an implicit desire to 'lighten' blacks through blood ties with whites. Hopkins wanted to emphasize those sets of social relations and practices which were the consequence of a social system that exercised white supremacy through the act of rape.[44]

Yet it seems that the myth of white supremacy has indeed produced an author who is most decidedly ambivalent about her own race:

> Surely the Negro race must be productive of some valuable specimens, if only from the infusion which amalgamation with a superior race must eventually bring.[45]

This confusion, ambivalence and intra-racial division continues in the works of African-American women writers for some time to come. A growing black middle class, desperate for economic inclusion and acceptance in a white world, embraced white western literary conventions. It must also be noted that white publishers would only be interested in literature that mirrored their own ideologies and stereotypes of black people. For the black novelist, the 'mulatta' image remained strong and it was not until the 1930s that black female writers felt free to break away from it.

●   ●   ●

In a span of approximately two hundred years, we have seen the black woman struggle to write, and the black woman writer struggle to be heard. During a century dominated by slavery, African-American women came to articulate their existence in autobiography, fiction, poetry and polemics. It is quite miraculous that these women wrote, spoke, sang and survived. But they did, and every day we are recovering voices from the past, to remind us that:

> If the first woman God ever made was strong enough to turn the world upside down all alone, these women together ought to be able to turn it back, and get it right side up again![46]

2: **Words to a White World**

Certainly colored people are living in homes that are clean, well-kept with many evidences of taste and refinement about them. They are many of them well educated, cultivated and cultured; they are well-mannered and, in many instances, more moral than the whites; they love beauty; they have ideals and ambitions, and they do not talk – this educated type – in the Negro dialect. All the joys and sorrows, and emotions the white people feel they feel; their feelings are as sensitive; they can be hurt as easily; they are proud. [1]

Angelina Grimké wrote this plea in 1920 for the acceptance of the 'better sort of black folks' into white middle-class America. She was one of four African-American women writers who bridged the gap between late nineteenth-century romanticism and the avant-garde forms of the early twentieth century. Grimké, along with Alice Dunbar Nelson, Anne Spencer and Georgia Douglas Johnson, comprised what is now considered the 'genteel school' of writing.

At the turn of the century, one of the outstanding spokesmen for the black intellectual community was W. E. B. Du Bois, graduate of Harvard and Berlin Universities. In his ground-breaking book of essays, *The Souls of Black Folks* (1903), he set forth his proposal for the 'Talented Tenth', a select group of African-Americans trained to lead the less fortunate of their race:

If ... the races are to live for many years side by side ... it will call for social surgery at once the delicatest and nicest in modern history. It will demand broad-minded, upright men, both white and black, and in its final accomplishment American civilization will triumph.... By refusing to give this Talented Tenth the key to knowledge, can any sane man imagine that they will lightly lay aside their yearning and contentedly become hewers of wood and drawers of water? [2]

Though he consistently refers to men in his writings, in practice Du Bois opened up possibilities for suitably educated women to join this élite. Interestingly, the women who became members of the élite were frequently of very light complexion, some easily mistaken for white, and their colour and education often left them isolated from the rest of the black populace. As Nathan Huggins suggests:

> If anything, this alienation was more accentuated among Negro intellectuals. There had been little in the public schools or colleges to give them a sense of their cultural past or the distinctiveness of their people.... The fact that the line back to the past was snarled... made the racial past hazy, distant and impossible to know.... The shame that black men felt about their past was a measure of how much they had drunk up the values of the white world around them.[3]

Alice Dunbar Nelson (1875–1935) was the first woman of the genteel school to gain prominence in America's literary world and the only one to earn a living by her journalism. She was born of black and white parentage in Louisiana in 1875. Married to, then divorced from, the celebrated 'dialect' poet, Paul Laurence Dunbar, she continued to use his name throughout her life. Aware of sexism, as well as racism, she knew that the Dunbar name had its rewards.

Her first book, *Violets and Other Tales* (1895), was published when she was only twenty years old. This volume is a veritable pot-pourri of literary forms and set a pattern that stayed with Ms. Dunbar throughout her career. As Gloria Hull observes:

> In *Violets*, a well-read, conspicuously talented young writer is trying on voices.... This first period of her life set some major patterns – racial ambiguity, Creole materials and themes, vocational pursuits... journalistic work, women's concerns... [and] racial activism.[4]

Ms. Nelson's political activism continued throughout her life, yet, in her published work, she rarely addressed racial themes. This is certainly true of her poetry, which remained 'untainted' by concerns of colour. In a letter to Paul Laurence Dunbar she expressed her wishes 'to maintain separation between race and imaginative literature.'[5] Her reasons for this are not clear. She may have feared that she would lose readers by confronting such disturbing realities. Or she may have felt that the subject was not appropriate to romantic writing. Nathan Huggins observes that: 'Like white children, black children were taught that the speech of their fathers was not proper English speech. They were encouraged to leave behind their dialects and regional and ethnic idioms. The tales that they had heard the old folks tell was not the stuff of culture.'[6] It is better, then, for Ms. Nelson to use the sonnet form and speak of things 'lovelier' than racism:

I had not thought of violets of late,
   The wild, shy kind that spring beneath your feet
In wistful April days, when lovers mate
   And wander through the fields in raptures sweet.
The thoughts of violets meant florists' shops,
   And bows and pins, and perfumed papers fine;
And garish lights, and mincing little fops,
   And cabarets and songs, and deadening wine.
So far from sweet real things my thoughts had strayed,
   I had forgot wide fields and clear brown streams;

. . . .

And now – unwittingly, you've made me dream
Of violets, and my soul's forgotten gleam.[7]

Although Alice Nelson's poetry appeared in many periodicals and anthologies, no collection was published. She did, however, publish a book of short stories, sketches and poems entitled *St. Rocque and Other Stories* in 1899. Colourful, polished and 'picturesque', it concerns itself only with the lives of creoles and whites in Louisiana, avoiding any racial conflicts. Such lines as, 'She walked with the easy spring that comes from a perfectly arched foot',[8] show the signs of a talented writer. The creole 'patois' enlivens the text:

> Pralines, madam? I lak you' face. What fo' you wear black? You' lil' boy daid? You tak' one, jes see how it tas'. I had one lil' boy once, he jus' grow twell he's big lak dis, den one day he tak' sick an' die.[9]

Nothing in these examples, however, indicates how fervently Alice Dunbar Nelson fought for the rights of her people. She was the first black woman to serve on the State Republican Committee of Delaware and, with her husband, founded the Wilmington *Advocate*, an African-American newspaper. Her column in the Pittsburgh *Courier*, 'From A Woman's Point of View', was widely read. Though still clinging to romanticism, a new Ms. Nelson emerges:

> The women of a race should be its pride . . . and this race of ours has much for which to pride itself. . . . For instance Jane Porter Barrett . . . found out, as so many colored women have found, that the girls of the race need all that can be done for them. Outcast. Homeless, forlorn. Misunderstood. . . . Whipped and reviled, when they need a friendly word, a chance to make a decent living.[10]

But Nelson's 'veiled' existence is fully unmasked in her recently discovered diary, *Give Us This Day*, written from 1921 to 1931. In it, we learn of her enduring physical and economic struggles, her love for women, her life in a supportive female-centred household, her fight for black causes and her ambivalence towards those darker than herself: 'Pauline did not want to go, being tied up with some ink-spot who had a Nash car.'[11] Although a traditionalist in her poetry and prose, her diary is of great importance for its revelations about black culture and black women's existence.

Released from the eye of the white critic and the expected forms of written expression, Ms. Dunbar was a free agent, writing as she pleased. What one finds is a fresh and spirited prose. Here, Alice D. Nelson often uses phrases or words indigenous to black speech and culture: 'Ethel Barrymore and her young daughter Ethel Colt in "Scarlet Sister Mary". Why would Ethel go Negro, *and* Gullah Negro? Well done, but as Dr. Johnson said of a woman preaching and a dog walking on its hind legs, "Who do it at all!"'[12] She is of course is referring to Johnson's infamous remark: 'It is not done well, but you are surprised to find it done at all.'

It is a pity that Alice Dunbar Nelson could not use this kind of writing in her published prose, for she then would have brought the full range of experience to her work. The only other black woman of the nineteenth century whose journal (written 1854–65), has been published, was Charlotte Forten. Both she and Alice Dunbar Nelson believed in the importance of their lives. Since they refused to be 'invisible', their chronicles have enriched our understanding of the black woman in America.

Angelina Weld Grimké (1880–1958), was born in Boston. Her father, Archibald Grimké, was of mixed racial background. She was named after her aunt, Angelina Grimké Weld, one of the two sisters who were famous for their fight for abolition and women's rights. The Grimké sisters introduced Archibald to the liberal, aristocratic Bostonian society in which his daughter was to grow up. Such people as William Lloyd Garrison, Charles Sumner, Wendell Phillips, Elizabeth Peabody and the journalist and orator Frederick Douglass, who was an escaped slave, were friends of the family.

Ms. Grimké started writing at an early age and her first story was published in 1900. Her poems began to appear in Boston publications around 1902. Like Dunbar Nelson's, they concerned themselves with neutral topics such as spring and romantic fantasies. When Grimké dared to submit a poem along clear racial lines, it was rejected. However, her play *Rachel* (1920) was written with a specific purpose and received a favourable response, although some blacks found it 'defeatist'. It concerns a young black woman who, after enduring racism for most of her life, decides not to marry or bear children and subject them to the racist world in which she lives. The programme states: 'This is the first attempt to use the stage for race propaganda in order to enlighten the American people relative to the lamentable condition of ten million of colored citizens in this free Republic.'[13]

Of all the literary forms used by Ms. Grimké, it is her poetry that is outstanding. The influence of the 'Imagist' school of poetry, led in America by Amy Lowell, shows in 'Dawn':

> Grey trees, grey skies, and not a star:
> Grey mist, grey hush:
> And then, frail, exquisite, afar,
> A hermit-thrush.[14]

This restrained Imagist technique means that black experience enters her poetry only indirectly. In 'At April', for instance:

> Toss your gay heads,
> Brown girl trees;
>
> . . . .
>
> Stretch your brown slim bodies;
>
> . . . .
>
> Who knows better than we,
> With the dark, dark bodies,
> What it means
> When April comes a-laughing and a-weeping
> Once again
> At our hearts?[15]

But the subject Ms. Grimké was most concerned with was her love of women. She was completely open in her adoration:

> I should like to creep
> Through the long brown grasses
> That are your lashes;
> I should like to poise
> On the very brink
> Of the leaf-brown pools
> That are your shadowed eyes;
>
> . . . .
>
> I should like to sink down
> And down
> And down...
> And deeply drown.[16]

In her poetry Grimké often avoided black themes but was fairly overt in her lesbianism. This may have been the reason why, although she appeared in anthologies like *The New Negro* (1925), she never had a volume of poetry published.

A lonely black woman, with no known lesbian friends or lovers, Angelina Grimké stopped writing after the 1920s. She died in 1958 at the age of seventy-eight, in the solitude of her New York City apartment. In an unpublished poem, she wrote:

> The days fall upon me;
> One by one, they fall,
> Like leaves.
>
> . . . .
>
> They cover me,
> They crush,
> They smother.
> Who will ever find me
> Under the days?[17]

Gloria T. Hull has aptly described this poem as Grimké's 'own problematic epitaph.'[18]

The poet Anne Spencer (1882–1975), a black Seminole Indian, wrote: 'I proudly love being a Negro woman – it's so involved and interesting. We are the PROBLEM – the great national game of TABOO.'[19]

Yet the subject of black women must have been taboo to most publishers, for few of her poems relate to African-American women, or even indicate that she is black. Introducing a selection of her work, the black writer and editor James Weldon Johnson showed his own ambivalence towards 'race conscious poetry', stating: 'Mrs. Spencer is unique... practically none of her poetry has been motivated by race.'[20]

But in her public life, Spencer's outrage at racism and sexism was decidedly bold: she wore trousers when no 'genteel' woman dared consider it; she kept a wall covered with original slave posters to remind her of a history that should never be forgotten and she walked to any destination rather than ride on Jim Crow buses.

And when she did speak about the lives of her sisters, she spoke vividly:

> Lady, Lady, I saw your face,
> Dark as night withholding a star
>
> . . . .

The chisel fell, or it might have been
You had borne so long the yoke of men.

Lady, Lady, I saw your hands,
Twisted, awry, like crumpled roots
Bleached poor white in a sudsy tub,
Wrinkled and drawn from your rub-a-dub.[21]

The writer of these lines appeared in anthologies, but never had a volume of her own work published. Over a number of years, Anne Spencer sent her poems to H. L. Mencken, the white critic, and all were rejected. Ms. Spencer never tried to publish her poems again.

Georgia Douglas Johnson (1886–1966), a traditionalist in poetic form, gave much more attention to African-American women, and her home became a salon for the writers of the Harlem Renaissance. She was the first black woman since Frances E. W. Harper, in 1854, to have a volume of poetry published, and she published four in her lifetime.

In her second volume, *Bronze, a Book of Verse* (1922), Ms. Johnson says: 'This book is the child of a bitter earth-wound. I sit on the earth and sing-sing out, and of my sorrow. Yet . . . I know that God's sun shall one day shine upon a perfected and unhampered people.'[22] Nevertheless, W. E. B. Du Bois in his foreword to the same book uses backhanded compliments to keep her in her place:

Those who know what it means to be a colored woman in 1922 . . . must read Georgia Douglas Johnson's *Bronze*. . . . Her word is simple, sometimes trite, but it is singularly sincere and true.[23]

Many of the poems found in *Bronze* are addressed to young children coming into a cruel and prejudiced world. With painful knowledge, a 'Black Woman' says to an unborn child:

Don't knock at my heart, little one,
    I cannot bear the pain
Of turning deaf-ear to your call
    Time and time again!
You do not know the monster men
    Inhabiting the earth,
Be still, be still, my precious child,
    I must not give you birth![24]

The dilemma of the octoroon, being neither black nor white, concerns Georgia Johnson, as it had concerned Harriet Wilson and Frances Harper and would later concern women novelists of the Harlem Renaissance:

> One drop of midnight in the dawn of life's pulsating stream
> Marks her an alien from her kind, a shade amid its gleam;
> Forevermore her steps she bends insular, strange, apart –
> And none can read the riddle of her wildly warring heart.[25]

Johnson's first volume, *The Heart of A Woman and Other Poems* (1918), shows her search for identity as a black woman poet. Knowing that racism alone did not restrict her life, she said:

> The heart of a woman falls back with the night,
> And enters some alien cage in its plight,
> And tries to forget it has dreamed of the stars
> While it breaks, breaks, breaks on the sheltering bars.[26]

Though inhibited by the practice of 'veiling' her meaning and by the romantic tradition in which she wrote, she nevertheless began to question her identity more than previous black women poets had done. In 'Cosmopolite', for instance:

> Not wholly this or that
> But wrought
> of alien bloods am I,
>
> . . . .
>
> Estranged, yet not estranged, I stand
> All comprehending;
>
> . . . .
>
> All understanding,
> Nor this nor that
> Contains me.[27]

It was Georgia Douglas Johnson's fate to remain 'estranged' from potential readers of her work. Gloria Hull tells how, after her funeral, when the car stopped in front of her home, a friend saw manuscripts being carried away with the garbage. Even those close to Johnson did not value her creativity enough to safeguard her writing for posterity.

• • •

Save your tears for a rainy day,
We are giving a party where you can play
With red mammas and too bad Sheabas
Who wear their dresses above their knees
And mess around with whom they please.
At a
SOCIAL PARTY
Given by
Mrs. Helen Carter & Mrs. Mandy Wesley[28]

In contrast to the relative freedom enjoyed in the first decade of the twentieth century by blacks in the North, ex-slaves in the South still lived in servitude. Disenfranchisement, lynchings, segregated schools and public facilities were the norm. When World War One cut off the supply of immigrants to the United States, there was a need for cheap labour in the industrial North. Fleeing from violence and to supposed new freedoms, blacks packed their bags and headed North: the 'Great Migration' was on.

Due to a group of astute African-American real-estate agents, an upper region of Manhattan became the largest black community in the world. It was known as Harlem from the early days of Dutch settlement. Black intellectuals, as well as artisans, came from all over the globe to gather there. It was a time of great excitement and change as African-Americans built a new home and a new image. In the capital of the publishing and theatrical world of America, black people saw a bright and hopeful beginning and they called it the Harlem Renaissance.

Alain Locke gave expression to these hopes in his introduction to *The New Negro* (1925), an anthology of poems and prose by contemporary black artists. He described the 'New Negro' as the 'advanced guard of the African peoples in contact with the Twentieth Century civilization',[29] who would be responsible for 'rehabilitating the race in world esteem....'[30]

African-Americans were no longer country people but city-dwellers. The stereotypes of plantation days – *Uncle Tom, auntie, mammy, Sambo, brute nigger* and *shufflin' clown* – were now out of date. But the white sophisticated eye of the jazz age had newer stereotypes to put in their place, such as *primitives* and *exotics*. This is evident in *Nigger Heaven* (1926), a novel by the rich white patron of black culture, Carl Van Vechten. (The title is explained by the fact that when the theatres of America were segregated blacks had to sit in the balcony.)

The assertive 'New Negro' writers were determined to correct these images. One of them was Jessie Fauset (1888–1961), who fought for a better representation of blacks in literature, though her efforts to do so were limited by the genteel tradition.

Jessie Fauset was educated in France as well as in America, therefore her world was wider and she was better informed than her poorer brothers and sisters. As the literary editor for W. E. B. Du Bois's *Crisis* magazine, she gave Langston Hughes his first opportunity to publish, along with many other new young writers of the era.

The most widely read of the Renaissance writers, Ms. Fauset was a much anthologized poet. Eschewing racial matters, her poems usually concerned themselves with the joys and pains of love:

> Lolotte, who attires my hair,
> Lost her lover. Lolotte weeps;
> Trails her hand before her eyes;
> Hangs her head and mopes and sighs,
> Mutters of the pangs of hell.
> Fills the circumambient air
> With her plaints and her despair.
> Looks at me:
> 'May you never know, Mam'selle,
> Love's harsh cruelty.'[31]

Fauset published four novels: *Chinaberry Tree* (1931), *Plum Bun* (1929), *There Is Confusion* (1924), and *Comedy, American Style* (1933). These are also European in construction, but are studies of the black middle class. Although the language spoken could be that of the white bourgeoisie, her concern is with the problems facing the 'best' of the Negro race, usually with emphasis on the mulatta heroine, coping with intra-racial struggles as well as with white racism. As Nathan Huggins observes: 'Jessie Fauset tried to project the Negro image in very conventional terms. Indeed, it was her intended purpose in writing novels to place the Negro in the context of standard American life.'[32]

W. E. B. Du Bois, along with other black intellectuals, hailed her work; in depicting the best of the Negro race, it showed what all African-Americans could become if given the chance. But Jessie Fauset knew how difficult it was to publish books about intelligent, hard-working middle-class black folks:

> I blame the publisher for not being a 'better sport'. Most of them seem to have an idée fixe. They, even more than the public ... persist in considering only certain types of Negroes interesting and if an author presents a variant they fear that the public won't believe it or won't 'stand' for it.[33]

Ms. Fauset's fiction is riddled with complex, 'strained' plot structure and disturbing 'foreign phrases'.[34] This may reflect the difficulty of disguising her anger, but it was also a way of showing her sophistication to a mainly white readership. It has been noted that: 'It was no easy task to handle that problem [racism] honestly within a conventional model which had strong stoical ingredients and which could not accommodate bitterness or anger at personal misfortune'.[35]

Jessie Fauset aims to express the frustration of middle-class blacks who, if it were not for their skin-colour, would be able to live full and enriching lives:

> 'Why should I shut myself off from all the things I want most – clever people, people who do things, ART,' – Her voice spelt it with a capital, – 'travel and a lot of things which are in the world for everybody really but which only white people, as far as I can see, get their hands on.'[36]

Many of Ms. Fauset's characters 'pass' as white, unlike Frances E. W. Harper's 'mulatta' heroines. 'Passing' allows them to enjoy the privileges of white middle-class Americans. But Ms. Fauset shows that the cost of this is self-deception and betrayal of one's own people.

Though all of Fauset's novels deal with the 'fair-skinned' African-American, her most successful, *Plum Bun*, shows the ridiculousness of 'passing' and the insanity of a world where colour is a criterion for ability and talent. The heroine Angela Murray is able to get ahead as a passing black. In a crucial scene, she shuns her darker sister in order not to reveal her own origins to her white boyfriend. Eventually she recognizes her complicity with their racism and frees herself from this hypocrisy. Fauset's message here, as in *Comedy, American Style*, seems to be: You must be who you are, or else there is destruction.

'Passing' was a wide-spread concern for many of the Harlem Renaissance writers, as well as for their white counterparts. The difference lay in *why* one passed; for Ms. Fauset, it was the economic and educational restrictions that blacks battled against. Yet, for another African-American novelist, passing not only dealt with the barriers of colour, but of sexuality as well.

Nella Larsen (1893–1963) was catapulted into the literary world of the Harlem Renaissance unexpectedly and disappeared as abruptly as her career began. She was the first black novelist to deal with the psychology of the fair-skinned middle class, to dare and confront the interior, the soul divided and searching. Although she was the author of only two novels, her taut, clear, poetic prose propelled her into the limelight. Not content to expose the evils of a racist society, Larsen laid open the dilemma of the bourgeois black in America.

Nella Larsen was born of West Indian and Danish parentage. When she was a young girl her black father disappeared and was assumed to be dead. Her mother then remarried a white bigot, and Ms. Larsen spent the rest of her life grappling with her identity. Her highly acclaimed novel, *Quicksand* (1928), addresses this issue by taking as its heroine a half-Danish woman,

Helga Crane, and having her teach at a black college called Naxos (an anagram of Saxon). Its major theme is not skin colour, but the problem of black female sexuality. Since African-American women were frequently portrayed in white literature as loose and free-living, it was difficult for Larsen to resist the stereotype, and yet show her heroine as a sexual being.

Helga Crane is caught in this dilemma of her own sexuality and spins round and round searching for, yet avoiding, her sensual self. Finally she leaves the college, discarding its mimicry of white ways and denigration of black culture. To free herself, she flees to Harlem, the Mecca of black minds and music. But she finds the black bourgeoisie also caught in its own narrow-minded view of the world:

> Nevertheless, she felt a slightly pitying superiority over those Negroes who were apparently so satisfied. And she had a fine contempt for the blatantly patriotic black Americans.[37]

Confronted with her acute sexual yearnings, but unable to give rein to them, she runs once again; this time to relatives in Denmark. There, in an all-white society, she becomes the 'exotic' beauty. Her aunt dresses her in flamboyant garb to emphasize her 'innate wild nature'. Unable to play the role, she refuses the hand of a famous Danish artist and returns to Harlem, where once again, she hopes to become whole:

> *These* were her people. Nothing, she had come to understand now, could ever change that.... How absurd she had been to think that another country, other people could liberate her from the ties which bound her forever to these mysterious, these terrible, these fascinating, these lovable, dark hordes. Ties that were of the spirit.[38]

Yet, Helga Crane still feels a separation from her people and the role she has to play as a black middle-class woman. Reunited, at a party, with her rejected fiancé, she bemoans the fate of black marriage and childbearing:

> Marriage – that means children, to me. And why add more suffering to the world? Why do Negroes have children? ... Think of the awfulness of being responsible for the giving of life to creatures doomed to endure such wounds to the flesh, such wounds to the spirit, as Negroes have to endure.[39]

But the denial of her sensuality proves difficult for her and she makes a sexual approach to the man whom she has always wanted, yet feared, since her teaching days. He rejects her and she is unable to cope. Half-crazed, Helga embarks on a mad, frantic search for 'solace'. She comes across a store-front church in Harlem: swept up in the religious fervour, she loses herself and gets 'happy'. Spiritually released, believing she has found what she needs, Helga Crane gives in to the advances of a poor, Southern preacher.

Wedding him the next day, she goes South where, she is convinced, she can do good and 'save' herself. Helga is scorned by the women there and after the painful and unassisted births of four children, is a broken woman. Relegated to a life of hard work, misery and friendlessness, she sinks into mental and spiritual 'oblivion'. It has been noted that this ending shows the author's inability to resolve the representation of black female sexuality in literature: 'However much Larsen criticizes the repressive standards of sexual morality upheld by the black middle class, finally she cannot escape those values.'[40]

Ms. Larsen's second novel, *Passing* (1929), also received wide critical acclaim. Alice Dunbar Nelson, in a review of the book, writes that: 'you are suddenly aware that you have been reading a masterpiece all along, and that the subtle artistry of the story lies in just this – its apparent innocuousness, with its universality of appeal.'[41] The title is somewhat misleading, for the obvious plot is about the dangers of leaving one's race to 'pass' into another; but as Deborah McDowell astutely points out in her introduction, the sub-plot, or the veiled meaning within the plot, has to do with 'passing' from accepted modes of sexual behaviour to the 'dangerousness' of love for another woman.

The two heroines are Irene and Clare. Irene, the narrator of the story, is light enough to pass, but only does so for 'entertainment': to get into better stores, theatres and the basic privileges afforded to the white populace. She lives in Harlem with her husband and sees herself as a 'race' woman. Yet Irene also strives for security over fulfilment of self: she strains to be the embodiment of all that was expected of the upper middle-class American woman.

Clare, Irene's poor friend from childhood, is also able to pass and does so with a vengeance. Economically down-trodden, she sees her only escape in becoming a 'white woman'. Marrying a rich, bigoted business man, her life is sexually barren, as is Irene's, though for different reasons. Irene, unable to let go of the rigid, bourgeois life-style she has set out for herself, loses the interest of her husband:

> Nor did she admit that all other plans, all other ways, she regarded as menaces, more or less indirect to that security of place and substance which she insisted upon for her sons and in a lesser degree for herself.[42]

Clare, on the other hand, must be very careful in sexual relations with her husband, for the possibility of a dark child would mean the utter destruction of her well-planned life.

After many years of separation, Clare notices Irene in a teashop, where both are 'passing'. During their conversation, Clare realizes how desperately she wants to be with her people again. The risk lies in Clare's coming up to Harlem and being discovered by her husband. But for Irene, the real danger was the sexual feeling that Clare engendered in her:

> Looking at the woman before her, Irene Redfield had a sudden inexplicable onrush of affectionate feeling. Reaching out, she grasped Clare's two hands in her own and cried with something like awe in her voice: 'Dear God! But aren't you lovely, Clare!'[43]

Fighting her attraction to Clare, she concludes that Clare's intrusion in her life is causing turmoil; not only to her emotions, but also in separating her from her husband. The idea of telling Clare's husband of his wife's trips to Harlem haunts Irene, but he inadvertently finds out and confronts his wife at a party:

> It was the smile that maddened Irene. She ran across the room . . . and laid a hand on Clare's bare arm. One thought possessed her. She couldn't have Clare Kendry cast aside by Bellow [her husband]. She couldn't have her free.[44]

Her freedom would be the final threat to Irene's economically and sexually secure position. Clare's death would kill the need for her, destroy the upheaval her presence presented. It is left to conjecture whether Clare falls to her death from a window, or is pushed by Irene:

> Gone! The soft white face, the bright hair, the disturbing scarlet mouth, the dreaming eyes, the caressing smile, the whole torturing loveliness that had been Clare Kendry. The beauty that had torn at Irene's placid life. Gone![45]

Death, either physical or spiritual, is the only solution Larsen offers her tragic heroines.

After the publication of *Passing*, Ms. Larsen was awarded a Guggenheim Fellowship in 1930: she was the first black woman ever to receive one. While planning a trip to France and Spain to do research for her forthcoming book, she was accused of plagiarising her short story 'Sanctuary'. Although her editor helped to vindicate her, she never recovered. 'Passing' into another life, she died in obscurity in Brooklyn in 1963.

As African-American women writers struggled to give voice to themselves they still had to negotiate the restrictive stereotypes offered by white society and the repressive nature of black patriarchy. But the 'tragedy' of the 'mulatta' had finally been played out in Larsen's novels, and black women would receive fuller and freer representation in the very near future. Gwendolyn Bennett, a poet of the early twentieth century, foresaw the change coming when she wrote:

> Oh, little brown girl, born for sorrow's mate,
> Keep all you have of queenliness,
> Forgetting that you once were slave,
> And let your full lips laugh at Fate![46]

3: A Jump at de Sun

Got one face for the world to see
'Nother for what I know is me,
He don't know
He don't know my mind.[1]

Duke Ellington was playing at the Cotton Club, Bessie Smith was singing the blues, the Charleston was the rage, heavy gin-drinking was *de rigeur* and Freudian psychoanalysis challenged the uptight white middle class. Victorian mores were out and the 'Negro' was in. During this heady 'jazz age', the Harlem Renaissance flourished and a woman from the all-black town of Eatonville, Florida, arrived there to 'jump at de sun'.

Big-boned, brave, 'bodacious' Zora Neale Hurston landed in Harlem in 1925 with only $1.50, one bag of manuscripts and a determination to 'wrassle me up a future, or die tryin'.[2]

Zora hailed from a different world. 'With the map of Florida on her tongue',[3] she came North to extol the lives of the 'Negro farthest down'.[4] No middle-class assimilationist theories for this one: if blacks were looking for their unique culture, the 'New Negro' could find it in his own Southern backyard. It was the songs, tales, language and creativity of the 'folk' that gave black existence its distinctiveness. For Zora, 'Folklore, is the arts of the people before they find out there is such a thing as art.'[5]

Born in 1891, 1901? (Zora changed her age when it suited her),[6] at 'hog-killin' time', her early life was one of affirmative black cultural values. Eatonville gave young Zora a belief in her brown-skinned being that few African-Americans had ever experienced. Her father was a preacher and the mayor of the town, who firmly believed that blacks had their place in American society. Her mother fostered Zora's learning and encouraged her. She did not want to 'squinch' Zora's spirit and turn her into a 'mealy-mouthed rag doll.'[7]

The heart and centre of Eatonville was the store-front porch. Anyone passing by could hear the 'lyin' sessions', 'dozens', songs and comments about the state of the world. This vital gathering place was the starting-point of Ms. Hurston's writing:

> It was a time for sitting on porches beside the road. It was the time to hear things and talk. These sitters had been tongueless, earless, eyeless conveniences all day long. Mules and other brutes had occupied their skins. But now, the sun and the bossman were gone, so the skins felt powerful and human. They became lords of sound and lesser things. They passed nations through their mouths. They sat in judgement.[8]

For her, the porch enshrined the black cultural tradition. But the warm and nurturing environment of orange trees and 'tale tellin' sessions were to end early in life for Zora. Devastated, when she was nine, by the death of her mother, Zora was packed off at fourteen to make it on her own: out of Eatonville and into racism.

First to Jacksonville, Florida, where she discovered what poverty could feel like, how people could be 'slave-ships in shoes'.[9] Frequently working as a maid, she finally landed a job as a wardrobe girl in a Gilbert and Sullivan repertory company. Zora found this experience educationally exhilarating and it took her away from the disheartening provincialism she had come to know.

Leaving the troupe, she enrolled at Morgan Academy in Baltimore, Maryland, to finish high school. Then, working part-time as a manicurist, waitress and maid to upper middle-class black families, she went on to receive a degree from Howard University, 'the capstone of Negro education.'[10]

During her stay in Washington, DC, she often visited the home of Georgia Douglas Johnson, where she met other black artists and intellectuals. Encouraged by Alain Locke, then a philosophy professor at Howard and soon to become a major force in the Harlem Renaissance, Zora published her first story, 'John Redding At Sea', in *Stylus*, Howard's literary magazine. Her work caught the attention of Charles S. Johnson, the editor of *Opportunity*, the journal of the National Urban League. Zora's next story, 'Drenched in Light', placed her among the ranks of the new creative spirits in Harlem. Her short story 'Spunk', originally published in Alain Locke's anthology, *The New Negro*, soon propelled her into the limelight. She submitted it, together with *Color Struck* (a play of Florida folk life) for the 1925 *Opportunity* contest, and both won prizes.

The only female amidst the brightest blacks of the era, among them Langston Hughes, Wallace Thurman, Bruce Nugent and Aaron Douglas, Zora deemed herself 'Queen of the Niggerati'. Her buoyant personality, plus her creative gifts sparked the interest of Annie Nathan Meyer, who helped to secure her a scholarship to Barnard College, and of Fannie Hurst, who would later hire her as a secretary and chauffeur 'companion'.

That was the beginning of a prolific writing career. Ms. Hurston left no stone unturned. She was one of the first black women writers to do it all: anthropologist, novelist (four), short story writer (twelve), dramatist (two musicals plus one libretto for a folk opera), folklorist (voodoo, 'lies', recipes, tales, songs, remedies and jokes), essayist, journalist, autobiographer, teacher and lecturer. The woman was serious!

'Spunk' contains the nucleus of most of Zora's work. Set in a small, black, Southern town, the story is told by the folks on the store-front porch as they act as chorus and pass judgement. Spunk, the main character, manipulative and boastful, comes to his end by a loss of nerve. This occurs through supernatural forces, which are often active in black folklore. After Spunk's violent death, Zora has her chorus settle back into the rhythms of life:

> The cooling board consisted of three sixteen-inch boards on saw horses, a dingy sheet was his shroud.
> The women ate heartily of the funeral baked meats and wondered who would be Lena's next. The men whispered coarse conjectures between guzzles of whiskey.[11]

Among the many other short stories of Ms. Hurston were 'The Gilded Six-Bits' (1933) and 'Sweat', first published in the one and only issue of *Fire!* (1926). The founders of this little magazine were Langston Hughes, Wallace Thurman and Zora Neale Hurston, and it was intended 'to burn up a lot of the old, dead, conventional Negro-white ideas of the past.'[12] Its contents were indeed incendiary to the black bourgeoisie; ironically, most of the copies were burned in a cellar fire.

Launched as a spirited 'tale-teller', short story writer and 'hand-chicken' expert (fried chicken eaten without cutlery), Zora turned her attentions to more scholarly matters. Under the tutelage of the acclaimed anthropologist, Dr. Frank Boas, Zora entered Barnard College to study the folklore of her people. Although African-Americans had collected black folklore before, Ms. Hurston came to the task with a decided advantage. She *was* the folk. Eatonville had moulded her and made her. Her easiness with the people and knowledge of their lives has given us the most enriching collection of African-American folklore to date.

Caught up in 'Barnardese', Zora's first attempts at collection in Florida were difficult. Zora the artist and Zora the scientist proved to be at odds. Boas wanted scientific fact, yet how could this be done when the basis of oral tradition was fiction?

Zora remained unclear until she met one of the most powerful and influential people in her life. Mrs. Osgood Mason was interested in African-American arts and culture, and was already Langston Hughes' patron. This 'Godmother', as she liked to be called, gave Zora the opportunity to continue collecting folklore, but exacted a painful price. The collections were to be

Mrs. Mason's exclusive property and she claimed the right to edit and to censor. Zora could not publish without Mrs. Mason's permission and was forbidden to contact any other persons concerning her work, 'Papa' Frank Boas included. 'Godmother' also demanded an obedience and loyalty so strong that it fostered not only child-like dependency, but smacked of a mistress-slave relationship. The fact that her 'wards' had to sit at her feet does not suggest a meeting of equals. Mrs. Mason once addressed her thus: 'Does a child in the womb speak?'[13] Well, speak she did:

> ... The Negro is a very original being. While he lives and moves in the midst of a white civilization, everything he touches is re-interpreted for his own use. He has modified the language, mode of food preparation, practice of medicine, and most certainly the religion of his new country.[14]

Formal severance of her relationship with Mrs. Mason in 1931–2 left Zora on her own again. She had gathered considerable folk material that she hoped to publish in book form. The Depression hard on her heels, Zora was grateful to be contacted by Nancy Cunard, then assembling her massive anthology, *Negro*. Did she have any articles on folklore? Zora jumped at the chance to demonstrate her rich array of material and, after asking Mrs. Mason for permission, she submitted them for publication in 1935.

She praised black religion and spirituals. She also set the record straight:

> These songs, even the printed ones, do not remain long in their original form. Every congregation that takes it up alters it considerably. For instance, *The Dying Bed Maker* ... has been changed to *He's a Mind Regulator*. ... The real Negro singer cares nothing about pitch. The first notes just burst out and the rest of the church join in – fired by the same inner urge. Negro songs to be heard truly must be sung by a group, and a group bent on expression of feelings and not on sound effects. ...[15]

Zora also points to the rich contributions that African-Americans have made to the English language:

> The Negro's greatest contribution to language is:
> (1) the use of the metaphor and simile; (2) the use of the double descriptive; (3) the use of verbal nouns.[16]

For example:

> 'You sho is propaganda', 'Low-down', 'She features somebody I know', 'I wouldn't friend with her' and 'She won't take a listen'.[17]

Zora wrote of the angularity of the black dancer and of African sculpture; the asymmetry in African art and in the blues poetry of Langston Hughes: 'I ain't gonna mistreat ma good gal no more, I'm just gonna kill her next time she makes me sore...'[18]

And above all, there was the tall tale:

> Once John D. Rockefeller and Henry Ford was woofing at each other. Rockefeller told Henry Ford he could build a gold road round the world. Henry Ford told him if he would he would look at it and see if he liked it, and if he did he would buy it and put one of his tin lizzies on it.[19]

These articles in *Negro*, which also include essays on 'Originality', 'Imitation', 'Absence of the Concept of Privacy', 'The Jook' and 'Dialect', give just a taste of the vast material gathered during her travels in the South. *Mules and Men* is a cornucopia: seventy-two folktales within the text. Not just a scholarly rendering of events, *Mules and Men* incorporates Zora, the narrator:

> I was just Lucy Hurston's daughter... and even if I had... a Kaiser baby [have a child by the Kaiser]... I'd still be just Zora to the neighbors.[20]

The introduction to *Mules and Men* helps to explain Zora's much misunderstood personality, as well as the use of the 'mask' or 'veil' by African-Americans in both life and in literature:

> You see we are a polite people and we do not say to our questioner, 'Get out of here'. We smile and tell him or her something that satisfies the white person because, knowing so little about us, he doesn't know what he's missing.... The Negro offers a feather-bed resistance....
>   The theory behind our tactics: 'The white man is always trying to know into somebody else's business. All right, I'll set something outside the door of my mind for him to play with and handle. He can read my writing but he sho' can't read my mind.[21]

The tales in *Mules and Men* display the complex communication systems set up by an oppressed, inventive people. To laugh at fate, outwit the oppressor and just generally 'keep on keepin' on' is what it was about then and now:

> *Well, once upon a time was a good ole time.*
> *Monkey chew tobacco and spit white lime.*

A colored man was walking down de road one day and he found a gold watch and chain. He didn't know what it was, so the first thing he met was a white man, so he showed the white man de watch and ast him what it was. White man said, 'Lemme see it in my hand.' De colored man give it to him, and de white man said, 'Why this is a gold watch, and de next time you find anything kickin' in the road put it in yo' pocket and sell it.'

With that he put the watch in his pocket and left de colored man standing there.

So de colored man walked on down de road a piece further and walked up on a little turtle. He tied a string to it and put de turtle in his pocket and let de string hang out.

So he met another colored fellow and the fellow ast him says: 'Cap, what time you got?'

He pulled out de turtle and told de man, 'It's a quarter past leben and kickin' lak hell for twelve.'[22]

With no means of support, living in Florida, in a one-room house and surviving on the fifty cents a week her cousin lent her, Zora Hurston's dedication to her craft was remarkable. Her first novel, *Jonah's Gourd Vine* (1934), was loosely based on the early years of her life, coupled with her folklore research.

The story revolves around John, a preacher who struggles with his moral duties and commitment to God. The lure of warm, womanly flesh defeats his 'calling' and causes his downfall. The novel's excellence is manifested in its poetic use of the spoken idiom. John's sermon lauds the ability of an uprooted people to hold onto their origins:

'Hey you, dere, us ain't no white folks! Put down dat fiddle! Us don't want no fiddles, neither no guitars, neither no banjoes. Less clap!'

So they danced. They called for the instrument that they had brought to America in their skins – the drum – and they played upon it. With their hands they played upon the little dance drums of Africa. The drums of kid-skin ... 'I, who am borne away to become an orphan, carry my parents with me.'[23]

Jonah's Gourd Vine is resplendent in rich imagery. So much so that white critics found it hard to believe that a black preacher could possess such gifts of language. Despite their ignorant scepticism, Zora's career as a novelist was launched.

The tide of black literature was turned with Ms. Hurston's second novel, *Their Eyes Were Watching God* (1937). The heroine, Janie Crawford, is the first black woman in American fiction who is not stereotyped as either a slut, a 'tragic mulatta', a mammy or a victim of racist oppression. This novel is a joyful black love story and is also about a black woman's search for herself. Casting off the legacy of her grandmother, who tells her: 'De nigger woman is de mule uh de world so fur as Ah can see',[24] and the husbands who treat her as a commodity, Janie stands as a symbol of self-affirmation and independence. Combining richness of metaphor, the humanizing of nature's elements, the celebration of black culture, the telling of folk-tales with an accurate and loving ear and the depiction of a positive heroine, Zora gave a new beginning to African-American literature and in Janie Crawford, she gave black women a fictional heroine with whom to identify.

Janie is raised by her grandmother, an ex-slave who wants a better life for her granddaughter whom she marries off to an older, propertied man. Janie's lonely and lacklustre marriage propels her into the arms of ambitious, self-centered Joe Starks and he sweeps her away to 'a town all outa colored folks.'[25] She anticipates a full and fruitful life, but her aspirations are thwarted when Joe, who 'always wanted to be a big voice',[26] becomes Mayor and landowner and she is muffled and marginalized as the Mayor's wife.

After twenty years of marriage, Joe Starks dies and Janie is left a wealthy woman, pursued by many suitors. She resists. She knows that life has more to offer. Since adolescence, she has ached for greater fulfilment; the blossoming pear tree has become a symbol to her of all the dreams and desires of love:

> She was stretched on her back beneath the pear tree... when the inaudible voice of it all came to her. She saw a dust-bearing bee sink into the sanctum of a bloom; the thousand sister-calyxes arch to meet the love embrace and the ecstatic shiver of the tree from root to tiniest branch creaming in every blossom and frothing with delight. So this was marriage.[27]

A young, gentle, easy-going spirit arrives in Janie's life in the form of Teacake: 'He could be a bee to a blossom – a pear tree blossom in the spring.'[28] In this equal relationship, Janie comes into her own. Even after Teacake's death, Janie remains whole: 'She pulled in her horizon like a great fish net. Pulled it from around the waist of the world and draped it over her shoulder'.[29]

Their Eyes Were Watching God exemplifies the very best in Zora's writing. Above all, she gave the black woman back to herself. In fact, she is speaking for all women when she says:

> Ships at a distance have every man's wish on board. For some they come in with the tide. For others they sail forever on the horizon, never out of sight, never landing until the Watcher turns his eyes away in resignation, his dreams mocked to death by Time. That is the life of men.

Now, women forget all those things they don't want to remember, and remember everything they don't want to forget. The dream is the truth...[30]

Zora's second book of folklore, *Tell My Horse* (1938), came out of her search for truth in the practices of voodoo in Haiti and Jamaica. Somewhat uneven, it nevertheless took away much of the sensationalism usually associated with investigations of voodoo practices. Her political under-standing of these islands was limited, but her awareness of the intra-racial problems of the time was acute:

So in Jamaica it is the aim of everybody to talk English, act English and *look* English.... The color-line in Jamaica between the white Englishman and the blacks is not as sharply drawn as between the mulattoes and the blacks. To avoid the consequences of posterity the mulattoes give the blacks a first-class letting alone.[31]

Living closely with the people of Haiti and Jamaica, Zora learned old and ancient folk traditions. In Jamaica, she witnessed the rituals of preparing a young girl for marriage. She also recorded stories of apparitions of the Maroons: slaves who had fled to the mountains and fought to remain free. In Haiti, she gained knowledge of the ways of the medicine man and visited an apparent zombie. During a voodoo ceremony, the question was put: 'What is the truth?'[32] Zora witnessed the answer when a Mambo priestess threw back her veil and revealed her vagina: 'The ceremony means that this is infinite, the ultimate truth. There is no mystery beyond the mysterious source of life.'[33]

Ms. Hurston's most ambitious work was *Moses, Man of the Mountain* (1939). Though this is based on the biblical story of Moses, his speech and that of many of the other characters seems to come straight from the Eatonville porch. Wedding folklore with legend, Zora creates a novel that is allegorical, and also satirical. The obvious theme is an oppressed people seeking freedom, yet veiled within the text are protests at the intra-racial divisions found within the black community.

In 1937, Freud published two controversial essays in *Imago*, suggesting that Moses was not Hebrew, but Egyptian. It has been suggested that Zora could have been influenced by these articles. She may, however, have come to the idea of a black Moses on her own, for Moses has always been firmly placed in African-American tradition. Zora tells us:

Then Africa has her mouth on Moses. All across the continent there are legends of the greatness of Moses.... And this worship of Moses as the greatest one of magic is not confined to Africa. Wherever the children of Africa have been scattered by slavery, there is the acceptance of Moses as the fountain of mystic powers.[34]

African-American slaves also adapted the biblical story of Moses leading his people from slavery to their own situation, for they saw themselves as the 'chosen people'. There are innumerable references to this in Negro spirituals: *'when Israel was in Egypt's land, they were oppressed so hard they could not stand'* or *'Didn't old Pharaoh get los', didn't Pharaoh's army get drowned?'* and *'Go down Moses . . . tell ol' Pharaoh, to let my people go'*.

Zora combines black folk legends, biblical history and her own creative vision to give us her version of the story of Moses:

> How about them Israelites? They're down there in Egypt without no god of their own and no more protection than a bare headed mule? . . . Those people . . . need help, Moses. And besides, we could convert 'em, maybe. That really would be something – a big crowd like that coming through religion, all at one time.[35]

Although Zora could not sustain all of the various elements in *Moses, Man of the Mountain*, she is strikingly successful at grafting modern fiction onto the black oral tradition. Here, for instance, she explores the problems of establishing an identity, with no antecedents, and in doing so uses repetition like a preacher:

> Moses had crossed over. He was not in Egypt. He had crossed over and now he was not an Egyptian. He had crossed over . . . He had crossed over so he was not of the house of Pharaoh. He did not own a palace because he had crossed over. . . . He did not have friends to sustain him. He had crossed over. He did not have enemies to strain against his strength and power. He had crossed over . . . He felt as empty as a post hole for he was none of the things he had once been. He was a man sitting on a rock. He had crossed over.[36]

Zora certainly had 'crossed over' from the small town of Eatonville, Florida to fame as a black American folklorist and writer, so much so that her publishers, J. B. Lippincott, asked her for an autobiography. In 1942, *Dust Tracks on a Road* was published, and Alice Walker believes that it was 'the most unfortunate thing that she [Zora] ever wrote'.[37]

By the time of its publication, Zora was beginning to show the strains of living on little money. Zora was a black woman in a white man's publishing world and the obliqueness of *Dust Tracks on a Road* could certainly be attributed to her editor's comment, 'Suggest eliminating international opinions as irrelevant to autobiography.'[38] 'Bodacious' Zora became careful: 'Rather than get across all of the things which you want to say you must compromise and work within the limitations (of those people) who have the final authority in deciding whether or not a book shall be printed.'[39] Lippincott deleted two complete chapters from the 1942 edition and one other was edited out of recognition.[40] Zora knew she had to watch her step.

Another factor that contributed to Zora's 'oddly false-sounding'[41] autobiography was her awareness of a white readership. Unable to assume a significant black audience, she is unwilling to offend her white one.

In the first quarter of the book, we feel the vividness of her childhood memories on her tongue. Yet, when a white man who has befriended her in youth says, 'Snidlits, don't be a nigger'[42], Zora comments: 'The word nigger used in this sense does not mean race. It means a weak, contemptible person of any race.'[43] Considering Zora's fervent belief in the greatness of her people, this kind of writing pinches the nerve. It is clear then that Zora knew her publishers and knew too that they had no real interest in knowing Zora.

For most of the work, self-revelation is side-stepped:

> What do I really know about love? . . . Love, I find is like singing. Everybody can do it enough to satisfy themselves, though it may not impress the neighbors as being very much. . . . Don't look for me to call a string of names and point out chapter and verse. Ladies do not kiss and tell anymore than gentlemen do.[44]

Likewise, black political issues are given no real discussion. Glibly, Zora says, 'While I have a handkerchief over my eyes crying over the landing of the first slaves in 1619, I might miss something swell that is going on in 1942.'[45]

Zora was misunderstood. In the 1930s and 1940s, when a new political consciousness was informing black literary protest against racism, Zora very rarely let white audiences know that they had the power to hurt her or make her feel less than a human being. This offended male contemporaries like Richard Wright, who saw her portrayal of blacks as naive 'Uncle Tomming'. Her separatist stance played into the hands of white racists and caused further chasms. Zora was not about to be allied with the 'sobbing school of Negrohood.'[46]

Her veiling of meaning is best exemplified in the last paragraph of *Dust Tracks on a Road*:

> I have no race prejudice of any kind. My kin-folks, and my 'skin-folks' are dearly loved. . . . In my eyesight, you lose nothing by not looking just like me. I will remember you all in my good thoughts, and I ask you kindly to do the same for me. Not only just me. You, who play the zig-zag lightning of power over the world . . . think kindly of those who walk in the dust. . . . Let us all be kissing-friends. Consider that with tolerance and patience, we godly demons may breed a noble world in a few hundred generations or so. Maybe all of us who do not have the good fortune to meet, or meet again, in this world, will meet at a barbeque.[47]

Is this 'barbeque' a friendly gathering or is it 'the fire next time'? Zora was the master 'trickster'. When sales of her books declined, Ms. Hurston returned to her home state. There, with very little money or recognition, she completed her last novel, *Seraph on the Suwanee* (1948). For the first time in her creative life, Zora abandoned the black folks that she knew. All the characters in this book are white. There is no doubt that she had the right to choose whatever subjects she pleased, but the effort was not successful. Although described as white, these folks sound just like the ones on Joe Clark's front porch. Try as she may, the Eatonville experience was inescapable. It had made for her most brilliant writing, but it didn't work coming from the mouths of Southern whites.

The book received fairly good reviews, but Zora's life had been very difficult of late and the toll was becoming apparent. Before moving South, she had been accused of molesting a young boy and though she was acquitted of the charge, some black newspapers had gone ahead and published the story. Devastated by this incident, Zora retreated further into her own world. No friends came to the rescue; no articles were written to refute such slander. Zora's good days were gone.

She continued writing until her health and money failed her. Eventually she was admitted to Saint Lucie County Welfare Home and three months later, on January 28, 1960, Zora died of 'hypertensive heart disease'.[48] She was buried in an unmarked grave in the city's segregated cemetery. Some twenty years later Alice Walker had a gravestone inscribed and placed near the site of her burial:

ZORA NEALE HURSTON

"A GENIUS OF THE SOUTH"

NOVELIST   FOLKLORIST

ANTHROPOLOGIST

1901   1960

Zora Neale Hurston's gifts to her people and the world have been prodigious. She has inspired countless African-American women writers, among them Alice Walker, Toni Morrison, Toni Cade Bambara, Sherley Anne Williams and many others. She praised her people and it is now only fitting to let 'the folk' praise her:

Listen: Zora came from Diddy-Wah-Diddy to Sugar Hill and back. She was bodacious but never astorperious. She knew full well that the Negro or Black

Esthetic could only be found in the everyday folks from 'Bam with every postman on his beat. She was hip to the fact that whether one had made-hair or naps, it was the essence of the culture that counted. Through most of her life, she struggled with the bear and had little more than a thousand on a plate, but she kept on keepin' on till the very end. And all the while, she was cookin' with gas and gettin' on some stiff time. She was strollin'. She was a solid sender. You dig?

4: Urban Realities

I remember
dark pissy stairways
broken elevators
compressed dreams
when pride was
covered by distraught
writings on cement walls

. . . .

Stone-love
Fuck-you-love
anybody's love
but there wasn't any love
when love had died unnaturally[1]

After the Depression set in, Harlem was no longer 'the home of happy feet', but a walk down the mean, hard streets. As the economy plummeted, the nation suffered and blacks more than most. Over-crowded, rat-infested, crumbling buildings owned by absentee landlords covered the landscape and poor, unemployed blacks were caught in a hostile game of survival. The plight of these times scarred Harlem forever.

The cry went out amongst black intellectuals and artists that no decent life could be lived under such conditions. The foremost African-American woman to concern herself with the literature of social protest was Ann Petry (1908 –), in her novel *The Street* (1946).

Although Ms. Petry came from a middle-class family in Connecticut, she spent a few years in Harlem as a journalist. Her firsthand experience enabled her to assess the conditions and the people of the most famous black section of America:

The rubbish had crept through the broken places in the fences until all of it mingled in a disorderly pattern that looked from their top-floor window like a huge junkpile instead of a series of small backyards...[2]

Streets like the one she lived on were no accident. They were the North's lynch mobs... the method the big cities used to keep Negroes in their place....[3]

The Street presents a harsh and cruel environment where there is no escape from dim hallways, rancid smells and horrid congestion. The competition for survival is fierce and Petry paints a picture of an alienated, disturbed people. She was determined to let the world know how urban blacks suffered at the hands of social and economic racism:

I try to show why the Negro has a high crime rate, a high death rate, and little or no chance of keeping his family unit intact in large northern cities....[4]

The Street has sold over a million copies since its first publication and won the Houghton Mifflin Award. It tells the story of Lutie Johnson, a young, respectable, African-American woman and her struggle to make a better life for herself and her family. Separated from her husband and child, she works long, hard hours, as a live-in domestic. Her husband is unable to find employment and it remains impossible to make ends meet. Lutie realises she must try something else. Overhearing her employers in conversation, she decides that she, too, can share in the 'American Dream':

It was a world of strange values when the price of something called Tell and Tell... had a direct effect on emotions. When the price went up everybody's spirits soared....

After a year of listening to them talk, she absorbed some of the same spirit. The belief that anybody could be rich if they wanted to and worked hard enough and figured it out carefully enough.[5]

In pursuit of the Dream, Lutie Johnson goes with her young son to New York. But, as a black woman without a husband or a supportive community, she can only be destroyed by the forces of urban America:

It was a bad street.... It wasn't just this street that she was afraid of or that it was bad. It was any street where people were packed together like sardines in a can.

And it wasn't just this city. It was any city where they set up a line and say black folks stay on this side and white folks on this side, so that black folks were crammed on top of each other... and forced into the smallest possible space until they were completely cut off from light and air.[6]

The power of this novel lies in the narrator's control of language. The demeaning, debilitating situations encountered by Lutie and her son are never romanticized and the depiction of the environment is relentlessly realistic.

Ms. Petry also strikes back at the stereotypes of the 'lazy black man' and the 'loose black woman' when she describes the situations that make any semblance of decent living almost impossible:

> It was any place where the women had to work to support the families because the men couldn't get jobs and the men got bored and pulled out and the kids were left without proper homes because there was nobody around to put a heart into it. Yes. It was any place where people were so damn poor they didn't have time to do anything but work, and their bodies were the only source of relief from the pressure under which they lived; and where the crowding together made the young girls wise beyond their years.[7]

Lutie Johnson's character refutes the myth of the Harlem Renaissance writers: that you can make it if you try. She also stands as a black heroine without any communal support. And, as a pretty, hard-working woman, wanted by black as well as white men, her beauty and her sentimental dream are her undoing.

Battling against the many odds that threaten her hopes of the 'good life', she finally gives vent to all her anger and frustration. To avoid sexual abuse, she, in effect, destroys herself. She kills a black man, who dares not love her and thus lose his highly paid position with the white 'underground' ruler of Harlem, who wants her also. Lutie Johnson then flees Harlem, leaving behind her son, who has been tricked into criminal acts and faces life in a detention home. The 'dream' becomes a nightmare. In the world of Petry's *The Street*, there is no escape.

Ann Petry wrote two other novels, *Country Place* (1947) and *The Narrows* (1953), as well as a book of short stories, *Miss Muriel and Other Stories* (1971). The first novel concerns itself with the hypocrisy of small town New England life and the latter with inter-racial love in another small Connecticut town. In all of these works, no one escapes economic determinism or racism. Lutie Johnson, especially, never had a chance:

> The trouble was with her. She had built up a fantastic structure made from the soft, nebulous cloudy stuff of dream. There hadn't been a solid, practical brick in it, not even a foundation. She had built it up of air and vapor and moved right in. So of course it had collapsed. It never existed anywhere but in her mind.[8]

●　　●　　●

In Louise Meriwether's novel, *Daddy Was A Number Runner* (1970), we feel there is a chance, however slim, of securing a better life than Harlem had to offer. This is a beautiful and disturbing account of a year in the life of a young black girl growing up in Harlem during the 1930s. James Baldwin stated in his foreword that: 'This book should be sent to the White House ... and to everyone in this country able to read.'⁹ Through Francie's eyes, we see a black girl's attempts to grow into a balanced woman in a world determined to deny her that growth.

Louise Meriwether (1923 –)based her novel on her own adolescence. Like Francie's, her family had their home in Brooklyn, until the Depression set in. Like Francie's, her father lost a fairly well-paid job, went to Harlem and became a number runner. The numbers are the black people's stock market, or as James Baldwin says: 'the game which contains the possibility of making a "hit" – the American dream in blackface.'¹⁰ The similarities in Meriwether's life and Francie's are not necessarily exact, but Ms. Meriwether's early experiences give special credence to Francie's story.

Francie lives in a world where black families, no matter how destitute, aid one another in the struggle to survive. Communal caring and concerns are evident throughout. But despite this, economic forces, corrupt white merchants and landlords as well as a decidedly distorted legal system help to destroy many of them.

We see this upside-down world through the eyes of Francie, without explanation or apology. As Nellie McKay points out in her sharp and sensitive afterword, when three black boys are accused of murder of a white child molester in their neighbourhood (their confession has been beaten out of them), we are left to decide where *real* justice begins. Francie has encountered the man many times, but is afraid to tell anyone, lest they think that she enticed him, or for fear of violence:

> Then there was the men on the roof showing off their privates and the man in the movies with his fumbling hands – that little bald-headed man who had stopped hanging around my roof and now followed me to the show.¹¹

Francie's mother, unaware of white child molesters in the world of little black girls, even in the neighbourhood shops, always asks her daughter to try and get a little extra to stave off starvation. Francie goes reluctantly, and says to the butcher:

> I want ten cents' worth of hamburger meat and my mother says to please give her a soupbone. 'Come to the end of the counter Francie, and let me see how big you are growing.' ... Mr. Morristein, in his scroungy white smock, patted my shoulder and his hands slipped down and squeezed my breast. ... I stood there patiently while his

hands fumbled over my body. Anytime I came to the butcher and no one else was there I had to stand for this nonsense.[12]

This passage is all the more disturbing by being in the first person, we experience what Francie experiences. At the butcher's, Francie gets meat to eat at the expense of her own flesh being handled. This irony emphasizes the double bind of poverty and sexual oppression that makes Francie mute. Her 'I stood there patiently' is especially poignant.

Although her father and brothers have been undone by the 'system', we know that because of her mother's strength, Francie will make it too. Although she is naive, she also possesses 'street-smarts'. The narrative remains plausible throughout and the theme brilliantly understated. In contrast to Lutie Johnson's vulnerable isolation, Francie's sense of belonging gives us hope for herself and for her people: 'I wanted to hug them all. We belonged to each other somehow.'[13]

•   •   •

Not all blacks in America suffered from the destructiveness of ghetto life. The black middle class, since the turn of the century, had been steadily growing. Dorothy West (1912 -), editor and friend to many of the luminaries of the Harlem Renaissance, portrays the lives of Boston's African-American bourgeoisie in her novel, *The Living Is Easy*. Written in 1948, it tells of Cleo Judson's rise from southern poverty to the black Boston élite. Married to a self-made business man with no cultural aspirations, Cleo Judson is well off, but always wanting more, she strives to be with 'the best'. Her husband is a dark man and she is a fair woman. In the world of aspiring blacks, he is considered beneath them. Through most of the novel, Cleo refers to him as 'Mr. Nigger'.

Cleo is a controlling, strong, determined woman. She wants desperately to have power within her community, but cannot. She sends for her sisters in the South whom she feels she can control. They also represent a sense of community not evident in the lives of black bourgeois Bostonians.

The power of this work is in its clear picture of middle-class African-Americans imprisoned and insulated within their own small, suffocating world. The inter-racial and intra-racial concerns of this class become very clear. Although not accepted by white 'society', they have no desire to relate to the black 'common folk'. With myopic vision, they construct their own hierarchy:

They did not consider themselves a minority group. The Irish were a minority group, the Jews, the Italians, the Greeks, who were barred from belonging by old country memories, accents and mores. These gentlewomen felt that they had nothing in common except a facial resemblance. Though they scorned the Jew, they were secretly pleased when they could pass for one. Though they were contemptuous of the Latins, they were proud when they looked European. They were not too dismayed by a darkish skin if it were counterbalanced by a straight nose and straight hair that established Indian origin. There was nothing that disturbed them more than knowing that no one would take them for anything but colored.[14]

Cleo Judson's world was a far cry from Lutie Johnson's or Francie's, but certainly just as disturbing. This is the only book of the period that depicts the lives of the better-off urban black woman and her alienation from her people and herself.

• • •

After fighting World War Two to save democracy, African-Americans turned their thoughts and energies to the 'democracy' not yet awarded them in their own country. During the 1950s, the Civil Rights Movement began in the South. Integration was in the forefront of many people's thoughts, and black literature, in works such as Ralph Ellison's *Invisible Man*, mirrored the times.

Alice Childress (1920 –), actress, director, screenwriter, playwright and novelist, did not embrace these assimilationist views when they were in vogue. She went against the grain of the times. Hers was a stance of black affirmation. This is evident in her first play, *Troubled in Mind* (1955), which received the first Obie Award for the best off-Broadway production.

Childress chose to write about everyday black folks, instead of achievers and accomplishers:

> I turned against the tide and to this day I continue to write about those who come in second, or not at all. . . . My writing attempts to interpret the 'ordinary' because they are not ordinary. . . . I concentrate on portraying have-nots in a *have* society. . . .[15]

The best example of this can be found in the stories of *Like On~ of the Family: Conversations from a Domestic's Life* (1956). In it we find sassy and proud Mildred telling of her adventures in the homes of various employers, to her friend Marge, who never speaks. Yet it is easy to intuit Marge's responses: Childress gives room and space for the reply.

In 'The Pocketbook Game', Mildred brilliantly reverses her employer's paranoia:

Marge... I tell you, it really keeps your mind sharp tryin' to watch out for what folks will put over on you.... Marge, she's got a big old pocketbook... and whenever I'd go there, she'd be propped up in a chair with her handbag double wrapped tight around her wrist, and from room to room she'd roam with that purse hugged to her bosom.... Yes, girl!... NO, there's *nobody* there but me and her....[16]

Mrs. E. asks Mildred to go see the super about fixing a faucet. She goes, then rushes back to the apartment:

Did you see the super?... 'No,' I says, graspin' hard for breath, 'I was almost downstairs when I remembered... *I left my pocketbook!*'[17]

In the title story, Mildred challenges the fabrication that many white employers use when they speak of their domestic workers as being 'Like One of the Family':

After I have worked myself into a sweat cleaning the bathroom and the kitchen... making the beds... cooking the lunch... washing the dishes and ironing Carol's pinafores.... I do not feel like no weekend house guest. I feel like a servant.[18]

Not only does Mildred converse about her work experiences, but also about other facets of her life: 'I Hate Half-Days Off', 'Ain't You Mad', 'We Need A Union Too', 'Dance With Me, Henry' and 'I Wish I Was A Poet'. There is much humour to be found in *Like One of the Family*, but its vision stays sharply focused on the economic and racial injustices of black women in America.

Alice Childress is a prodigious writer, with nine books, ten plays, three television productions plus numerous publications in periodicals to her credit. The works range from *The Wedding Band* (1966), about an inter-racial love affair, to *Florence* (1949), a one act play about an encounter between a black woman and a white woman in the waiting-room of a segregated train station. The newly 'liberated' white woman is having a chat with a black acquaintance, whose daughter is trying to break into show business in New York City:

Mama: Could I ask you something?
Mrs. Carter: Anything...
Mama: Florence is proud... but she's having it hard.... Could you help her out some, mam? Knowing all the folks you do... maybe....[19]

Ironically, Mrs. Carter offers to help by getting a friend who is a director to hire Florence as a domestic: 'I'll just tell her... no heavy washing or ironing ... just light cleaning and a little cooking ... does she cook?'[20]

By forcing the reader/audience to look at the injustices of black American life, Ms. Childress gives no easy portrayals or solutions. But by voicing these realities, she makes us aware of the many sides of racism and prejudice and challenges blacks, as well as whites, to change it.

• • •

> In the streets out there, any little white boy from Long Island or Westchester sees me and leans out of his car and yells – 'Hey there, *hot chocolate!* ... YOU! Bet you know where there's a good time tonight....'
>
> Follow me sometimes and see if I lie. I can be coming from eight hours on an assembly line or fourteen hours in Mrs. Halsey's kitchen. I can be all filled up that day with three hundred years of rage so that my eyes are flashing and my flesh is trembling – and the white boys in the streets, they look at me and think of sex.... Baby, you could be Jesus in drag – but if you're brown they're sure you're selling![21]

These words are uttered by a domestic, a mother and a professional woman, in an unfinished work by the journalist and playwright, Lorraine Hansberry (1930–1965).

Ms. Hansberry was the youngest, the fifth woman and the only black American to win the New York Drama Critics Circle Award for Best Play of the Year. She received that honour for *A Raisin in the Sun* in 1959 at the age of twenty-nine, and five years later she died of cancer. During that short span of time, her literary achievements were considerable, as was her untiring fight for the equality of blacks in America. Martin Luther King, Jr. said that: 'Her commitment of spirit ... her creative literary ability and her profound grasp of the deep social issues confronting the world today will remain an inspiration to generations yet unborn.'[22]

From a middle-class home, frequented by black leaders, writers and musicians, Ms. Hansberry learned early of evils inflicted on blacks worldwide. Although her somewhat privileged life was not fraught with the strains of survival in America's so-called ghettos, she immersed herself in that world and witnessed its results:

> You stand watching him for a long time. And an old woman comes and stands beside you and she asks you what was wrong with him, such a strong, young man. You tell her he was killed, shot. The cops, she asks – did a cop do it? And you say, yes, it was a cop.... And she shakes her head. He was *very* young, she says.... And she says she guesses it don't

make no difference about going to school then.
And you are quiet.[23]

Her most highly acclaimed work, *A Raisin in the Sun*, has become an American classic. The play concerns itself with the Youngers, a black family having to come to grips with whether to leave the ghetto and integrate into a white neighbourhood, or to take money from a white representative of that neighbourhood and 'stay in their place'.

The conflicting views of each member of the family charge the action and it is not until the very end of the play that we know what that decision will be:

Ruth: Lena, no! We gotta go. Bennie – tell her.... Tell her we can still move.... We got four grown people in this house – we can work.... I'll work twenty hours a day in all the kitchens in Chicago... I'll strap my baby on my back if I have to and scrub all the floors in America... but we got to move.... We got to get out of here.... What did you call that man for, Walter Lee?

Walter: Called him to tell him to come over to the show. Gonna put on a show for the man.... You see, Mama, the man came here today and he told us that them people out there where you want us to move – well they so upset they willing to pay us not to move out there.

Ruth: You talking 'bout taking them people's money to keep us from moving in that house?

Walter: I ain't talking 'bout it, baby – I'm telling you that's what's going to happen.

Mama: Son – I come from five generations of people who was slaves and sharecroppers – but ain't nobody in my family never let nobody pay 'em no money that was a way of telling us we wasn't fit to walk the earth. We ain't never been that poor. We ain't never been that dead inside.[24]

Hansberry's deft orchestration of a variety of complex themes adds to the richness of the play: portrayal of the African-American family, their lifestyles, speech-patterns, wit and strength coupled with theories of Pan-Africanism.

In a letter to her mother, Lorraine Hansberry explains what she hoped to achieve by writing *A Raisin in the Sun*:

Mama, it is a play that tells the truth about people, Negroes and life and I think it will help a lot of people to understand how we are just as

complicated as they are... but above all, that we have among our
miserable and downtrodden ranks – people who are the very essence of
human dignity.[25]

Lorraine Hansberry's short life left many projects incomplete, among
these the African play she was working on when she died, *Les Blancs* – a
powerful response to Jean Genêt's *Les Nègres*. Her ex-husband, Robert
Nemiroff prepared this for production in 1970 and also adapted segments of
her letters, essays and unfinished works into an 'autobiography': *To Be
Young, Gifted and Black* (1969). Although Adrienne Rich questions this
'major lens through which Hansberry's life has been viewed',[26] it is still an
exciting glimpse of her rich talents and profound dedication to her people.

Praised by many and criticized by others, Lorraine Hansberry's work
elicits controversy and celebration. It is unfair to judge while there is so
much to be discovered from her unavailable papers. Mama, from *A Raisin in
the Sun*, sagely suggests:

> When you starts measuring somebody, measure him right, child,
> measure him right. Make sure you done taken into account what hills
> and valleys he come through before he got to wherever he is....[27]

•   •   •

The life of African-Americans in an urban setting is only one of the many
areas that Margaret Walker (1915 –), poet and novelist, incorporates in her
sweeping work, *For My People* (1942). This work chronicles the history of
blacks from rural slavery to city tenements. Ms. Walker won the Yale
Younger Poets Award for it, the first black person to do so.

In this volume, Ms. Walker experiments with modern and traditional
poetic forms, many based on black jazz and blues rhythms. In it, she speaks
for all the suffering and joy that blacks have experienced in America:

> For my people everywhere singing their slave songs repeatedly; their
>   dirges and their ditties and their blues and jubilees, praying their
>   prayers nightly to an unknown god, bending their knees humbly to
>   an unseen power;
>
> . . . .
>
> For my people lending their strength to the years, to the gone years
>   and the now years and the maybe years, washing ironing cooking
>   scrubbing sewing mending hoeing plowing digging planting

pruning patching dragging along never gaining never reaping never
knowing and never understanding;

. . . .

For my people thronging 47th Street in Chicago and Lenox Avenue
in New York and Rampart Street in New Orleans, lost disinherited
dispossessed and happy people filling the cabinets and taverns and
other people's pockets needing bread and shoes and milk and land
and money and something – something all our own; 28

Ms. Walker not only gives a grand panorama of the lives of blacks in the
United States, but sharply focuses on the significance of black women's
history and endurance:

My grandmothers were strong.
They followed plows and bent to toil.

. . . .

They touched earth and grain grew.
They were full of sturdiness and singing.

. . . .

My grandmothers are full of memories

. . . .

With veins rolling roughly over quick hands
They have many clean words to say.
My grandmothers were strong.
Why am I not as they?29

In a conversation with the poet Nikki Giovanni, Margaret Walker
identifies the base line for all her writing:

In anything I write, you can expect my main character will be a
woman. I'm interested in the black woman and feel that the black
woman's story has not been told, has not been dealt with adequately.30

In her novel, *Jubilee* (1966), Margaret Walker gives a perspective on
Southern life in the nineteenth century very different from that of Margaret
Mitchell's *Gone With The Wind*. The central character is Vyre, a female
slave, and we see plantation life, war and the Reconstruction through her
eyes. By revising the stereotype of *mammy* and *mulatta*, Walker corrects the
false myths that flourish in epic novels of the Civil War, and where a white

writer like Mitchell sees humiliation and defeat, the black writer records the eventual triumph of Emancipation.

In Ms. Walker's other volume of poetry, *Prophets for a New Day* (1970), she looks to the future and captures the spirit of the Civil Rights Movement. She had seen long before, in *For My People*, the inevitable raising of the black fist:

> I can remember wind-swept streets of cities
> on cold and blustery nights, on rainy days;
> heads under shabby felts and parasols
> and shoulders hunched against a sharp concern;
> seeing hurt bewilderment on poor faces,
> smelling a deep and sinister unrest
> these brooding people cautiously caress;
> hearing ghostly marching on pavement stones
> and closing fast around their squares of hate.[31]

5: Birth in a Narrow Room

> *Being you, you cut your poetry from wood.*
> *The boiling of an egg is heavy art.*
> *You come upon it as an artist should,*
> *With rich-eyed passion, and with straining heart. . . .*[1]

Black people settled into the madness of ghetto life after the Second World War and imbued it with as much inventiveness as they could. Angry and astonished that white American society still relegated them to second-class citizenship, even after losing life and limb in the war, they summoned their energies to bring magic to a mundane, maligned existence.

Charlie Parker and others played a new music, 'be-bop', with the wizardry of sorcerers. It was a music to stun, to show that the 'minstrel' days were over and that black music was no longer to be mimicked. Black musicians turned their backs on 'entertainment' and played the blues with a new urgency and complexity. It was an African-American art form, distinct and defiant.

And into these days of an emergent black art, came the first African-American to receive the Pulitzer Prize: the poet, Gwendolyn Brooks.

Gwendolyn Brooks, born in Topeka, Kansas in 1917, wrote about the beauty and bewilderment of America's post World War II urban blacks with compassion, poetic innovation and a sharp, sensitive eye.

Her highly stylized work has always been concerned with 'plain black folks'. Initially using Western poetic traditions, she infused these forms with the sounds, colours, confusions, dilemmas and dreams of the city-dwelling black American. She heightened the events of everyday life with the African belief that each task in living requires artistry. And in her later works, instead of putting black 'content' into white literary forms, she evolved new structures from African-American oral tradition.

In her first volume of poetry, *A Street In Bronzeville* (1945), Gwendolyn Brooks delved deeper into black urban life than the 'realists' and 'naturalists' of the period. We are aware of the racism that these people encounter, but we are also involved with their dreams, their imaginations. As we become acquainted with the characters in *A Street In Bronzeville*, their habits, foibles and fears are closely examined. We know not only who they are, but in effect, how the restrictions of racism have made them that way.

> We are things of dry hours and the involuntary plan,
> Grayed in, and gray. 'Dream' makes a giddy sound, not
>   strong
> Like 'rent', 'feeding a wife', 'satisfying a man'.
>
> But could a dream send up through onion fumes
> Its white and violet, fight with fried potatoes
> And yesterday's garbage ripening in the hall,
> Flutter, or sing an aria down these rooms
>
> ....
>
> We wonder. But not well! not for a minute!
> Since Number Five is out of the bathroom now,
> We think of lukewarm water, hope to get in it.[2]

In this work, we meet domestic employers, whores, lonely old people, women at the beauty parlour, battered black American soldiers; we are witness to wife-beatings, funerals and the emotional devastation of an abortion. We are aware that Brooks inhabits this world of 'Bronzeville' and feels its pain, fury and hopelessness:

> Abortions will not let you forget.
> You remember the children you got that you did not
>   get,
> The damp small pulps with a little or with no hair,
> The singers and workers that never handled the air.
>
> ....
>
> Believe me, I loved you all.
> Believe me, I knew you, though faintly, and I loved, I
>   loved you
> All.[3]

The poetic styles of *A Street In Bronzeville* range from the sonnet to the blues. The use of the ballad and the Negro spiritual is also evident, giving depth and dignity to a seemingly simple story:

He was born in Alabama.
He was bred in Illinois.
He was nothing but a
Plain black boy.

Swing low swing low sweet sweet chariot.
Nothing but a plain black boy.[4]

This poem, 'of De Witt Williams on his way to Lincoln Cemetery' is a dirge for every young black man whose life has been denied. As we join the funeral procession, his past life becomes vivid and engaging:

Don't forget the Dance Halls–
Warwick and Savoy,
Where he picked his women, where
He drank his liquid joy.

Born in Alabama.
Bred in Illinois.
He was nothing but a
Plain black boy.

Swing low swing low sweet sweet chariot.
Nothing but a plain black boy.[5]

Living among poor blacks, Gwendolyn Brooks often witnessed a confused people, brainwashed, berated and hating their skin colour. In 'the ballad of chocolate Mabbie', we see the hopes of a black girl shattered by her own kind:

It was Mabbie without the grammar school gates.
And Mabbie was all of seven.
And Mabbie was cut from a chocolate bar.
And Mabbie thought life was heaven.

She waits for a young man who is to meet her after school:

Out came the saucily bold Willie Boone.
It was woe for our Mabbie now.
He wore like a jewel a lemon-hued lynx
With sand-waves loving her brow.

It was Mabbie alone by the grammar school gates.
Yet chocolate companions had she:
Mabbie on Mabbie with hush in the heart.
Mabbie on Mabbie to be.[6]

In another poem, the anxiety of having 'bad' hair is made lucid:

Gimme an upsweep, Minnie,
With humpteen baby curls.
'Bout time I got some glamour.
I'll show them girls.

Think they so fly a-struttin'
With they wool a-blowin' 'round.
Wait till they see my upsweep.
That'll jop 'em back on the ground.

. . . .

Long hair's out of style anyhow, ain't it?
Now it's tie it up high with curls.
So gimme an upsweep, Minnie.
I'll show them girls.[7]

In Ms. Brooks's earlier poetry, we feel a tension between the idiom and
the European poetic framework. Black critics of the time argued that the
content did not fit the form, but this contrast often made for exceptionally
taut writing. For, by juxtaposing the two, we see the division between the
black world and the white. Telescopic attention to the detail of the lives of
her people set against formal structure made a startling statement. Witness
these excerpts from 'The Sundays of Satin-Legs Smith':

Now, at his bath, would you deny him lavender
or take away the power of his pine?
What smelly substitute, heady as wine,
Would you provide? life must be aromatic.

. . . .

A bit of gentle garden in the best tradition? Maybe so.
But you forget, or did you ever know,
His heritage of cabbage and pigtails,
Old intimacy with alleys, garbage pails.

. . . .

Let us proceed. Let us inspect, together

. . . .

The innards of this closet. Which is a vault
Whose glory is not diamonds, not pearls,

. . . .

But wonder-suits in yellow and in wine,
Sarcastic green and zebra-striped cobalt.

. . . .

Ballooning pants that taper off to ends
Scheduled to choke precisely.
                      Here are hats
Like bright umbrellas; and hysterical ties
Like narrow banners for some gathering war.[8]

In 1949, Gwendolyn Brooks was awarded the Pulitzer Prize for her second volume of poetry, *Annie Allen*. Du Bois' 'two warring souls in one body'[9] become evident, as Ms. Brooks tries to reconcile the expectations of a white literary world with an honest representation of her people. She remained committed and concerned, but this volume's highly formalized poetic structure all but alienated her from the people she wrote about. Yet within this collection there are still references to the oral traditions of African-Americans:

Lay it on lightly, lay it on with heed.
Because it took that stuff so long to grow.[10]

Annie Allen is divided into three sections. In 'Notes From the Childhood And The Girlhood', we learn of young Annie's home, parents and the moral lessons she must learn. The second section, 'The Anniad' is a long 'mock-heroic' poem in rhymed, seven-line stanzas that describes Annie's maturing into young adulthood. This section ends with a new invention of Gwendolyn Brooks, the sonnet-ballad, Shakespearean in its rhythm and feel. The last section, entitled 'Womanhood' bears a similarity in theme and construction to *A Street In Bronzeville*.

The opening poem prepares us for a more concentrated reading than that of her previous work. Here, she sets the tenor of the life of a little black girl growing up somewhere in America:

Weeps out of western country something new.
Blurred and stupendous. Wanted and unplanned.
  Winks. Twines, and weakly winks

. . . .

Now, weeks and years will go before she thinks
'How pinchy is my room! how can I breathe!

> I am not anything and I have got
> Not anything, or anything to do!'[11]

In 'The Anniad', Gwendolyn Brooks skilfully portrays an adolescent's painful realization of the unjust world that erodes the promise of her youth, leaving her only with the burden and bafflement of blackness:

> Think of sweet and chocolate,
> Left to folly or to fate,
> Whom the higher gods forgot,
> Whom the lower gods berate;
> Physical and underfed
> Fancying on the featherbed
> What was never and is not.
>
> . . . .
>
> Think of thaumaturgic lass
> Looking in her looking-glass
> At the unembroidered brown;
> Printing bastard roses there;
> Then emotionally aware
> Of the black and boisterous hair,
> Taming all that anger down.[12]

Without shrill statements or polemical poses, the rage and disillusionment in this volume are easily apparent. Gwendolyn Brooks's ability to observe without sentimentality or bitterness, as well as her capacity to engage with the subject, governs the writing and makes evident her artistry.

In the last section, 'Womanhood', Gwendolyn Brooks's mastery of fresh and striking combinations, as well as her use of alliteration, signals the beginning of what will mark much of her future poetry:

> First fight. Then fiddle. Ply the slipping string
> With feathery sorcery; muzzle the note
> With hurting love; the music that they wrote
> Bewitch, bewilder. Qualify to sing
> Threadwise. . . .[13]

But further into the poem, her plea to 'the children of the poor', comes in stronger strains, harsher phrases:

> . . .Be remote
> A while from malice and from murdering.
> But first to arms, to armor. Carry hate
> In front of you and harmony behind.[14]

Throughout *Annie Allen*, Gwendolyn Brooks sees racism as the cause of African-American poverty. To counteract these obstacles, blacks must stop searching for 'external' answers and find strength and pride within themselves and each other. Her last words in this volume are a form of protest; a quiet urging:

> ...Rise.
> Let us combine. There are no magic or elves
> Or timely godmothers to guide us. We are lost, must
> Wizard a track through our own screaming weed.[15]

•   •   •

An autobiographical novel... is a better testament, a better thermometer, than a memoir can be. Who, in presenting a 'factual' account, is going to tell the absolute, the inclusive, the horrifying or exquisite, the 'incredible Truth?'... An 'autobiographical novel' is nuanceful, allowing. There's fact-meat in the soup, among the chunks of fancy...[16]

These are the words of Gwendolyn Brooks, from a discussion of her third book, the autobiographical novella, *Maud Martha* (1953). While Brooks's first two volumes were well received and reprinted, *Maud Martha* was widely reviewed, but allowed to go out of print. Mary Helen Washington has suggested that 'it was given the kind of ladylike treatment that assured its dismissal.'[17] It was certainly not taken as seriously as James Baldwin's dramatic account of a young black man's life, *Go Tell It On The Mountain*, which was published in the same year.

Maud Martha lacks the sensational elements of Baldwin's novel. What it gives us instead is a brilliantly poetic treatment of a black girl growing into womanhood in urban America. Brooks carefully explores the rituals and patterns of an ordinary life, the life of the many and examines the racism that is experienced in 'small droplets' rather than in drastic encounters. Life is much of 'make do'[18] and the simple things have great import:

> What she liked was candy buttons, and books, and painted music (deep blue, or delicate silver)... and dandelions.... Yellow jewels for everyday.... She liked their demure prettiness second to their everydayness; for... she thought she saw a picture of herself, and it was comforting to find that what was common could also be a flower....
> And could be cherished![19]

Here was a life untouched, as were most black lives at the time, by the beginnings of integration in America. Concentration is on the black family and community and the limits of Maud's small sphere. Her revelations about herself, her lighter-skinned husband and the 'colour' problems that still beset her world are poignantly presented here:

> But it's my color that makes him mad.... What I am inside, what is really me, he likes okay. But he keeps looking at my color, which is like a wall. He has to jump over it in order to meet and touch what I've got for him. He has to jump away up high in order to see it. He gets awful tired of all that jumping.[20]

Although Maud Martha's life is confining, she helps to create a new one through her imagination. As Barbara Christian notes, no other heroine in black literature thus far, had ever been given this gift.[21] What is often bleak at first glance can spring forth into glorious beauty:

> The school looked solid. Brownish-red brick, dirty cream stone trim. Massive chimney, candid, serious....
> Up the street... blew the children.... It was wonderful. Bits of pink, of blue, white, yellow, green, purple, brown, black, carried by jerky little stems of brown or yellow or brown-black, blew by the unhandsome gray and decay of the double-apartment buildings....[22]

In her daily existence, Maud Martha seasons her life with artistry, sees she is a valuable and unique individual, creating herself:

> What she wanted was to donate to the world a good Maud Martha. That was the offering, the bit of art, that could not come from any other.
> She would polish and hone that.[23]

The momentum of the Civil Rights Movement was gaining national attention, and in her next volume of poetry, *The Bean Eaters* (1960), Gwendolyn Brooks addresses this political situation. 'A Bronzeville Mother Loiters in Mississippi. Meanwhile, A Mississippi Mother Burns Bacon' is a complex response to the murder of Emmett Till, a young black boy who was killed by white racists for whistling at a white woman. His murderers were acquitted.

This long poem is written in free verse but continually alludes to ballad form. That is one of the ways in which Brooks opens up an ironic gap between the romantic imagination of the Mississippi mother and the horrific reality that the Bronzeville mother must experience. For instance, in the fantasy of the white Southern woman, she is a princess and her husband the prince who saves her from the supposed advances of a 'dark villain' – now a lynched black boy:

> Herself: the milk-white maid, the 'maid mild'
> Of the ballad. Pursued
> By the Dark Villain. Rescued by the Fine Prince.
> The Happiness-Ever-After.
> That was worth anything.
> It was good to be a 'maid mild'.
> That made the breath go fast.[24]

In the twisted, sick minds of this couple, fantasy finally fades and reality reveals itself:

> Then a sickness heaved within her. The courtroom Coca-Cola,
> The courtroom beer and hate and sweat and drone,
> Pushed like a wall against her.
>
> . . . .
>
> But a hatred for him burst into glorious flower,
> And its perfume enclasped them – big,
> Bigger than all magnolias.[25]

Gwendolyn Brooks continues this theme in 'The Last Quatrain of the Ballad of Emmett Till'. She also turns her attention to the troubled and violent reaction to integration of Southern schools, in poems such as 'The Chicago Defender Sends a Man to Little Rock'.

Another theme that echoes throughout this volume is black Americans' quest for identity and 'a relief from aimlessness'.[26] She chronicles the various ways her people search for security: flashy clothes, religion, careless living, integration of the races, and identification with white movie stars. These escapes, when pursued to excess, can only lead to failure:

> THE POOL PLAYERS.
> SEVEN AT THE GOLDEN SHOVEL.

> We real cool. We
> Left school. We
>
> Lurk late. We
> Strike straight. We
>
> Sing sin. We
> Thin gin. We
>
> Jazz June. We
> Die soon.[27]

Gwendolyn Brooks has said of these pool players: 'They are supposedly dropouts.... These are people who are ... saying, "Kilroy is here. We *are*." But they're a little uncertain of the strength of their identity.... I want to represent their basic uncertainty.'[28]

Focusing on the 'integrationist' fervour of the times, Ms. Brooks sees little hope in blacks 'escaping' into white neighbourhoods. In 'The Ballad of Rudolph Reed', a black man wants to move his family out of the ghetto where he listens to 'roaches/Falling like fat rain' and into a white suburb. This family is 'oaken' and tough. When they move in, the whites 'would look, with a yawning eye/that squeezed into a slit' and finally they throw a rock into the Reeds' window, wounding Rudolph's daughter, Mabel. He retaliates with a pistol and knife, wounding four white men before he is killed. But the family will not be moved:

> Small Mabel whimpered all night long,
> For calling herself the cause.
> Her oak-eyed mother did no thing
> But change the bloody gauze.[29]

Critics began to see a shift in Gwendolyn Brooks's work during this period. In an interview, George Stavros asked her if her poetry was becoming more 'socially aware'. She responded: 'Many people hated *The Bean Eaters*; such people would accuse me of forsaking lyricism for polemics, despised *The Bean Eaters* because they said it was "getting too social. Watch it, Miss Brooks!"'[30]

By 1968, there was a change in Gwendolyn Brooks's approach to her art, as there was a decided change in the Nation. A strong sense of black nationalism was capturing all African-Americans and Ms. Brooks realized there was a 'whirlwind occurring':

> In 1967 I met some 'new black people' who seemed very different from youngsters I had been encountering.... They seemed proud and so committed to their own people.... The poets among them felt that black poets should write as blacks, about blacks, and address themselves *to* blacks. I had never thought deliberately in such terms....[31]

Gwendolyn Brooks did not 'watch it' and, in *In The Mecca* (1968), her technical skills are used to achieve a more accessible kind of expression. In the tenement houses on which these poems are based, the words of the inhabitants precede her own:

'How many people live here? ... Two thousand? oh, more than that.
There's 176 apartments and some of 'em's got seven rooms and they're
all full.'
    – A MECCAN

'... there's danger in my neighborhood...'
    – RICHARD 'PEANUT' WASHINGTON[32]

We enter the world of 'The Mecca': 'Now the way of the Mecca was on
this wise.'[33] The first poem is an account in free verse, blank verse and rhyme
of Mrs. Sallie Smith's search for her missing daughter, Pepita, and the
various neighbours that she meets in 'The Mecca' in her attempt to find her.
Some stand strong against the difficulties of life in this tenement, while
others are lost, unconcerned, driven-down and obsessive. 'Way-out
Morgan' who collects guns, is readying himself for 'the Day of Debt-pay',
preparing to avenge the many injustices in his life: the lawless beatings, and
the mob-rape of his sister in Mississippi. There is also 'The prophet', who
promotes a fanatical religion, and Edie Barrow, who laments the loss of her
white boyfriend. Few care about the lost child; they have their own ravaged
dreams to contend with. And the family of Sallie Smith struggle with the
strain of poverty, loss and longing:

> And they are constrained. All are constrained.
>   And there is no thinking of grapes or gold
>   or of any wicked sweetness and they ride
>   upon fright and remorse and their stomachs
>   are rags or grit.[34]

We find that Pepita has been killed by a 'Meccan' and is lying under a cot 'in
dust with roaches'. Ms. Brooks's summation of these events gives credence
to her compassion and craft:

> She never went to kindergarten.
> She never learned that black is not beloved.
> Was royalty when poised,
> sly, at the A and P's fly-open door.
> Will be royalty no more.
> 'I touch' – she said once – 'petals of a rose.
> A silky feeling through me goes!'
> Her mother will try for roses.[35]

But rising out of saddened, stilled dreams, comes the voice of a new black poet:

> Don Lee wants
> not a various America.
> Don Lee wants
> a new nation
> under nothing;
>
> . . . .
>
> wants
> new art and anthem; will
> want a new music screaming in the sun.[36]

In the second half of the work, there are poems dedicated to civil rights causes and leaders; Medgar Evers, Malcolm X: 'Original./Ragged-round./Rich-robust.'[37] In 'Two Dedications' there is a parallel drawn between two types of 'art' and two types of 'lives'. 'The Chicago Picasso' is experienced thus:

> But we must cook ourselves and style ourselves for Art, who
> is a requiring courtesan.
> We squirm.
> We do not hug the Mona Lisa.
> We
> may touch or tolerate . . .[38]

In contrast, 'The Wall' depicts the unveiling of a black neighbourhood mural:

> Black
> boy-men on roofs fist out 'Black Power!
> Women in wool hair chant their poetry.
>
> . . . .
>
> All
> worship the Wall.[39]

Gwendolyn Brooks's resonant reshaping of her art and her life can be experienced in this volume when she says:

> This is the urgency: Live!
>
> . . . .

It is lonesome, yes. For we are the last of the loud.
Nevertheless, live.

Conduct your blooming in the noise and whip of the whirlwind.[40]

In the Mecca was the last of her books to be published by Harper and Row, with whom Brooks had a twenty-three year association. From now on, her work would be published by the black-owned Broadside Press.

During these years, she started a poetry workshop in Chicago with a group of young people, including gang youths, college students and teen-age organizers of the area. This, along with her trips to Kenya, Tanzania and Ghana, in the early seventies, helped to strengthen her sense of the disparity between the lives of African-Americans and Africans. Although Harper and Row continued to express interest in her writing, Gwendolyn Brooks made a conscious decision to work within a black context. She also acknowledged the difficulty of having African-American literature assessed by the uninformed:

How are you going to force white critics to learn enough about us? Most of them have *no* interest in us or our work. So how are you going to make them sensitive?[41]

In 1969 *Riot* was published by Broadside Press. A tremendous change in style is apparent and an urgency of message is in the forefront. There is daring and defiance here:

But, in a thrilling announcement, on It drove
and breathed on him: and touched him. In that breath
the fume of pig foot, chitterling and cheap chili,
malign, mocked John. . . .

John Cabot went down in the smoke and fire
and broken glass and blood, and he cried 'Lord!
Forgive these nigguhs that know not what they do.'[42]

In 1970 another book of verse, *Family Pictures*, appeared, and in 1972, her autobiography, *Report From Part One*. Nellie McKay has remarked that: 'Black women autobiographers have always extended the boundaries and modified the patterns within the black male tradition . . . to leave their own mark on African-American narrative.'[43] This is certainly true of *Report from Part One*. It is prefaced by tributes from two writers who were both friends of Gwendolyn Brooks, George Kent and Don L. Lee (Haki Madubuti). From this starting point, Brooks's inventive re-workings of autobiographical narrative take it in highly original directions. Skilfully constructed, lean and concise, it consists of various sections covering the fifty-five years of her life. From childhood remembrances (including her own mother's account of Gwendolyn's childhood written as she felt 'Gwen' would have seen it), to her 'African Fragment' (a look at Ms. Brooks's confrontation with her homeland), Gwendolyn Brooks emerges as a new woman with a heightened political consciousness. Also included are three interviews, photographs of family and friends, and the book concludes with the appendices 'Marginalia' and 'Collage'.

Although this is an autobiography, its presentation is not only of *self*, but of the black communal *family* as well. Her commitment to a 'one-ness', a 'wholeness', of the African-American family and community is witnessed throughout. And although she sympathizes with the white feminist movement, she has cautioned 'black women not to "turn on" black men.' 'Blacks', she writes, 'need *all* their strength – male and female, *operating together*.'[44] Nevertheless, she acknowledges the importance of identity and individualism for the black American woman:

> Black Woman must remember, through all the prattle about walking or not walking three steps behind or ahead of her 'male', that her personhood precedes her femalehood; that, sweet as sex may be, she cannot endlessly brood on Black Man's blonds, blues, and blunders. She is a person in the world – with wrongs to right, stupidities to outwit, *with* her man when possible, on her own when not. She will be there, like any other, once only. Therefore she must, in the midst of tragedy and hatred and neglect, in the midst of her own efforts to purify, mightily enjoy the readily available: sunshine and pets and children and conversation and games and travel (tiny or large) and books and walks and chocolate cake....[45]

The year 1975 saw another volume of poems: *Beckonings*. In it she urges blacks to become aware of their culture and identity and to cease 'following'. This volume also takes a hard look at the lack of community involvement and the alienation caused by the ravages of racism in urban life:

> The Boy died in my alley
> without my Having Known.
> Policeman said, next morning,
> 'Apparently died Alone.'
>
> 'You heard a shot?' Policeman said.
> Shots I hear and Shots I hear.
> I never see the Dead.

. . . .

I have known this Boy before, who
ornaments my alley.
I never saw his face at all.
I never saw his futurefall.
But I have known this Boy.[46]

Gwendolyn Brooks's new role as a poet was to be an integral part of the community, going to public places where she could speak directly to the people:

I want to write poetry that will appeal to many, many blacks, not just the blacks who go to college but also those who have their customary habitat in taverns and the street.[47]

In a recent interview with Claudia Tate, we learn she is ready to do just that: 'I write my poems on scraps of paper because I want to carry them. . . . I'm likely to read them at a moment's notice.'[48]

Gwendolyn Brooks's style of poetic presentation has altered dramatically in her writing career, but her compassion for the lives of blacks has always been constant. Her hopes for the future of African-Americans lies in the entire black community, whom she addresses with outstretched arms:

I tell you
I love You
and I trust You.
Take my Faith.
Make of my Faith an engine.
Make of my Faith
A Black Star. I am Beckoning.[49]

6: Black Talk, Black Judgement

Nigger
Can you kill
Can a nigger kill a honkie

. . . .

Can you kill nigger
Huh?

. . . .

A nigger can die
We ain't got to prove we can die
We got to prove we can kill
Can you kill

. . . .

Can you kill the nigger
in you[1]

It was the 1960s and the American nation was in turmoil. African-Americans were fuelled with fury as they sang, marched, picketed, rioted and died for freedoms not yet afforded them. On the hundredth anniversary of the Emancipation Proclamation of 1863, black people cried out for change and they wanted it NOW. Still oppressed, black Southerners suffered from separate and unequal schools and segregated public facilities and transportation. Unemployment for African-Americans was at a critical level. Black urban neighbourhoods were overcrowded and their inhabitants undernourished. Martin Luther King, Jr., Baptist minister and advocate of Gandhi's theories of non-violent resistance, became the leader of the Civil Rights Movement. The white Southerners' response to organized 'sit-ins', 'bus-boycotts' and 'freedom marches' by both blacks and whites, was to startle the nation and the world. Children were bombed, beaten, hosed and attacked by dogs. Thousands were jailed and many killed.

Sirens seared the hot summer air as cities burned: WATTS HARLEM BEDFORD-STUYVESANT PATERSON ELIZABETH PHIL-ADELPHIA CHICAGO ATLANTA BOSTON TAMPA CINCINNATI BUFFALO MEMPHIS CLEVELAND MIAMI. Screams of horror went up as the country's leaders, both black and white, were felled by assassinations. With the loss of John F. Kennedy, Malcolm X, Martin Luther King and Robert Kennedy, it became all too apparent that the way to freedom was not to be found in 'the law of the land' or by turning the other cheek.

The time of integration was over. A new 'Black Nationalism' arose and challenged assimilationist beliefs. Malcolm X, leader of the Black Muslims, had preached self-sufficiency and separatism. Black people returned to their communities, their roots, to Africa. New pride in 'Blackness' was apparent everywhere: Afros, dashikis, beads, the taking of African names, 'soul food' and the need to 'legitimize' black values and the lives of common black people. Aretha Franklin sang 'Respect' and 'Ain't No Way For Me To Love You' and James Brown set the rhythm and tone: 'Say It Loud, I'm Black And I'm Proud'. 'A Change Is Gonna Come' came and African-Americans looked for new ways to define themselves and to combat the racist injustices still rife throughout the land.

African-American artists and intellectuals returned to 'the streets' to address the concerns of their people. They set up their own theatres, journals and publishing houses. Poetry became the means by which these artists reached the African-American masses. It was a poetry for the urban black, with an emphasis on oral traditions and a decided polemical stance. Impervious to white critics, blacks looked to themselves for approval and affirmation. As Gwendolyn Brooks stated in her introduction to *Jump Bad, A New Chicago Anthology*, 'True black writers speak as blacks, *about* blacks, to blacks.... They give to the ghetto gut.'[2]

The 'Revolution' had begun. The Black Panthers advocated self-defence and picked up guns, and black 'revolutionary' poets picked up their pens:

> let uh revolution come. uh
> state of peace is not known to me
> anyway

. . . .

> where pee wee cut lonnel fuh fuckin wid
> his sistuh and blood baptized the street
> at least twice ev'ry week and judy got
> kicked outa grammar school fuh bein pregnant
> and died trying to ungrow the seed

. . . .

let uh revolution come.
couldn't be no action like what
i dun already seen.[3]

The revolution was not just in politics but in poetic language. Early in the century, the modernist revolution had overthrown traditional poetic forms in favour of free verse. In the fifties and sixties, white Beat poets, influenced by jazz, had turned poetry from an academic pursuit into a performance art. Black poets not only injected political content into these new forms, but adapted them to black talk. In the poem just quoted, we see spelling that imitates pronunciation, as in 'uh' for *a*, or 'wid' for *with*. Also, the omission of capital letters and punctuation signifies the poet's rebellion against grammatical convention.

Black vocabulary was also used in deliberate reflection of the way people spoke. The speech was there for a reason: 'The "jive" language... while presented in a way that whites look upon simply as a quaint ethnic peculiarity, is used as a secret language to communicate the hostility of blacks for whites, and a great delight is taken by blacks when whites are confounded by the language.'[4] Another critic explains:

Blacks clearly recognized that to master the language of whites was in effect to consent to be mastered by it through the white definitions of caste built into the semantic/social system. Inversion... words and phrases... given reverse meanings and functions [became] the defensive mechanism which enabled blacks to fight linguistic, and thereby psychological entrapment.[5]

This kind of word-play has been used by blacks for centuries, and is part of the story-teller's art. 'Folk Fable', a poem by Jewel Latimore (Johari Amini) (1935 –), uses the technique to comment on past, present and future, all within the same narrative framework.

but the niggas wadn't hip & wadn't hipped
until they was copped.
too.
to work in the mines on the moon

. . . .

& the ships has promises had names

. . . .

like JESUS & HEAVEN & FREEDOM
to take the niggas to a new world

. . . .

> when they was shipped to the moon
> mainland sold
> to companies who
> was biddin
>
> . . . .
>
> the chasemanhattan bank
> supervised the auctions[6]

When Ms. Latimore speaks of 'the niggas' being 'copped' (taken) to 'work in the mines on the moon', she is not only making reference to America's recent landing on the moon (1969), but that there in the future, as now here on earth, the same racist, hierarchical system would be set up. The word 'ships' immediately takes us back to the slavers that brought Africans to the 'New World'. And the reference to the stock market brings to mind the slave auctions. The implication is that blacks continue to be bought and sold by corporate capitalism. By using this 'time-play', her message to African-Americans is that, unless the system is changed, they will forever remain in 'slavery'.

Carolyn Rodgers (1942 –) has commented: 'Black poetry is becoming what it has always been but has never quite *beed*.'[7] She also sets out the categories: 'signifying, teachin'/rappin', covers-off, spaced (spiritual), bein' (self-reflective), love, shoutin' (angry/cathartic), jazz, du-wah and pyramid (getting us together/building/nationhood).'[8] Thus, the blues, the shout, the field-holler, the rhythms of jazz, the rappin', the dozens, the double-entendre, black urban English and all other aspects of African-American cultural life were embodied in the poetry of the sixties.

Poets gathered in taverns, on street corners, in parks, at universities and anywhere else they could readily reach the people. Mari Evans, in 'Vive Noir!' wrote for the voices of thousands:

> i
> am going to rise
> en masse
> from Inner City
> > sick
> > of newyork ghettos
> > chicago tenements
> > I a's slums
>
> . . . .
>
> > I'm tired
> > of hand me downs
> > shut me ups

> pin me ins
> keep me outs
>
> . . . .
>
>   now
>   i'm
> gonna breathe fire
> through flaming nostrils BURN
>   a place for
>
>   me[9]

This poem shares Rodgers's sense in 'let uh revolution come', that the future can be no worse than the past, but Evans is determined to make a space for positive change. Poetry was recognized as a means of raising consciousness, and even women who did not identify themselves primarily as writers used poetry as a form of self-expression. Here is Erika Huggins, one of the leaders of the Black Panther Party, in her 'Poems from Prison':

> tall
> skinny
> plain i am
> erika, 22,
> fuzzy hair
> droopy eyes
> long feet
>   i love people
>
> . . . .
>
>   love love
> i am a revolutionary
> nothing special
>   one soul
>   one life willing
>   to give it
>   ready to die[10]

● ● ●

Nikki Giovanni (1943–) was the most widely read woman among the revolutionary writers. The feelings of the time found a voice in her:

> Poetry is the culture of a people. We are poets even when we don't write poems; just look at our life, our tenderness, our signifying, our

sermons and our songs.... The new Black Poets, so called, are in line with this tradition. We rap a tale out, we tell it like we see it; someone jumps up maybe to challenge, to agree. We are still on the corner – no matter where we are – and the corner is in fact the fire.... I don't think we younger poets are doing anything significantly different from what we as people have always done. The new black poetry is in fact just a manifestation of our collective historical needs.[11]

Born in Knoxville, Tennessee and growing up in Cincinnati, she was greatly influenced by her grandmother, Louvenia Terrell Watson. Grandmother Watson was an assertive, militant woman who 'had no truck' with the white folks and imbued Nikki with an enduring sense of responsibility to her own people.

Ms. Giovanni entered Fisk University in 1960 and there she founded a chapter of SNCC (Student Non-Violent Coordinating Committee) and also took part in the Fisk Writers Workshop, directed by the highly respected black author, John O. Killens.

From these community involvements came her first two published volumes of poetry: *Black feeling, Black talk* (1967) and *Black judgement* (1968). The first book contains works of black consciousness-raising and homages to African-Americans who aided in her development as a writer. This poem uses alliteration and chanting to get her message across:

> Bitter Black Bitterness
> Black Bitter Bitterness
> Bitterness Black Brothers
> Bitter Black Get
> Blacker Get Bitter
> Get Black Bitterness
> NOW[12]

Fired with the pent-up anger of generations, Ms. Giovanni wasn't afraid to confront reality as she perceived it. She unequivocally explained why black people 'be's' that way during these difficult times ('honkie' means a white person):

> Honkies always talking 'bout
> Black Folks
> Walking down the streets
> Talking to themselves
> (they say we're high –
> or crazy) –
>
> But recent events have shown
> We know who we're talking
> to[13]

Her hard-hitting rhetoric struck home. It was out front, not circuitous or oblique. The people understood and responded. But there were still those who wanted to play it 'safe'. Sometimes reproachful, Ms. Giovanni would confront these 'jivers and shuckers': 'The Black Revolution is passing you by negroes...', she writes, 'Tomorrow was too late to properly arm yourself....'[14]

Although much of the volume contained words of a 'fighting spirit', often a lament could be heard within the protests, a song of sorrow, of loss:

it's so hard to love
people
who will die soon

the sixties have been one
long funeral day
....

it's so easy to love
Black Men
they must not die anymore

and we must not die
with america[15]

Not all of Nikki Giovanni's poetry in this volume is imbued with anger, pain and rage. Her ability to see humour, enabled her 'to laugh to keep from cryin', as in this imaginary love-scene between herself and a 'brother':

one day
you gonna walk in this house

....

you'll sit down and say 'The Black...'

....

while i rest your hand against my stomach
you'll go on – as you always do – saying
'I just can't dig...'
while i'm moving your hand up and down
and i'll be taking your dashiki off

....

and i'll be licking your arm

....

and unbuckling your pants

. . . .

and taking your shorts off
then you'll notice
your state of undress
and knowing you you'll just say
'Nikki,
isn't this counterrevolutionary . . .?'[16]

In her second volume, *Black judgement*, we begin to see the germination of ideas that Ms. Giovanni will sustain in later works: the conflict of the public, political self versus the private, artistic one. We find here a more introspective African-American woman, reassessing and re-evaluating her life. In one instance, she shows that black poverty doesn't necessarily equal black misery:

childhood remembrances are always a drag
if you're Black

. . . .

and if you become famous or something
they never talk about how happy you were to have
your mother
all to yourself

. . . .

because they never understand
Black love is Black wealth[17]

But her youthful reminiscences could not override the urgency of the times. In an answer to an acquaintance's query as to why Nikki didn't write poems about nature and 'odes' to love, Ms. Giovanni replied:

i wanted to write
a poem
that rhymes

. . . .

maybe i shouldn't write
at all
but clean my gun
and check my kerosene supply

perhaps these are not poetic
times
at all[18]

These first two volumes placed Nikki Giovanni, along with Don L. Lee
and Sonia Sanchez, in the limelight of critical acclaim of the new black
poetry. There were some African-American critics that deemed it 'hate'
poetry, but for the most part, it was praised by the black populace.

Her third work, *Re-Creation,* resembled her two previous collections, with
major emphasis on black revolution. Yet one begins to see the emergence of a
more profound questioning of self within the framework of the black
revolution:

i used to dream militant
dreams
. . . .
i used to dream radical dreams
. . . .
then i awoke and dug
that if i dreamed natural
dreams of being a natural
woman doing what a woman
does when she's natural
i would have a revolution[19]

As Suzanne Juhasz observes, '"Militant" and "radical" are poised here
against "natural".... Somehow the black woman must be true to herself as
she *is* to be both a poet and a revolutionary, for the nature of the revolution
itself is in question.'[20]

Her fourth book of poetry, *My House,* was published in 1972. There is a
change of direction in this volume that had only been hinted at previously.
Her thoughts turn from external issues to concerns of self, family and home.
As the 'revolution' continued, it sapped energies and saddened hearts. Nikki
Giovanni now wanted peaceful solutions and began to modify her more
offensive position. Here we see her confrontation with an old white woman
and the emotional response it engenders:

if she weren't such an aggressive bitch she would see
that if you weren't such a Black one
there would be a relationship but anyway – it doesn't matter
much – except you started out to kill her and now find
you just don't give a damn cause it's all somewhat
   of a bore
so you speak of your mother or sister or very good friend

and really you speak of your feelings which are too
    personal
for anyone else
to take a chance on feeling[21]

Nikki Giovanni continued to write poetry; *The Women and the Men*
(1975), *Cotton Candy on a Rainy Day* (1978) and *Those Who Ride the
Nightwinds* (1983).

In *Those Who Ride the Nightwinds*, she employs a new and innovative
poetic form. Much of the volume is written in short paragraphs with
punctuations which are reminiscent of 'telegraphic communication'.

I wrote a good omelet... and ate a
hot poem
after loving you[22]

In 1971, her autobiography, *Gemini: An Extended Autobiographical
Statement on My First Twenty-Five Years of Being a Black Poet* appeared. In
it we find a more individualistic, mature woman. Her creative powers are
honed here, giving us a much more serious look at her life, and her
revolutionary stance. Comprising political, polemical and poetic essays, this
volume has more depth than her earlier works.

The various topics touched upon vary widely, but all encompass Ms.
Giovanni's life and experiences: 'On Being Asked What It's Like To Be
Black', 'A Revolutionary Tale', 'Don't Have a Baby till You Read This', 'A
Spiritual View of Lena Horne', and 'The Weather as a Cultural
Determiner'. Also included are the warm and poignant characterizations of
family members, especially her grandmother, in '400 Mulvaney Street'.

Gemini is Giovanni's continuing search for herself, her coming around to a
more humanist world view: 'The state of the world we live in is so
depressing. And this is not because of the reality of the men who run it but it
just doesn't have to be that way. The possibilities of life are so great and
beautiful that to see less wears the spirit down.'[23] And she recognizes the
creative force that has enabled African-American women to continue in a
world set against their survival:

We black women are the single group in the West intact.... We are,
however (all praises), the only group that derives its identity from
itself. I think it's been rather unconscious but we measure ourselves by
ourselves, and I think that's a practice we can ill afford to lose.[24]

As well as her prolific output of verse, Nikki Giovanni has published two
'conversations', with James Baldwin and Margaret Walker. In these probing
and often explosive talks, we see 'the old and the new' theorists of black life

and literature searching to find a common ground. Margaret Walker's much more pronounced pacifist politics of change are challenged by the young and impatient author: 'It's unacceptable. I wrote a poem once that said, "what 'always is' is not the answer. What never will be, must come." '[25]

●   ●   ●

There were many other poets of the 'Revolution' and one of the most outstanding of the time was Sonia Sanchez (1934 –). Her poetry was like a laser, bringing sharp and startling truths to her readership. In a selection from her first book of poetry, *Homecoming* (1969), Ms. Sanchez chastised all black performers who were more concerned with 'crossing-over' than 'getting-over'. Her particular target here is the black pop group, the Supremes, and she connects the betrayal of their racial origins with the acceptance of white masters:

> the supremes done gone
> and sold their soul
> to tar
>   zan and other
> honky/rapers
>
>   They sing rodgers
>
> and hart songs
> as if we didn't
> have enough andrew
> sisters spitting their
> whiter than mr.
> clean songs in our faces.
> YEAH.
>   the supremes
>
>   done gone
>
> and bleached out
>
>   their blk/ness
> and all that is heard
> is
>   me. tarzan
>   u.   jane
> and
>   bwana.
>   bwana.
>   bwana.[26]

In this poem, Ms. Sanchez also links the sexism of the Tarzan story with the racism of white colonialism. (*Bwana* means master or father in Swahili.)

Poet, educator, activist, playwright, teacher and champion of black causes world-wide, Sonia Sanchez has continually addressed herself to her people, be it by 'revolution' or re-evaluation.

In her earlier works, she states that she owes a great debt to the late Malcolm X. In razor-sharp poetic style, she takes a strong militant stance:

> its time
> > an eye for an eye
> > a tooth for a tooth
> > don't worry bout his balls
> they al
> > > ready gone.
> > > > git the word
> out that us blk/niggers
> > are out to lunch
> and the main course
> is gonna be his white meat.
> > > yeah.[27]

Sonia Sanchez was not only concerned with content and commitment. Often incorporated in her work is the concept of 'sound', which obviously cannot be reproduced here. But, 'to Blk/record/buyers' gives us an idea:

> don't play me no
> righteous bros.
> > white people
> ain't rt. bout nothing
> no mo...
> > > > but
> play blk/songs
> > to drown out the
> shit/screams of honkies
> AAAH. AAAH.   yeah.   AAAH.   brothers.
> > andmanymoretogo.[28]

In the 1960s, Sonia Sanchez joined other political activists, among them, Amiri Baraka, Ed Bullins, Huey Newton, Eldridge Cleaver and Ron Karenga in efforts to change America's higher educational system and helped to introduce 'Black Studies' programmes. She travelled throughout the country giving lectures and readings as testament to her beliefs. As an educator, she has taught at numerous universities in the United States and continues to do so, as well as being a member of various international organizations for the liberation of oppressed peoples.

With twelve volumes of poetry, among them *We A BaddDDD People* (1970), *A Blues Book for Blue Black Magical Women* (1973) and *homegirls & hand grenades* (1984), as well as five plays in print, Sonia Sanchez continues to address problems of black liberation.

She witnesses a new and insidious killer of African-Americans that has come to take the place of lynchings and guns: heroin. The 'killing' continues, but with much more subtlety:

> the first day i shot dope
> was on a sunday.
>
>   i had just come
>
> home from church
>
>   got mad at my mother
>
>   . . . .
>
>   and as the sister
>   sits in her silent/
>   remembered/high
>   someone leans for
>   ward gently asks her:
>   sister.
>   did u
>   finally
>   learn how to hold yr/mother?[29]

As the 'Revolution' gained momentum in the mid-sixties and early seventies, there was the belief that all black men and women were unified in their fight for freedom. But there was an undertone, a feeling of betrayal that black women began to experience in respect to their 'macho-revolutionary' brothers. This new attitude was disturbing and in 1970, Sonia Sanchez, for one, began to question it:

>   Sisters
> git yr/blk/asses
> out of that re/
>   volution/
>   ary's
> bed.
>
> . . . .
>
>   and that so/
> called/brother there
> screwing u in tune to
>   fanon

                    and fanon
        and fanon
                        ain't no re
                                vo/lution/
                                ary

                                    . . . .

    cuz. u show me
    a revolutionary/fuck &
    i'll send my ass   C.O.D.
    to any Revolutionary.
                        u dig?[30]

Within the 'Black Power Movement', it was becoming clear that one of the main concerns of the African-American male was to, as Huey Newton (Minister of Defence, Black Panther Party) proclaimed, 'recapture his balls'.[31] Black women were to understand and console their men. As Eldridge Cleaver (Minister of Information, Black Panther Party) stated, 'I, the Black Eunuch, divested of my Balls, walk the earth with my mind locked in Cold Storage.'[32] This is quite a puzzling statement when we consider his actions in *Soul On Ice* (1969) where he tells us, 'I became a rapist. . . . I started out by practising on black girls in the ghetto . . . – and when I considered myself smooth enough, I crossed the tracks and sought out white prey.'[33] The frustrations and 'denials' experienced by the African-American male, are used here to excuse violence against women that most blacks would censure. However, black women in support of 'their man' would sometimes condone truly questionable behaviour. Artie Seale, a female Black Panther states: 'Black men in our communities are being castrated. . . . Black men have to turn to their families for the release of their frustrations . . . Black men beat their women because they aren't sure who is to blame for their frustration [because] Black men are made to feel less than a man. . . .'[34]

This was the tenor of the times. The black woman was to walk 'ten paces behind her man' and Stokely Carmichael of SNCC said at a 1964 meeting that the 'best position for a woman in the organization was prone.'[35] As Jacqueline Jones observes in *Labor of Love, Labor of Sorrow*, 'too often male Black Power advocates – from activists to scholars – wanted their female kin to get out of the white man's kitchen and back into their own.'[36] Many of the tenets of the Black Muslims were embraced by the Black Panther Party and one of them was that 'baby-making' was essential to ward off the 'genocide' of African-American people. The march of 'Black Manhood' was yet again muffling and marginalizing an already maligned and misrepresented group: African-American women.

Fareedah Allah (Ruby C. Saunders) embraced the beliefs of her black Muslim brothers and changed her 'way of acting' accordingly:

HUSH! YO' MOUTH
IT IS TIME TO BE QUIET
AND SOFT SPOKEN
WELL MANNERED
REFINED
SPEAKING SELDOM
AND ONLY WHEN NECESSARY

. . . .

CLOSE YOUR BIG UGLY MOUTH
CAN'T YOU SEE HOW UGLY YOU BE
YOU'RE BAD   ALRIGHT
YOU LOOK BAD!
YOU SOUND BAD!

YOU MAKE THE MAN FEEL SO SMALL
HE HAS TO KICK YOU   KICK YOU
BEAT YOU   BEAT YOU
LEAVE YOU   LEAVE YOU
LEAVE YOU TO KEEP FROM KILLING
YOU
THE MOTHER OF HIS BABIES[37]

But some African-American women poets had a resounding response to
this submissive posture. They were not ashamed of being seen as 'Sapphire',
the loud-mouthed, gaudily dressed, bossy black woman. Carolyn Rodgers
wrote:

they say,
that i should not use the word
muthafucka anymo

. . . .

they say,
that i must and can only say it to myself
as the new Black Womanhood suggests
a more reserved speaking self. they say
that respect is hard won by a woman
who throws a word like muthafucka around

. . . .

But anyhow, you all know just like i do

. . . .

there's plenty of MEAN muthafuckas out
here trying to do the struggle in and we all know
that none of us can relax until the last m.f.'s
been done in[38]

The schism which had appeared between black men and women was
beginning to widen – African-American women in the movement realized
that they were not only fighting the white male oppressor, but the black male
oppressors as well. Angela Davis explained her own position:

> I ran headlong into a situation which was to become a constant
> problem in my political life. I was criticized very heavily, especially by
> male members...for doing a 'man's job'. Women should not play
> leadership roles, they insisted. A woman was to 'inspire' her man and
> educate his children. The irony of the complaint was that much of
> what I was doing had fallen to me by default.[39]

While the poet Amiri Baraka (Leroi Jones) asserted that 'Nature had
made women submissive, she must submit to man's creation in order for it to
exist'[40], James Baldwin and Nikki Giovanni disputed such assumptions.
Baldwin, along with most of his black brothers, maintained that the woman's
role in this civilization is to 'understand the man's point of view' and aid him
in recapturing his manhood. Nikki's response was: 'Black men say, in order
for me to be a man, you walk ten paces behind me. Which means nothing. I
can walk ten paces behind a dog. . . . If that's what the black man needs, I'll
never get far enough behind for him to be a man. I'll never walk that
slowly.'[41]

The results of the 'Revolution' had not turned out as hoped and posed new
problems for the African-American man and woman to resolve. Although
some political goals were achieved, the air was laden with fatigue and
frustration. Bell Hooks speculated that:

> Black male leaders of the movement made the liberation of black
> people from racist oppression synonymous with their gaining the right
> to assume the role of patriarch, of sexist oppressor. By allowing white
> men to dictate the terms by which they would define black liberation,
> black men chose to endorse sexist exploitation and oppression of black
> women. They were not liberated from the system but liberated to serve
> the system.[42]

Abused, misunderstood, unrecognized and unappreciated, African-
American women suffered a time of questioning and pain. After giving their
lives, their love, their talent and their tenacity, they were relegated to the
'back-bench' or forgotten about entirely. Carolyn Rodgers wrote:

we live with fear.
we are lonely.
we are talented, dedicated, well read
   BLACK, COMMITTED,

we are lonely.

we understand the world problems
Black women's problems with Black men
   but all
we really understand is
   lonely.[43]

In this anguished time of introspection, the African-American writer realized that in order to be 'herself' in the present, she had to re-capture and re-define her past. Most previous representations by white authors and black male writers were suspect and all relationships hindering that process of re-definition, were relinquished. The time of 're-birth' had come:

Not circumstance; history
keeps us apart. I'm black. You black. And
how have niggas proved they men? Fightin
and fuckin as many women as
they can. And even when you can do
all the things a white man do you may
leave fightin behind but fuckin stay
the same.

For us it's havin babies and how
well we treats a man and how long we
keep him. And how long don't really have
that much to do with how well. I just
can't be a woman to yo kinda man.[44]

7: A Deeper Reckoning

The black woman had nothing to fall back on; not maleness, not whiteness, not ladyhood, not anything. And out of the profound desolation of her reality she may very well have invented herself.[1]

The 'Revolution' over, blacks settled into new jobs and old injustices. They nursed their wounds, counted their gains and contemplated their losses. African-Americans entered the corporate world, and white performers aped the sounds of 'black soul music'. The television and movie industries gave blacks new stereotypes: 'bad-assed niggers' like Superfly, while Broadway set the stage for 'good-time' musicals, such as 'Bubbling Brown Sugar' and 'The Wiz'. But with few exceptions, the complexity of African-American women's lives was still not being addressed.

In a town in upstate New York in the late 1960s an African-American woman sat down and wrote a novel about a little black girl who wanted blue eyes. Published in 1970, it was to alter the portrayal of black women in literature.

Toni Morrison, Pulitzer prize winning author, was born Chloe Anthony Wofford, in Lorain, Ohio. Growing up in The Depression, she knew her parents to be strong-willed and self-reliant, and her community a nurturing one. Yet, Ms. Morrison felt the constraints of small town living, and made her way Eastward. She attended Howard University in Washington, DC and then Cornell University for graduate work.

After teaching at Howard and other universities, Ms. Morrison ventured into publishing. As a senior editor for Random House, she aided the careers of several black writers, and while she pursued her editorial career, her first novel emerged.

Toni Morrison was troubled by the representation of black women's lives in the literature of the 'black revolutionary era': 'I felt a sense of loss, a void. Things were moving too fast in the early 1960s–1970s . . . it was exciting but it left me bereft.'[2]

A fair amount of African-American women's writing was being published, but mostly in the 'immediate and accessible' forms of poetry and drama. Few authors had taken on the task of writing about the diverse and complex lives of black women within the black community as well as holding that community responsible for its own actions. Barbara Christian observed that:

> By 1970, when Toni Morrison's *The Bluest Eye* [was] published, black women writers' stance toward their communities had begun to change. The ideology of the sixties had stressed the necessity for Afro-Americans to rediscover their blackness, their unity, in their blackness. As positive as that position was to the group's attempt to empower itself, one side effect was the tendency to idealise the relationship between black men and women, to blame sexism in the black community solely on racism or to justify a position that black men were superior to women.[3]

Ms. Morrison, a voracious reader and astute observer of the lives of her people, gave voice to the black women that had been side-stepped by the writing of the day:

> The writing was a result of a sustained progress of reading. I thought of myself as a reader, not a writer. I wrote it [*The Bluest Eye*] because I had not read it before. There were no books about me. I didn't exist in all of the literature I had read ... When I reached this moment, the writing was important because I had to bear witness to what was not recorded. This person, this female, this black, did not exist 'centre-self'.[4]

Few black writers were confronting the 'interiority' of African-American lives. Many were concerned with addressing a white audience, yet keeping that audience nescient by obscuring the complicated emotional under-pinnings of black life. They contented themselves with a surface depiction of black existence, and this careful stance robbed African-Americans of a more probing and representational literature. Toni Morrison explains:

> It once seemed important in literature to make the best presentations of ourselves so that they, the other, would see us in our best light. For me, it made the literature different in a way. The emotional landscape could not exist if I had in mind as I wrote presenting the best possible front to a mainstream civilization. I was not interested in the perceptions of the mainstream because I knew what they were. What

was interesting to me were the things that were hidden, interiorized, private – having it read by people like me.[5]

Toni Morrison has written all of her books for a black readership, but the writing contains such specificity that all who read her are totally engaged. She has stated: 'I write for black women'[6], and it is the women of her family who have remained a strong and sustaining force for her.

She acknowledges her debt to them:

> I remember my grandmother and my great-grandmother. I had to answer to these women, had to know that whatever I did was easy in comparison with what they had to go through.[7]

They also gave her a special gift: 'They taught me how to dream ... [and] they were interested. ...' This freedom shapes and informs all of Ms. Morrison's writing. Nature stands as a metaphor for human interaction and reality rests comfortably beside the fantastic. And the sense of the storyteller must always be in evidence:

> I have to rewrite, discard and remove the print-quality of language to put back the oral quality where intonation, volume and gesture are there.[8]

> To make a story appear oral, meandering, effortless, spoken – to have the reader *feel* the narrator without *identifying* that narrator or having him knock about and to have the reader work with the author in the construction of the book – is what's important. What is left out is as important as what is there.[9]

Toni Morrison's commitment to her people, their lives and their art is evidenced in all that she has written. Her work stems from the deep realization that she must explore the past and re-address it, in order for African-Americans to understand themselves and the world they live in today:

> If anything I do in the way of writing novels (or whatever I write) isn't about the village or the community or about you, then it is not about anything ... which is to say ... the work must be political. ... It seems to me that the best art is political and you ought to be able to make it unquestionably political and irrevocably beautiful at the same time.[10]

●　　●　　●

> *Pretty eyes. Pretty blue eyes. Big blue pretty eyes . . . Alice has blue eyes.*
> *Jerry has blue eyes. Jerry runs. Alice runs. They run with their blue*
> *eyes. . . . Four pretty blue eyes. Blue-sky eyes. . . . Morning-glory-blue-*
> *eyes. Alice-and-Jerry-blue-storybook-eyes.* [11]

This excerpt from Toni Morrison's first novel, *The Bluest Eye*, is the painful kernel of a black girl's dream of acceptance in a world that does not want her. Pecola Breedlove's aching need to become what she is not is the cord that eventually pulls her into madness.

Toni Morrison's experimental telling of this contemporary fable is done with brilliant impressionistic brush-strokes, bringing not only Pecola's fractured life into focus, but also the lives of her community.

Ms. Morrison begins the novel with her interpretation of a well-known children's primer:

> Here is the house. It is green and white. It has a red door. It is very pretty. Here is the family. Mother, Father, Dick and Jane live in the green-and-white house. They are very happy.[12]

As we continue reading, the words are repeated, but are now placed on the page to signify a state of confusion and incoherency:

> Hereisthehouseitisgreenandwhiteithasareddooritisverypretty.[13]

The incomprehensibility of this passage signals the blurred and battered sense of self-worth experienced by the Breedloves, and in varying degrees the community itself:

> The Breedloves did not live in a storefront because they were having temporary difficulty adjusting to the cutbacks at the plant. They lived there because they were poor and black, and they stayed there because they believed they were ugly.[14]

Toni Morrison divides each section of the book into the four seasons, Autumn, Winter, Spring and Summer, 'a child's flow of time'.[15] Within each of these sections, the action that occurs is in direct opposition to what the seasons bring to mind. In this world of 'inversions', 'There were no marigolds in the fall of 1941',[16] and Spring does not hold the promise of youthful budding for Pecola, but the last hopes of blossoming. Her father was a man so unloved he was 'free' to make himself up:

> Cholly was truly free. Abandoned in a junk heap by his mother, rejected for a crap game by his father, there was nothing more to lose. He was alone with his own perceptions and appetites, and they alone interested him.[17]

Powerless and confused, he gives Pecola the only gift of love he has left: he rapes and impregnates her.

This is one of the many examples employed by Ms. Morrison to show how black people's loss of their own sense of self is manifested in a world of reversals; for Mrs. Breedlove, romance is substituted for love and standards of white 'beauty' for worthiness. Living in an industrial mid-western city, she is cut off from a supportive community. Her loss is exemplified in the metaphor of discovering a rotten tooth while watching the 'platinum prettiness' of Hollywood stars on the movie screen:

> *The onliest time I be happy seem like when I was in the picture show . . .*
> *The screen would light up, and I'd move right on in them pictures. White*
> *men taking such good care of they women, and they all dressed up in big*
> *clean houses . . . I 'member one time I went to see Clark Gable and Jean*
> *Harlow. I fixed my hair up like I'd seen hers on a magazine . . . It looked*
> *just like her. Well, almost just like . . . I taken a big bite of that candy, and*
> *it pulled a tooth right out of my mouth . . . There I was . . . trying to look*
> *like Jean Harlow, and a front tooth gone. Everything went then.* [18]

What went was Pauline Breedlove's ability to love or appreciate herself, and therefore her family. Her disengagement with the crying needs of her daughter is portrayed in a scene where Pecola spills a blueberry cobbler onto the clean kitchen floor of her mother's white employer. Pauline's destructive dismissal of her daughter, and the comforting warmth then lavished upon her employer's child, hasten Pecola's quiet descent into madness.

Pecola becomes the pariah of the community, just as blacks are pariahs in a white world. The pivotal character is Pecola, and the voices of the community are but softer echoes of the insanity that finally engulfs her. The townspeople all 'wiped their feet on her', as a means of warding off their own insecurities: Geraldine, in her immaculate middle-class home, who staves off 'funkiness' and blackness; Maureen Peal, the cream-coloured school-mate who thinks herself superior to Pecola, and Soaphead Church, a light-skinned immigrant from the British West Indies who reveres whiteness. His misanthropy for his own kind enables him to understand Pecola's need for 'blue-eyes', for whiteness. As the 'conjure-man' of the town, he 'gives them to her', thereby completing the cycle of her insanity.

The story is told by Claudia, friend of Pecola's and witness to her destruction. She and her sister Frieda are only saved from a similar fate by a strong and supportive family unit.

In *The Bluest Eye*, Toni Morrison weaves a multi-layered vision of a community who have lost their cultural bearings. Circular in construction, the themes appear, then re-appear, to be expanded and played upon, just as jazz musicians approach their music. And like the jazz soloist or black preacher, Ms. Morrison leaves the air expectant after a statement. She says said there were 'spaces and places' for the reader to come in, to participate.[19]

She tells us that:

> The preacher's job was to make me stand up and say something. Jazz musicians and blues singers wanted their audience to respond in some way; it was not a solitary thing that the performers did and the audience received passively.[20]

In this beautiful, disturbing and probing first novel Toni Morrison tells not only the story of a black girl's desperate attempt at self-definition, but also brings out the need for the black community to embrace their own culture and beliefs. For in not doing so, not only do they 'lose' their Pecolas, they lose themselves.

●   ●   ●

> A joke. A nigger joke. That was the way it got started. Not the town, of course, but that part of the town where the Negroes lived, the part they called the Bottom in spite of the fact that it was up in the hills. Just a nigger joke . . .[21]

In Toni Morrison's second novel, *Sula* (1973), we enter the world of the Bottom, the black section of town up in the hills of Medallion, Ohio. Again, we witness a state of reversals. The Bottom, land promised to a slave by his master as a reward of freedom, is the antithesis of its meaning. The master, realizing that the bottom land was fertile and the top land unyielding, tricked the slave into acceptance of the hilly land by stating that 'When God looks down, it's the bottom. That's why we call it so. It's the bottom of heaven – best land there is.'[22]

The basic theme of the work concerns the friendship of two girls growing into womanhood; Sula Peace and Nel Wright. But by framing their story in the community of the Bottom, we have the setting that moulds them into who they are. Once again, the community is the context within which these women search for self-definition. Barbara Christian sees it thus: 'The novel is not only about Nel Wright and Sula Peace, it is most emphatically about the culture that spawns them.'[23] And this culture, this place and the people who inhabit it, give us some of the most intriguing and complex characters to unfold in black American literature. Toni Morrison explained this to Robert Stepto:

> When I wrote *Sula*, I was interested in making the town, the community, the neighborhood, as strong a character as I could without

actually making it 'The Town, they'... because the most extraordinary thing about any group, and particularly our group, is the
fantastic variety of people and things and behavior.[24]

Smoothly, the novel 'spirals' from the years 1919 to 1940, with an epilogue
in 1965. Seemingly chronological, 'time collapses' and events come before
and after the years specified, giving focus to particular events that shape that
year:

The structure then, so apparently neatly defined by the march of time,
by chronological pattern, is always transforming itself, for in fact, we
do not move forward in a straight line... it is as if we were hearing an
African folk-tale – mythological in tone – in which content revitalizes
an empty terminological system. The then is in the now; the now is in
the then; and the teller spins ever-intricate webs of connectiveness...[25]

Throughout the novel, the townspeople grapple with Nature and the
forces of Evil. And Death, in some form, introduces each section of the work.
After the explanation of the 'beginning' and 'ending' of the Bottom, we are
introduced to our first character, Shadrack. Shell-shocked veteran of World
War I, he returns home and 'struggle[s] to order and focus experience' by
'making a place for fear as a way of controlling it.'[26] He does so by yearly
declaring 'National Suicide Day', and, in this act, metaphorically embodies
the townspeople's reaction to life: 'Not to protest God's will but to
acknowledge it and confirm once more their conviction that the only way to
avoid the Hand of God is to get in it.'[27]

In *Sula*, the forces of Nature are essential and are inextricably linked to
life, death and time. Images of water, fire, earth and wind pervade the novel
and are signals or omens of events as well as relating to the personalities of
characters. An example of this can be seen in Sula, who is often portrayed in
relationship to water. When Toni Morrison said in an interview that she
herself was a 'conduit'[28] for the tales of the tribe, she spoke in earnest. In
choosing the name Sula, she just thought it 'was a nice colored girl's name',[29]
only to find out from the Africanist Melville Herscovitz that in Tui (a dialect
of the Ashanti language) 'Sula' means water.

To the community of the Bottom, the force of 'Evil' was not to be worked
with, nor were attempts made to alter it; it was to be survived:

In spite of their fear, they reacted to an oppressive oddity, or what they
called evil days, with an acceptance that bordered on welcome. Such
evil must be avoided, they felt, and precautions must naturally be
taken to protect themselves from it. But they let it run its course, fulfill

itself, and never invented ways either to alter it, to annihilate it or to prevent its happening again. So also were they with people.[30]

But rather than focus on the 'Evil' that denied them their rights and removed them from full entrance into a larger society, they located it in a character who, arguably, is one of the most thought-provoking and controversial heroines ever to emerge in American literature: Sula Peace.

Born into a household where 'women simply loved maleness, for its own sake',[31] Sula comes from a line of decidedly non-conformist women. Her grandmother, Eva Peace, is a domineering woman who gave life and took it away. Forced to take drastic measures to save her children from starvation after her husband has abandoned them, she purposely loses a leg on the railroad track in order to collect insurance. And, witnessing her son succumb to heroin addiction, burns him to death rather than have him 'crawl back in [her] womb'.[32] But her actions bring disastrous reactions, for her daughter Hannah accidentally burns to death.

Sula, branded as different, born with 'a birthmark that spread from the middle of the lid toward the eyebrow, shaped something like a stemmed rose', lives free to become all and anything in a world of chaos:

> Sula... wedged into a household of throbbing disorder constantly awry with things, people, voices and the slamming of doors, spent hours in the attic behind a roll of linoleum galloping through her own mind.[33]

Finding in her friend Nel Wright the opposite of her own existence, she is drawn to the differences. But there was a special knowledge they both shared:

> Because each had discovered years before that they were neither white nor male, and that all freedom and triumph was forbidden to them, they had set about creating something else to be.[34]

As Sula grows into womanhood, she fights against the prescribed role for black women of the community to 'make someone else', and because there is no other definition in her life, 'she's like water and assumes the shape of whatever holds her.'[35] Toni Morrison sees this as a metaphor for the talented black woman whose gifts are not taken seriously:

> In a way, her strangeness, her naïveté, her craving for the other half of her equation was the consequence of an idle imagination. Had she paints, or clay, or knew the discipline of dance... had she anything to engage her tremendous curiosity and her gift for metaphor, she might have exchanged the restlessness and preoccupation with whim for an

activity that provided her with all she yearned for. And like any artist with no art form, she became dangerous.[36]

Nel Wright, child of a home where the mother 'drove her daughter's imagination underground',[37] chooses the life expected of her and defines herself only through matrimony and motherhood. Her treasured friendship with Sula is destroyed, as is her marriage, when Sula sleeps with her husband, as she does with all the men in town:

> She went to bed with men as frequently as she could. It was the only place where she could find what she was looking for: misery and the ability to feel deep sorrow.[38]

The townspeople had always tolerated Sula's uniqueness, but because she treated their women's husbands as faceless, nameless non-entities, and because she put her mother in a home, they said that she had done the unpardonable: slept with white men. They armoured themselves against such evil and used her as a scapegoat, but 'did nothing to harm her'.[39]

In Ms. Morrison's view, the concept of the black 'community' is one in which difference is accepted, even if it is not condoned. She explains:

> There is no other place in the world [Sula] could have lived without being harmed. Whatever they [the community] think about Sula, however strange she is to them, however different, they won't harm her. Medallion is a sustaining environment even for a woman who is very different. Nobody's going to lynch her or call the police. They call her bad names and try to protect themselves from her evil; that's all. But they put her to very good use, which is a way of manipulating her.[40]

In one of the most haunting novels of African-American literature, Toni Morrison considers the thwarted freedom of a black woman, a community's fear of change and experimentation, and above all the importance of female friendship. As Ms. Morrison says of Sula: 'When Nel misses her, we miss her.'[41] Nel's belated discovery of Sula's importance to her is a startling and sorrowful cry:

> All that time ... I thought I was missing Jude [her husband]. ... We was girls together ... Oh Lord, Sula, ... girl, girl, girlgirlgirl.'
> It was a fine cry – loud and long – but it had no bottom and it had no top, just circles and circles of sorrow.[42]

This concept of female friendship, unfortunately, was frightening for some. Ms. Morrison elaborates:

> I went someplace to talk about *Sula* and there were some genuinely
> terrified men in the audience, and they walked out on me and told me
> why. They said, 'Friendship between women?' Aghast... You
> wouldn't think anybody grown-up would display his fear quite that
> way.... But it was such a shocking, threatening thing in a book, let
> alone what it would be in life.[43]

Yet Toni Morrison knew that for black women friendship was a vital part
of their lives and must continue to be so:

> The term sister, has a deep old meaning – it was valid, never secondary.
> Black women had to be real and genuine to each other, there was no
> one else.... There was a profound and real need there [pre-Agency
> days]... for survival. [And] there is such a thing as 'the other'... The
> friend that is the other, and women must hang on to that.... What was
> valued was their friendship... it was spiritual, of first order priority.[44]

● ● ●

By the time *The Bluest Eye* had been published and during the writing of
Sula, Toni Morrison was being asked by newspapers and journals, especially
the *New York Times*, to comment on black culture and literature. She
reviewed twenty-eight books for the *New York Times Book Review* and wrote
'What the Black Woman Thinks About Women's Lib' for the *Times
Magazine*. Always concerned with black history, she contributed an essay
for the bicentennial issue of the *New York Times Book Review*, entitled 'Slow
Walk of Trees (as Grandmother Would Say) Hopeless (as Grandfather
Would Say)', discussing African-American history and its relationship to
her own family's history. And it is the importance of re-assessing black
history that informs Ms. Morrison's third novel, *Song of Solomon*.

> O Sugarman done fly away
> Sugarman done gone
> Sugarman cut across the sky
> Sugarman gone home...[45]

Sung by a character in the novel, these words are the thematic basis for the
Song of Solomon. Throughout African-American history, there have been
folk-tales of how Africans, trapped by slavery, 'flew away' to home and
freedom. This myth could be found anywhere black Americans were in
bondage.

Early on in the novel Ms. Morrison intertwines the fantastic so deftly with the 'realistic' that it becomes all the more believable. The use of the fantastic has a solid and edifying basis for Ms. Morrison:

> I could blend the acceptance of the supernatural and a profound rootedness in the real world at the same time with neither taking precedence over the other. It is indicative of the cosmology, the way in which Black people looked at the world. We are a very practical people, very down-to-earth.... But within that practicality we also accepted what I suppose could be called superstition and magic, which is another way of knowing things.... And some of these things were 'discredited knowledge' that Black people had; discredited only because Black people were discredited.... That kind of knowledge has a very strong place in my work.[46]

In this work, the world of inversions is still in evidence, where African-Americans change the names of given properties since their 'correct' names have no significance in their lives. For example, in this Michigan town, Mercy Hospital's name has been changed in the black community to No Mercy Hospital, for blacks are not allowed treatment there.

The story's central character is Milkman Dead, a young black man whose loss of spiritual being (as exemplified in his name), is reborn when he goes on a quest for gold that eventually becomes a quest for self. In this novel, Ms. Morrison has a male protagonist, but 'female' characters figure strongly in the shaping of Milkman's self-realization.

The construction of *Song of Solomon* differs from her two previous works, but its structure, like theirs, is shaped by the story:

> I was trying to push this novel outward; its movement is neither circular nor spiral. The image in my mind for it is that of a train picking up speed; and that image informs the language....[47]

The language is steeped in the sonority of black expression. The narrative is alive and memorable; the conversations of black characters resound with authenticity.

Song of Solomon is about black history and the pressing need for African-Americans to be aware of that history in order to become 'whole'. It is also a novel about names and naming. For African-Americans, names have great significance and are approached with much sensitivity. Their names were not their names, therefore most black Americans received 'new' names related to their personalities or their physical make-up. Since slavery denied them their real names, Toni Morrison points out 'the trauma of having no one to speak your language and being named haphazardly – the way you name a horse. [Nicknames are] both an outrage and a means of resistance.'[48]

Most characters in this narrative are given names that are closely connected with their personalities, and Ms. Morrison shows us how we can receive names or own them. In the first instance, the Dead family received their name as the result of a white man's mistake:

> 'When freedom came. All the coloured people in the state had to register with the Freedmen's Bureau... Papa was in his teens and went to sign up, but the man behind the desk was drunk. He asked Papa where he was born. Papa said Macon. Then he asked him who his father was. Papa said, "He's dead"... the Yankee wrote it all down, but in the wrong spaces... and in the space for his name the fool wrote, "Dead" comma "Macon". But Papa couldn't read so he never found out what he was registered as till Mama told him.'[49]

Having been twice removed from their real name, they 'own' their first names. Carrying on a family ritual, they choose the names of their children blindly from the Bible, as Milkman's grandfather did because he could not read.

Milkman's story is a journey from materialism and selfishness to 'rootedness'.[50] He is the only son of the wealthiest black in town, and his mother, a woman bereft of marital love, lavishes an almost incestuous affection on him.

> She called her son to her. When he came into the little room she unbuttoned her blouse and smiled. He was too young to be dazzled by her nipples, but he was old enough to be bored by the flat taste of mother's milk, so he came reluctantly, as to a chore, and lay as he had at least once each day of his life in his mother's arms....
>
> She felt him. His restraint, his courtesy, his indifference, all of which pushed her into fantasy. She had the distinct impression that his lips were pulling from her a thread of light. It was as though she were a cauldron issuing spinning gold.[51]

His father, a dealer in real estate, is a man possessed by money: 'Own things. And let the things you own own other things. Then you'll own yourself and other people too.'[52]

With a family affording him no passage to the past, thereby rendering his present empty, he is just a young man looking for the next party. Guitar, his life-long friend, moves further away from him, for Milkman has no interest in the welfare of his people. Spurred on by the Civil Rights struggle, Guitar joins 'The Days', a group of black men pledged to avenge the random killing of African-Americans by doing the same to whites.

Milkman's only link with the fecundity of his past comes from his aunt Pilate, a woman born without a navel. Toni Morrison explains the meaning of this:

> It meant that Pilate could be 'inside and outside' at the same time. She was innocent wisdom.[53]

Fabulist in concept, this character represents the real and rewarding properties that enable Milkman to find his ancestors, and thereby himself. 'Outside' the community, Pilate is the one who personifies black culture and history. She stands as a symbol of what must be understood before blacks can have self-understanding. 'Pilate is Morrison's most complex and concentrated image of an African-American in touch with the spiritual resources of African-American folk traditions.'[54] And she is surely one of Toni Morrison's most vivid characters:

> When she was neither singing nor talking, her face was animated by her constantly moving lips. She chewed things. She kept things in her mouth – straw from brooms, gristle, buttons, seeds, leaves, string, and her favourite . . . rubber bands India rubber erasers. Her lips were alive with small movements. If you were close to her, you wondered if she was about to smile or was she merely shifting a straw from the baseline of her gums to her tongue . . .[55]

Pilate is endowed with a sense of self and culture, but her daughter Reba and her grand-daughter Hagar do not possess this strength. Removed from the rural basis of black culture, yet outside the urban community, they are afloat in a world of false values and consumerism.[56] Reba is lucky at contests, but gives most of her winnings away to men, just as freely as she gives herself. Hagar, obsessed with the love of Milkman, tries, but fails, to become a part of consumer society, in an effort to win him back.

> She bought a Playtex garter belt, I. Miller No Color Hose, Fruit of the Loom panties, and two nylon slips . . . one pair of Joyce Fancy Free and one of Con Brio ('Thank heaven for little Joyce heels'). . . . The cosmetics department enfolded her in perfume, and she read hungrily the labels and the promise. Myurgia for primeval woman who creates for him a world of tender privacy where the only occupant is you, mixed with Nina Ricci's L'Air du Temps. . . . Hagar believed she could spend her life there among the cut glass, shimmering in peaches and cream, in satin. In opulence. In luxe. In love.[57]

Milkman, in his search for riches, travels South, where he learns endurance, courage, selflessness, and the answer to 'the riddle' of his family's history, as sung in a children's song. With the help and the love of Pilate, he becomes 'whole' and responsible to his community.

In a reversal of roles, Milkman has become socially conscious and caring, while Guitar has changed into a gold-seeker and killer. Milkman stands unafraid in the face of possible death for he knows that his grand-daddy could 'fly'. With this knowledge, he symbolically transcends death by embracing flight:

> As fleet and bright as a lodestar he wheeled toward Guitar and it did not matter which one of them would give up the ghost in the killing arms of his brother. For now he knew what Shalimar knew: If you surrendered to the air, you could *ride* it.[58]

In *Song of Solomon*, Toni Morrison gives us a fable of freedom; liberation can only come with the knowledge of who you are. And with that knowledge, there is no question, no denial that you can 'soar'.

Toni Morrison became a major American writer with the publication of *Song of Solomon*. It received good reviews and it was the first black novel to be chosen as a main selection for the Book-of-the-Month Club since Richard Wright's *Native Son*. Some critics, however, thought it was less outstanding than her previous work. Margo Jefferson, in a *Newsweek* article, wrote that the selection for the book club was like 'an Academy Award denied an actress for her best performance and given several years later for a lesser one'.[59]

Although *Song of Solomon* was not as inventive and penetrating as her previous novel, *Sula*, it was more accessible, and received the fiction award of the National Book Critics Circle. Toni Morrison had gained national attention and was to hold the prestigious Albert Schweitzer Chair in Humanities at the University of the State of New York; she now holds a distinguished Chair at Princeton University.

•   •   •

'There is nothing in her parts for you. She has forgotten her ancient properties.'[60]

Tar Baby, Toni Morrison's fourth novel, is a cautionary tale of black contemporary life. Set in a small Caribbean island and in the cities of New York and Paris, *Tar Baby* embraces a wider geographical scope than her previous works. She also introduces white characters, who represent the thematic tensions of this novel.

The title is based on the African-American folktale about a farmer's efforts to catch a rabbit which steals from his garden. He makes a tar baby, alluring and sticky, and places it in his cabbage patch. This tale stands as an allegory for the dilemma of blacks who are lured and caught by the world of white values, but Toni Morrison adds another layer to this tale. In an interview with Thomas Le Clair she said:

> I found that there is a tar baby in African mythology. I started thinking about tar. At one point, a tar pit was a holy place, because tar was used to build things. It came naturally out of the earth; it held things together. For me, the tar baby came to mean the black woman who can hold things together.[61]

In this novel, these two concepts harbour all that the heroine is, and cannot be.

Jadine, a beautiful, black fashion model, is an orphan who has been raised by her aunt Ondine and uncle Sydney, servants to the white candy manufacturing heir, Valerian Street. Educated and worldly, Jadine's privileged existence has been made possible by the monetary support of Valerian, including an education at the Sorbonne. Moulded by white values and materialism, Jadine is the modern, hard-edged black woman, whose credo for survival is: 'Talk shit, take none.'[62]

The heroine Jadine represents the African-American tar baby, but is unable to take on the qualities of the African version of this folk-tale. She herself remains trapped in a state of contradiction. M. E. Mobley explains:

> [Toni Morrison]... focuses on the connotations of entrapment that are usually associated with the Afro-American version of the narrative. On the other hand, she also focuses on the not-so-familiar positive connotations found in the African version of the tale. Both sets of connotations deepen the portrait of Jadine as the tar baby that entraps Son, and as the woman who cannot sustain a relationship because she lacks the ancestral power of being able to 'hold things together'.[63]

The main setting for the novel is Valerian's estate on the Isle de Chevaliers, a small West Indian island named after blind African horsemen. They were brought as slaves but never became enslaved, and were believed to be still riding in the hills. Valerian represents the 'colonizer', or the power of white Western society. His young wife, Margaret, from a lower class, finds her only sense of self-worth in her beauty, which is now beginning to fade.

Ondine and Sydney consider themselves 'Philadelphia Negroes', a cut above the 'Yardbirds and Marys' who are the poor black people of the island. Perfect, skilled servants, they raise the young Jadine without respect for, or understanding of, the culture of her own people.

'Picasso *is* better than an Itumba mask. The fact that he was intrigued by them is proof of *his* genius, not the mask-maker's.'[64]

Into this compressed 'hot-house' of polite ritual, comes Son; black, on the run, he represents the values of rural African-American culture. Son's presence disturbs the household and causes the veneer of accepted roles to topple. Margaret's 'secret' is exposed as Ondine tells of Margaret's abuse to her son when he was a child. Jadine finds herself falling in love with a 'wild' black man, and both Ondine and Sydney show their hypocrisy when they come to the aid of their master instead of their own kind.

Fleeing the island, Jadine and Son go to New York, where, to Son,

> The black girls ... were crying. ... Crying girls split into two parts by their tight jeans, screaming at the top of their high, high heels ... crying on buses ... at traffic lights and behind the counters of Chemical Bank. ... It depressed him, all that crying, for it was silent and veiled by plum lipstick and the thin gay lines over their eyes.[65]

Jadine's hope is to make Son an achiever, a modern middle-class black man. But Son wants to go back home to Eloe, a black village in Florida, where he remembers the 'short street of yellow houses with white doors which women opened wide and called out, "Come on in here, you honey you...."'[66] But when they go to Eloe, it is a world of poverty, and Jadine feels restricted and uneasy there.

At odds with each other, and with what each represents, their relationship fails. Jadine cannot, will not, accept Son's dream vision of a happy life together in Eloe:

> 'I was learning how to make it in *this* world. The one we live in, not the one in your head. Not that dump Eloe; *this* world.'[67]

In denying anything positive in her culture, she is a woman besieged and haunted. In a Parisian supermarket, she sees an extraordinarily beautiful African woman, dressed in yellow, embodying the 'ancestor'. Jadine follows her. The response of the woman is to spit at Jadine. Thus, she is, in turn, denied by her culture, her heritage, her people.

Unable to enter Son's world, or at least to find a compromise, Jadine returns to Paris to marry a white man she does not love. Son, on the other hand, decides that he cannot be without Jadine, and goes in pursuit of her. He asks the islanders to get him back to the Isle de Chevaliers, so he may find out where she has gone. Set afloat in a small boat, he ends up on the wild side of the island. The persuasive presence of 'ghostly ancestors' lures him to this place where 'the men are waiting for [him]'; free of Jadine, he turns to the past, to the African horsemen, where 'the mist lifted and the trees stepped back a bit as if to make the way easier for a certain kind of man.'[68]

In this novel, where Nature fights against man's control, where trees dance and bees do not sting, Ms. Morrison gives us her most fabulous setting:

> The champion daisy trees were marshalling for war. . . . During the day
> they tossed their branches; at night they walked the hills.[69]

Nature is responding to the discord and disharmony found in the characters
of this narrative. And within this fabulistic world, Toni Morrison asks a very
sobering question: can black people sustain wholeness in a materialistic
society? With more and more African-Americans becoming assimilated into
mainstream white society, what happens to the culture they leave behind?
Most critics felt that Morrison found the answer to her own question
problematic. In her past novels, there was revelation, there was growth and
learning. In this particular work, Jadine remains ensconced in the world of
'making it' and Son lives in, and returns to, the past. Through all the many
strong and moving speeches that Ms. Morrison gives to these characters,
neither one hears the other. We wonder if the ability of African-Americans
to remain themselves, yet move within a wider world, is in danger. Toni
Morrison, in an interview with Nellie McKay, gives her opinion:

> I think there is a serious question about black male and black female
> relationships in the 20th century. I just think that the argument has
> always turned on something it should not turn on: gender. I think that
> the conflict of genders is a cultural illness. Many of the problems
> modern couples have are caused not so much by conflicting gender
> roles as by the other 'differences' the culture offers. . . . Jadine and Son
> had no problems as far as men and women were concerned. They knew
> exactly what to do. [But their problems] hinged on what they felt about
> who they were, and what their responsibilities were in being black.
> The question for each was whether he or she was really a member of
> the tribe.[70]

In *Tar Baby*, Toni Morrison's authorial voice often invades and overtakes
the narrative. In her previous works, we entered Morrison's world and
participated but in this novel we remain outside, due in part to its allegorical
nature. Despite its occasional rococo language and somewhat stereotypical
characters, Ms. Morrison still manages to hold our attention and engage our
imaginations. Above all, she continually makes us think. The message is a
dismal and disheartening one, but the dilemma of the contemporary
African-American is not for Toni Morrison alone to resolve. Maybe, in *Tar
Baby*, she is not asking for reader participation, but begging for a real
engagement in solving the problems she presents.

●   ●   ●

> I will call them my people, which were not my people, and her beloved, which was not beloved. (Romans 9:25)

With this epigraph, Toni Morrison carries us into 124 Bluestone Road, a house on the outskirts of Cincinnati, Ohio, in 1873, racked with the painful past of slavery.

Beloved, Ms. Morrison's Pulitzer Prize-winning novel, is a harrowing narrative of reclamation and love. Her craft as an artist shines luminously here. *Beloved* is undoubtedly one of the greatest American novels of all time.

Purported by Ms. Morrison to be a 'ghost story', it is much, much more than that. She dares to delve into a past that African-Americans would rather forget, and deftly leads us through and beyond that painful place to peace. And it is 'rememory' (Ms. Morrison's word) that we must experience in order to take on that past and go forward.

Although historical in content, this is not an historical novel. In most of the preceding literature about slavery, the narratives were awash with moralizing and guilt. In historical texts, the atrocities of slavery were rendered in such a way as to make them seem 'flat', almost statistical. The characters in *Beloved* are far from the usual slave depictions: bad whites, good blacks. Each person carries his or her own complexity: Sethe, the slave-mother who 'owns' her child by taking its life; Paul D, unable to understand Sethe's actions, initially perceives her as a slave-owner would: 'You got two feet, Sethe, not four'[71]; Amy, the white indentured servant, who is there to remind us that nineteenth-century child labour and its attendant abuses caused poor whites to suffer as well as blacks; and the townspeople, who, out of pride, do not forewarn Sethe of her owner's imminent approach. All of *Beloved*'s characters grapple with moral decisions that must be made in order to survive in a mad world. And Toni Morrison emphatically states that *Beloved* is not about slavery in any conventional sense:

> [A novel] can't be driven by slavery. It has to be the interior life of some people, a small group of people, and everything that they do is impacted on by the horror of slavery, but they are also people.[72]

By this specificity, we feel what slaves feel, see what they see. The slave, this 'non-name', becomes real, becomes familiar, becomes human. This in itself is a triumph.

The novel is based on the case of Margaret Garner, a runaway slave mother, who, when caught, rather than have her children taken into slavery, tries to kill them. She does kill one child, and this becomes a *cause célèbre* for the abolitionists, and the beginning of *Beloved* for Ms. Morrison:

> I found an article in a magazine of the period, and there was this young woman in her 20s, being interviewed– oh a lot of people interviewed her... and she was very calm, she was very serene. They kept

remarking on the fact that she was not a madwoman, and she kept saying, 'No, they're not going to live like that. They will not live the way I have lived.'[73]

In the hands of this brilliant storyteller, Sethe's history slowly unfolds. A woman desperately trying to keep 'the past at bay', a runaway slave from the ironically named Sweet Home farm in Kentucky, she comes to live in 124 Bluestone Road, the home of her husband's mother, Baby Suggs. Sending three children ahead of her and pregnant with another, she arrives and tastes freedom. But twenty-eight days after, when faced with recapture and enslavement for her children, she cuts the throat of one and tries to kill the others. This moment of wrenching agony is told to us through the eyes of 'schoolteacher', a Mengele-like character, who now runs Sweet Home, and studies his slaves' physical characteristics to prove scientifically that they are animals:

> Inside, two boys bled in the sawdust and dirt at the feet of a nigger woman holding a blood-soaked child to her chest with one hand and an infant by the heels in the other. She did not look at them; she simply swung the baby toward the wall planks, missed and tried to connect a second time, when out of nowhere ... the old nigger boy, still mewing, ran through the door behind them and snatched the baby from the arch of its mother's swing.
>
> Right off it was clear, to schoolteacher especially, that there was nothing there to claim.[74]

Eighteen years later, the sad and yearning spirit of the slain child has taken over the house. Un-named in life, this 'crawling-already?' baby seeks retribution and rocks the house in her search for it. But the family has learned to live with the spirit, except for Sethe's two sons, Howard and Buglar, who, after almost being killed, never let go of each other's hands during childhood. With the sons driven away, only Baby Suggs, Sethe and her daughter Denver are left to contend with the spirit. Denver welcomes it, for she is an adolescent alone, without friends, for the family has been spurned by the townspeople because of Sethe's act. But Baby Suggs knows that they are not the only ones keeping company with a poltergeist:

> 'Not a house in the country ain't packed to its rafters with some dead Negro's grief.'[75]

This grief pervades the house and renders it grey. Baby Suggs dies wanting some colour; 'Bring a little lavender in, if you got any. Pink, if you don't.' But it is colour that brings on 'rememory' for Sethe. For pink is the colour of 'crawling already?''s tombstone, which Sethe had engraved with the only word she could pay for, and the price was high:

The welcoming cool of unchiseled headstones; the one she selected to lean against on tiptoe, her knees wide open as any grave. Pink as a fingernail it was, and sprinkled with glittering chips. Ten minutes, he said. You got ten minutes I'll do it for free.

Ten minutes for seven letters. With another ten could she have gotten 'Dearly' too? . . . Dearly Beloved. But what she got, settled for, was the one word that mattered. She thought it would be enough . . . his young son looking on, the anger in his face so old; the appetite in it quite new. That should certainly be enough.[76]

So Beloved is named after the second of seven words that Sethe heard the preacher say at her funeral. And it is naming, as well as 'rememory', that threads its way through this novel. These characters are not 'slaves', but people who give themselves back to themselves by the process of naming. Baby Suggs, known to her master as Jenny, and called so, is never asked if that is her name. This blithe disregard is revealed in even the most 'caring' of masters:

'Mr. Garner . . . why you call me Jenny?'
'Cause that's what's on your sales ticket, gal. Ain't that your name? What you call yourself?'
'Nothing, . . . I don't call myself nothing.' . . .
'What did you answer to?'
'Anything, but Suggs is what my husband name . . . Suggs is my name, sir. From my husband. He didn't call me Jenny.'
'What he call you?'
'Baby.'[77]

As readers, we are given only pieces of the past, bit by bit, as the mystery unravels. We know something terrible has happened in this house, but we are only given so much at a time, only, it seems, as much as Sethe and the other characters can endure remembering. The past continually intrudes into the present, so shifts of time are constantly ebbing and flowing, as waves, crashing to shore, leaving new and altered configurations. To Sethe, the present is always the past:

Then something. The plash of water . . . and suddenly there was Sweet Home rolling, rolling, rolling out before her eyes, and although there was not a leaf on that farm that did not make her want to scream, it rolled itself out before her in shameless beauty. It never looked as terrible as it was and it made her wonder if hell was a pretty place too. . . . Boys hanging from the most beautiful sycamores in the world.

It shamed her – remembering the wonderful soughing trees rather than the boys. Try as she might to make it otherwise, the sycamores beat out the children every time and she could not forgive her memory for that.[78]

Into Sethe's present walks Paul D, 'the last of the Sweet Home men', one of the gentlest and most loving male characters in black literature since Teacake, in Zora Neale Hurston's *Their Eyes Were Watching God*: 'He had become the kind of man who could walk into a house and make the women cry.... There was something blessed in his manner.'[79] He had desired Sethe at Sweet Home, as did all the men, but she chose to marry Halle. They were called men at Sweet Home, rather than boys, by their master Mr. Garner, and given choices and freedoms not usually afforded slaves: they could carry arms and have opinions. But these 'men' lived without women:

> And so there they were: Paul D Garner, Paul F Garner, Paul A Garner, Halle Suggs and Sixo, the wild man. All in their twenties, minus women, fucking cows, dreaming of rape, thrashing on pallets, rubbing their thighs and waiting for the new girl....[80]

And after the death of their 'kind' master, when the farm is run by schoolteacher, they realise that their manhood could be 'given' and taken away at will:

> Nobody counted on Garner dying. Nobody thought he could. How 'bout that? Everything rested on Garner being alive. Without his life each of theirs fell to pieces. Now ain't that slavery or what is it?[81]

Paul D, upon entering Bluestone Road 124, experiences the spirit and eventually destroys it by breaking up the house. But soon thereafter, a young girl, with no remembered past and no lines on her hands, enters their lives and calls herself Beloved. Through her, the past bubbles up and boils over, as Sethe and Paul D are moved to confront it. Sethe's 'rememory' takes her back to her rape by schoolteacher's nephews with 'mossy teeth', and her subsequent escape to Cincinnati. Beaten during the 'taking of her milk', pregnant and lost, she is befriended by a poor white girl on her way to Boston to look for velvet. In aiding Sethe's birth, Amy discovers the unleashed hatred upon Sethe's back:

> 'Come here, Jesus.... It's a tree.... A chokecherry tree. See, here's the trunk – it's red and split wide open, full of sap, and this here's the parting for branches. You got a mighty lot of branches. Leaves, too,

look like, and dern if these aren't blossoms. Tiny little cherry blossoms, just as white. Your back got a whole tree on it. In bloom. What God have in mind, I wonder.'[82]

Nudged by the force of Beloved's spirit, Paul D swirls in the sea of the past: Halle's 'buttered face', Sixo's 'crisped body', the 'breakfast' of white foreskins in the Georgia Prison camp and the black woman, 'jailed and hanged for stealing ducks she believed were her own babies.' All this 'rememory' floods his mind; the beaten and battered lives of black people:

> He had seen Negroes so stunned, or hungry, or tired or bereft it was a wonder they recalled or said anything. Who, like him, had hidden in caves and fought owls for food; who, like him, stole from pigs... buried themselves in slop and jumped in wells to avoid regulators, raiders, patrollers, veterans, hill men, posses and merrymakers.[83]

Sethe's 'rememory' also reels recklessly before her: her mother taken from her when she was a baby, branded by the mark 'on her rib... a circle and cross burnt right in the skin', who was left to hang so long that even the marks were unrecognizable.[84] And her mother's smile: 'You know what? She'd had the bit so many times she smiled. When she wasn't smiling she smiled, and I never saw her own smile.'[85]

Toni Morrison, in an interview, discussed the inherent meanings of the bit, a device used on slaves, similar to that used on horses:

> It was the physical obscenity of having this thing in your mouth – it was inhuman. [They used it because] they thought slaves were animals. And to stop you from talking – silence – having no language, not being able to express anything. Imposing this should destroy you. All human qualities should evaporate.[86]

Ms. Morrison was 'overwhelmed by the heroism of these ordinary people'. She says of this torture that: 'It was always startling that it wasn't successful.' And those that did survive never forgot the ones that didn't:

> The people of the broken necks, of fire-cooked blood and black girls who had lost their ribbons.

> What a roaring.[87]

This 'roaring' is embodied in Beloved, ghost of the 'crawling already?' baby, and the voice for millions of black people who lost their lives in slavery and its aftermath.

For those who managed to carry on, life is only made possible by shutting off some part of themselves. As they look back upon their lives and ask, 'What *are* these people?'[88], who systematically take mothers away from children, husbands away from wives, families away from each other; maim, whip, hang, shackle, beat, rape, burn and 'silence' – they chose caring carefully:

> Risky, thought Paul D, very risky. For a used-to-be-slave woman to love anything that much was dangerous.... The best thing, he knew, was to love just a little bit; everything, just a little bit....[89]

Yet Sethe loves fully and embraces Beloved as her lost child. But it is not only Beloved seeking reclamation, it is also the need of Sethe and Denver. A threnody, they speak as one:

> You are my sister
> You are my daughter
> You are my face; you are me...
> You are my Beloved
> You are mine
> You are mine
> You are mine[90]

This seems a most implausible story, but Toni Morrison is so skilled at bringing together imaginative reality and documentary realism that the reader is never left disbelieving. Her use of African-American folklore is unsurpassed – for blacks do believe in ghosts. Certainly a walk on America's Southern soil can cause a black person to hear the cries of ancestors and feel the earth heave with their longing and discontent.

Ms. Morrison's use of language in *Beloved* is, by turns, rich, rounded, lean, linear, colourful, clean, sharp and sensual. And the form of the novel is truly innovative, in that we are given only fragments of the story, as the lives of these people are also fragmented. As Judith Thurman wrote in her review in *The New Yorker*:

> *Beloved* is not primarily a historical novel, and Morrison does not attempt... to argue the immorality of slavery on rational grounds.... She treats the past as if it were one of those luminous old scenes painted on dark glass... and she breaks the glass, and recomposes it in disjointed and puzzling modern form. As the reader struggles with its fragments and mysteries, he keeps being startled by flashes of his own reflection in them.'[91]

●   ●   ●

On January 24, 1988, a letter was published in the *New York Times Book Review*. Signed by forty-eight prominent African-American writers and academics, it thanked Toni Morrison for her 'forward movement of our literature, our life.'

It came at a time when blacks had lost one of their most renowned writers, James Baldwin. He died, never having received 'the keystones to the canon of American literature: the National Book Award and the Pulitzer Prize.' Grieved by this slight and saddened by the fact that *Beloved* had been passed over by the National Book Award committee, they put forth their own affirmation of her creative genius:

> In grateful wonder at the advent of *Beloved*, your most recent gift to our community, our country, our conscience, our courage flourishing as it grows, we here record our pride, our respect and appreciation for the treasury of your findings and invention.[92]

● ● ●

'This is not a story to pass on', writes Ms. Morrison, on the last page of *Beloved*.[93] She was aware that, in African-American folklore, there 'were no songs, no stories about the trauma of that voyage – nothing came down orally from my generation.'[94] But Toni Morrison does tell the story, and we are blessed by her bravery and hushed by its horror. But this is finally a novel about love – healing and restorative. And it is with immense love that Toni Morrison has given her people *Beloved*:

> We flesh; flesh that weeps, laughs ... Love it. Love it hard. Yonder they do not love your flesh. They despise it. They don't love your eyes ... And O my people they do not love your hands ... Love your hands! Love them. Raise them up and kiss them. Touch others with them, pat them together, stroke them on your face 'cause they don't love that either. *You* got to love it, *you*! ... And no, they ain't in love with your mouth ... What you say out of it they will not heed. What you scream from it they do not hear ... And the beat and beating heart, love that too ... For this is the prize.[95]

8: The Silenced Speak

Remember me?
I am the girl
with dark skin
whose shoes are thin
with the wounded eye
and the melted ear
with rotted teeth
I am the dark
rotten-toothed girl
with the wounded eye
and the melted ear.

I am the girl
holding the babies
cooking their meals
sweeping their yards
washing their clothes
Dark and rotting
and wounded, wounded.

I would give
to the human race
only hope.

I am the woman
with the blessed
dark skin
I am the woman
with teeth repaired
I am the woman

> *with the healing eye*
> *The ear that hears*
>
> *I am the woman: Dark,*
> *repaired, healed*
> *Listening to you.*
>
> *I would give*
> *to the human race*
> *only hope.*
>
> *I am the woman*
> *offering two flowers*
> *whose roots*
> *are twin*
>
> *Justice and Hope*
>
> *Let us begin.*

(Alice Walker, 'Remember')[1]

By the late 1960s, African-American women writers had begun the task of reclamation: the renaming and reclaiming of black women's history and selfhood. Two authors chose to do this by reassessing the lives of black women in the South. Often misrepresented in literature, and 'silenced' in life, the landscape of their lives for the most part remained uncharted. Alice Walker and Maya Angelou, both raised in the South, gave voice to the black woman, who, in African-American literature, had rarely 'spoken' since Janie Crawford in *Their Eyes Were Watching God*.

● ● ●

The Great Migration lured millions of blacks away from the soil of sorrow, to Northern and Midwestern America. Some remained in the small towns of the South that were nearly decimated by this mass movement. And often, it was a very difficult decision: 'If I stay here any longer, I'll go wild.... There ain't enough people here I know to give me a decent burial.'[2]

Of those who did remain, almost all tried to form a tight and cohesive community that would enable them to endure the 'slave' work of sharecropping, Jim Crow laws, no voting rights, the Ku Klux Klan, rampant racism and persistent poverty.

Black women, working in fields or in some white woman's home, tried to keep up their spiritual strength to see them through. Some were able to persevere; others, beset by racism, saw themselves and their families demolished by it. Yet most managed to keep alive the sustaining rituals that were the basis of African-American life. Through song, sharing, sewing, quilting, gardening, cookery, planting, tale-telling and abundant good humour, they brought beauty to a tainted land.

These poor, black women were sustained by the richness of their culture, even if the larger world dismissed its existence. The only times they heard their voices ring out were in church, across a field or yard, in someone's kitchen or, quite often, in a small private place in their minds.

Through the literature of Alice Walker and the autobiographies of Maya Angelou, a voice has been given to that 'small place', and those silenced women have been allowed to speak. Complex, contrary, battered and brave, the lives of those black Southern women instruct and inform us; but above all, they inspire.

● ● ●

Our mothers and grandmothers...moving to a music not yet written. And they waited. They waited for a day when the unknown thing that was in them would be made known.... [3]

Alice Walker, poet, essayist and novelist, has consistently 'made known' the intense and intricate essence of America's most 'put-upon' women. With great clarity and painful honesty, she has examined the degree of freedom afforded these women and explored how they develop and cope within their communities. She has also deciphered the patterns of racism which, when not fully comprehended by blacks, can destroy both self and family.

Born in 1944, the eighth and last child of a sharecropping family in Eatonton, Georgia, Alice Walker soon learned of the ravages of racism. Stories of lynchings in the recent past stayed with her from childhood. Her family was considered poor, but economic poverty had little to do with poverty of spirit:

Somebody knew, I suppose, that we were poor. Somebody knew, perhaps the landowner who grudgingly paid my father three hundred dollars a year for twelve months' labor. But we never considered ourselves to be poor.... And because we never believed we were poor, and therefore worthless, we could depend on one another without shame. [4]

At the age of eight, Alice Walker lost the sight of one eye when her brother accidentally shot her with an air gun. This experience caused her to feel 'outcast and ugly'. Timid and somewhat removed, Alice Walker became an observer of life. She began to notice the dynamics of relationships, kept a notebook, and wrote poetry. Those formative years in the South left a lasting impression. Her acute inner vision allowed her to examine not only the relationships of people but also their relationship to nature. Ms. Walker feels that through their hardships, African-Americans have managed to keep a part of their African heritage, which she describes as animism:

> A belief that makes it possible to view all creation as living, as being inhabited by spirit. This belief encourages knowledge perceived intuitively.[5]

Alice Walker has also considered the plight of the poor, talented, Southern black woman, who had no outlet for her art. She contemplates the anguish that must have seared her soul:

> What did it mean for a black woman to be an artist in our grandmother's time? In our great-grandmother's day? It is a question with an answer cruel enough to stop the blood.[6]

But the future generation held some hope, and one of the greatest achievements of Ms. Walker was to acknowledge and exalt the everday tasks of the black Southern woman. Excluded from a viable means of artistic expression, these women made art from the most meagre of materials. With no 'room of their own', no education, no leisure nor luxury, these women made magnificence from miserly scraps and nature's bounty. Alice Walker did not have to go far to find this evidence of creativity, for it was in her mother's own backyard:

> What she planted grew, as if by magic, and her fame as a grower of flowers spread over three counties. Because of her creativity with her flowers, even my memories of poverty are seen through a screen of blooms – sunflowers, petunias, roses, dahlias, forsythias, spirea, delphiniums, verbena... and on and on.[7]

Alice Walker left Eatonton, Georgia, to attend Spelman College in Atlanta, the first university for black women in America. While there, she found herself at odds with the major goal of the college: to turn black girls into ladies. Walker found this 'ideal' in direct opposition to the kind of woman she had admired and grown up with in the South: hardworking, self-sufficient and strong.

However, the Civil Rights Movement at Spelman caught her enthusiasm. The members of SNCC (Student Non-Violent Coordinating Committee) made a dramatic impression on Alice Walker, and she was to honour the movement and its participants in the title poem of her first book of poetry, *Once* (1968).[8]

Having left Spelman, Alice Walker transferred to Sarah Lawrence College. While on vacation in Africa, she became pregnant. Unable to find an abortionist on her return to America, Ms. Walker considered suicide. She read books on the subject and spent long hours reviewing her past and recalling relationships with her family and community. Realizing their love for her, she decided to live, but not to have the child. Her celebration of renewed life was to take its form in writing. She wrote poem after poem, and placed them under the door of the then writer-in-residence at Sarah Lawrence, the distinguished radical poet Muriel Rukeyser, because she wanted 'someone to read them'.[9]

Ms. Rukeyser sent them to her agent and these poems of love, death, Africa and the civil rights struggle were brought together in *Once*. They signal the beginning of Ms. Walker's inquiry not only into racism but also her own personal struggle and the sexism that tried to inhibit it.

Events at both colleges were instrumental in forming Walker's position concerning blacks in America. At Spelman, she realized the discrepancy between being a lady and the kind of woman needed to participate fully in the Civil Rights Movement. It became apparent to Ms. Walker that for a black woman to involve herself effectively in the struggle, she could not be restricted. Such narrowness would make the development of a cohesive and cogent movement impossible.

She also realized that black men and women risked death in their fight for freedom. The theme of regeneration, of a freer life coming through death, is one she was to examine in her novel *The Third Life of Grange Copeland*.

Ms. Walker's experience of pregnancy had brought her close to the subject of death, as well as a fuller understanding of 'how alone woman is, because of her body'.[10] This time of reflection enabled her to appreciate the need for unity among women, and was the starting point for her version of feminism, which she calls 'womanism'.

After graduation from Sarah Lawrence, Alice Walker returned to the South, at the height of the Civil Rights Movement. From the late 1960s to the mid-1970s, Ms. Walker worked with blacks for voter registration and welfare rights. She collected folklore and recorded the lives of Southern black people.

While there, she met and married Mel Levanthal, a white civil rights lawyer. They moved to Mississippi and broke the state law, for at that time, white and black people were not allowed to live together. Some blacks, as well as whites, were disturbed by the marriage, and it would influence the negative response of some black critics to her writing. Alice Walker's reply to those who disagreed with her decisions was resolute:

In order to be able to live at all in America I must be unafraid to live anywhere in it, and I must be able to live in the fashion and with whom I choose. Otherwise, I'd just as soon leave. If society (black or white) says, then you must be isolated, an outcast – then I will be a hermit.[11]

This feeling of being an outsider has been a part of Ms. Walker's life, in varying degrees, since childhood. Barbara Christian concludes that these feelings made it possible for Alice Walker to confront issues in the black community in ways that did not conform with the general beliefs of the day. For example, Ms. Walker was one of the first black women writers to explore the problems of sexism, when most other blacks were declaring that racism was the cause of all the ills of African-American people.[12]

Ms. Walker's stance as an outsider has enabled her to look at the black community and depict its intricacies with clarity and compassion. For those who tried to restrict her voice, or that of any other black woman, she wrote:

Be nobody's darling
Be an outcast.
Take the contradictions
Of your life
And wrap around
You like a shawl,
To parry stones
To keep you warm.

Watch the people succumb
To madness
With ample cheer;
Let them look askance at you
And you askance reply.

Be an outcast;
Be pleased to walk alone
(Uncool)
Or line the crowded
River beds
With other impetuous
Fools.

Make a merry gathering
On the bank
Where thousands perished

For brave hurt words
They said.

> Be nobody's darling;
> Be an outcast.
> Qualified to live
> Among your dead.[13]

This poem, with its echoes of Langston Hughes's democratic voice, is from Alice Walker's second volume of verse, *Revolutionary Petunias* (1973). Comprised of memories of the South and her family, and reflections on her childhood, these poems also consider the effects of the Civil Rights Movement from an internal rather than external perspective. Ms. Walker has said that 'the whole book is a celebration of people who will not cram themselves into any ideological or racial mode.'[14]

Alice Walker gave the volume its name because of the symbolism in the prolific nature of this small and unheralded blossom; 'you just put them in any kind of soil and they bloom their heads off – exactly . . . like black people tend to do.'[15]

The title poem is a key to the whole work. It concerns Sammy Lou, a poor black Southern woman. She is considered 'incorrect' by her more informed revolutionary brothers and sisters, for nowhere in her life is there evidence of 'blackness'. She goes to church, respects God, is against violence in principle and names her children after presidents. But she is also a woman, who when hit enough, hits back: Sammy Lou kills the white man who murdered her husband. Yet, even in this act, she remains 'incorrect' to her very end, by loving flowers: 'Don't yall forget to *water* /my purple petunias.'[16]

In this as well as other poems in the volume, Alice Walker treads forbidden paths by questioning black revolutionaries' belief in violence and their contempt for the 'backward' blacks of the South. Ms. Walker believes that these people are in fact the backbone of African-American culture, most especially the women, whom she praises for their strength, love and vision:

> They were women then
> My mama's generation
> Husky of voice – Stout of
> Step
> With fists as well as
> Hands
> How they battered down
> Doors
> And ironed
> Starched white
> Shirts
> How they led
> Armies
> Headragged Generals
> Across mined

Fields
Booby-trapped
Ditches
To discover books
Desks
A place for us
How they knew what we
Must know
Without knowing a page
Of it
Themselves.[17]

The movement of these lines, whose words 'step' down the page, suggests the influence of William Carlos Williams, whose poetry was in turn influenced by the jazz idiom. Alice Walker has acknowledged Williams, Hughes and Arna Bontemps as models for her own writing. She has also found inspiration in the work of black women, especially Margaret Walker and Gwendolyn Brooks, and this is evident in the subject-matter of the poem just quoted.

Good Night, Willie Lee, I'll See You in the Morning (1979), is the title of Ms. Walker's third book of poetry. Named after the last farewell Alice Walker's mother gave her father at his funeral, this volume concerns itself with personal relationships and how they can alter social structures. The central associations are between men and women, and are, for Walker, the basis for the transformation of society. Moving from loss to hope, Ms. Walker sees love in a healthier light, but also realizes that love can only be attained through the acceptance and love of self. From the pained questioning of 'Did This Happen to Your Mother? Did Your Sister Throw Up a Lot?', Alice Walker dismally announces that 'love has made me sick',[18] but is unable to alter the destructive pattern she is in.

By moving through the history and lives of many known and unknown black women, Alice Walker confronts her own vulnerabilities and strengths. For instance, in 'On Stripping Bark From Myself',[19] she recognizes the importance of self-love.

By the end of this volume, Ms. Walker comprehends the healthy properties of love and its openness to forgiveness:

each time I order her to go
for a ruler and face her small
grubby outstretched palm
i feel before hitting it
the sting in my own
and become my mother
preparing to chastise me
on a gloomy Saturday afternoon

> long ago. and glaring down into my own sad
> and grieving face i forgive myself
> for whatever crime i may
> have done. as i wish i could always
> forgive myself
> then as now.[20]

In her fourth volume of poetry, *Horses Make a Landscape Look More Beautiful* (1984), Alice Walker considers the themes of friendship, racism, sexism, her relationship with her daughter, and the threat of nuclear destruction and world pollution. She also acknowledges the collusion of American capitalism in South African oppression:

> The diamonds on Liz's bosom
> are not as bright
> as his eyes
> the morning they took him
> to work in the mines
> The rubies in Nancy's
> jewel box (Oh, how he
> loved red!)
> not as vivid
> as the despair
> in his children's frowns.
>
> Oh, those Africans!
>
> Everywhere you look
> they're bleeding
> and crying
> Crying and bleeding
> on some of the whitest necks
> in your town.[21]

In 'We Alone', Alice Walker admonishes those who do not know that the gold they wear is the product of someone's 'chain' and suggests alternative adornments of 'feathers, shells and sea-shaped stones'.[22]

Ms. Walker also realizes that black people must work to save African-American writing from oblivion: '*Each one, pull one back into the sun*'[23], for without this effort, black literature will be lost and forgotten. But as Alice Walker so evocatively expresses it in 'These Days', there will be nothing to save if actions are not taken now to counter world destruction.[24]

In her poetry, Alice Walker considers the lives of black people, from the small, silent towns of the South to the cities of a wider world. She examines their triumphs, their trials, and their tenacious endurance. But it is the

Southern woman who speaks most fervently in these works, and this voice will continue to speak out in Ms. Walker's two volumes of short stories.

•   •   •

> So many of the stories that I write, that we all write, are our mothers' stories. Only recently did I fully realize this: that through years of listening to my mother's stories of her life, I have absorbed not only the stories themselves, but something of the manner in which she spoke, something of the urgency that involves the knowledge that her stories – like her life – must be recorded.[25]

Alice Walker found inspiration for her writing not only from her mother's stories, but also from the work of many writers, both women and men. She admired Dostoevsky, because he 'found truth where everyone else seemed afraid to look.'[26] Jean Toomer was important to her, as we shall see, but above all there was Zora Neale Hurston, whom Ms. Walker helped to recover from oblivion. Walker's essays, 'Zora Neale Hurston' and 'Looking for Zora', gave an extraordinary African-American artist back to her people, and paved the way for the re-publication of Hurston's work throughout the world.

Alice Walker's first collection of stories, *In Love and Trouble* (1973), is centred in the lives of black Southern women, who, moved by an inexplicable will, often challenge the abuses they suffer and the restrictions placed upon them. Some of these stories are based on tales told to her by her mother, such as 'The Revenge of Hannah Kemhuff', where the spell of voodoo is used as a revenge against oppression, and 'Strong Horse Tea', which shows the plight of poor blacks when the white medical profession does not come to their aid.

The most brilliant and telling tale in the collection is 'Everyday Use', which contrasts superficial 'media blackness' with an understanding of, and respect for, black cultural heritage. The focus for this discussion is a patchwork quilt. Quilt-making can be seen as a paradigm for the effects of the African diaspora:

> Weaving, shaping, sculpting or quilting in order to create a kaleidoscopic and momentary array is tantamount to providing an improvisational response to chaos. . . . It constitutes survival strategy and motion in the face of dispersal. A patchwork quilt, laboriously and affectionately crafted from bits of worn overalls, shredded uniforms, tattered petticoats, and outgrown dresses stands as a signal instance of a patterned wholeness in the African diaspora.[27]

Dedicated to 'your grandma', 'Everyday Use' considers the question of high art and functional art and its misuse within a black communal context. The story starts with the return of Dee (who now calls herself Wangero) to her Southern home, because 'black roots' are in style. While in the North, Dee (Wangero), has become a revolutionary; she wears her hair in an Afro and dresses in African clothing. She is received by her poor uneducated mother and sister, who embarrass her. Dee, having initially scorned a quilt made by her grandmother, which her mother thought she might use at college, returns for it, but wanting it only as a form of art, an artefact to be framed. What was once unusable to Dee has now become fashionable. Her sister Maggie, though she does not know the definitions of culture or heritage, embodies their true essence by loving her grandmother and respecting her ability to make beautiful quilts. As Barbara Christian has said: 'Maggie has accepted the *spirit* that was passed on to her.'[28] And Maggie can also *make* quilts.

The full irony of the situation is felt when Dee says of her sister: '"Maggie can't appreciate these quilts! . . . She'd probably be backward enough to put them to everyday use."'[29]

By juxtaposing these two ideas of usefulness and pricelessness, Ms. Walker confronts the concept of cultural heritage. Her conclusion is that by having culture as some kind of abstraction, it becomes a commodity, rather than a functioning expression of a people. It has also been pointed out that,

> Because [Alice Walker] used, as the artefact, quilts that were made by southern black women, she focused attention on those supposedly backward folk who never heard the word heritage but fashioned a functional tradition out of little matter and much spirit.[30]

You Can't Keep a Good Woman Down (1981), Alice Walker's second collection of short stories, continues the theme of the black woman's fight against restriction and abuse. But unlike the previous volume, where the heroines struggled 'in spite of themselves', these women demand the right to challenge any restrictions put upon them.[31]

All the stories have a contemporary setting and deal with topical issues such as pornography, abortion, sado-masochism, inter-racial rape and a greater knowledge of black ancestry. Once again, Ms. Walker emphasizes the correlation between personal action and political intent. In the story 'Porn', Walker shows the degradation caused by black and white, male and female stereotypes. This story also demonstrates how pornographic depictions have eroded the quality of black women's lives.

Alice Walker paved new passages in African-American literature by dealing with these highly sensitive and disturbing contemporary issues. She also introduced innovative forms in which to discuss them.

'Advancing Luna - and Ida B. Wells' is one example of innovative structure. In it, Alice Walker considers the implications of inter-racial rape during the Civil Rights Movement. When her young, black Southern heroine, who believes that 'all black people [are] superior', is told by her white friend that she was raped by a black man, it is almost impossible for her to comprehend. Startled, she is left to question her own beliefs and assumptions: 'Who knows what the black woman thinks of rape? Who has asked her? Who *cares*?'[32]

The narrator then has a dialogue with the great anti-lynching crusader Ida B. Wells, to show the historical connection between rape, lynching and racism, still so deeply rooted in American society. Giving us no easy answers to this overwhelmingly complex subject, Ms. Walker uses two endings, 'Afterthoughts', 'Discarded Notes' and a Postscript, where the author and the narrator merge as one.

In these two volumes of short stories, Alice Walker has illuminated the problems that have pervaded the lives of black women throughout history. In the first collection, the characters are trapped and remain thwarted by their restricted options in life. In the second, the heroines push forward, gaining a clearer understanding of themselves and a more liberated existence. Concurring with many other African-American women writers, Alice Walker believes that freedom comes from knowledge. And the knowledge needed is cognizance of black history. Without it, African-Americans will be a duped and divided people. This is the theme of her dramatic and disturbing first novel, *The Third Life of Grange Copeland*.

●   ●   ●

The Third Life of Grange Copeland (1970) is set in a small town in Georgia, and depicts the lives of one family, the Copelands, over a period of sixty years. We witness their struggle with, and terror of, the racism that permeates their lives and is respossible for the patterns of destruction that they inflict upon each other.

In this novel, Alice Walker challenges black Americans by posing the question of responsibility: how can oppressed blacks take control of their own lives? Ms. Walker feels it is through an understanding of a system, and the individual's position within that structure, that African-Americans will be able to emerge 'whole'. Barbara Christian considers Walker's central theme in this, and other novels:

> The question of responsibility for personal action and societal change is one recurrent motif in the complex quilts that Walker makes out of thrifty sentences, knotted questions, tight metaphors, terse sections.

Her novels continually stitch a fabric of the everyday violence that is committed against her characters and that they commit upon one another in their search for regeneration, and regeneration is what black people desire.[33]

Through three generations of Copelands, we witness violence in its many horrific manifestations: wife-beating, suicide, infanticide, murder and spiritual subjugation.

The novel's central character is Grange Copeland, who, believing what society has told him, considers himself worthless. He not only reels in self-destruction but eventually destroys his own family. His son, Brownfield, inherits this sense of worthlessness, and repeats, in varying degrees, the same patterns. It is only in Grange's final realization of responsibility that his family's future holds a glimmer of promise. In giving up his own life to save that of his grand-daughter, Ruth, Grange envisions a better life for her through sacrifice and regeneration. In one of the few scenes in the novel where Grange is able to relate honestly with his son, he expresses the main thesis of Ms. Walker's work:

'I know the danger of putting all the blame on somebody else for the mess you make out of your life . . . And I'm bound to believe that that's the way white folks can corrupt you even when you done held up before. 'Cause when they got you thinking that they're to blame for *everything* they have you thinking they's some kind of gods! . . . Then you begins to think up evil and begins to destroy everybody around you, and you blames it on the crackers. *Shit!* Nobody's as powerful as we make them out to be. We got our own *souls*, don't we?'[34]

But it is a long, arduous and violent journey as the Copelands search, in vain, for their own souls. Ms. Walker renders this tormented procession with disquieting insight.

This novel is rife with violence and its characters are filled with extraordinary self-hatred. It is hard to imagine one family perpetuating such twisted hatred upon one another, but I feel that Alice Walker emphasized this pattern to bring home a truth about the 'global' black family. Some critics felt that Ms. Walker only helped to intensify the myths about black men's violent natures and their abuse and neglect of their women. Even if Ms. Walker's polemical stance is somewhat over-emphatic in this work, it needs to be acknowledged that such problems did and do exist within the black community.

Alice Walker ends this novel mysteriously. Although Grange has died for Ruth's freedom, she is also left alone to fend for herself, and we wonder if she will survive 'whole'. So, the question of regeneration remains unclear. As

Barbara Christian comments:

> The paradox of death-giving-life remains. We wonder if it must be so.[35]

Yes. We wonder.

•   •   •

Alice Walker's second novel, *Meridian* (1976), investigates the impact of social change on individuals who are instrumental in effecting it. The novel is set in the South, from the beginnings of the Civil Rights Movement through to its violent aftermath and eventual decline.

Complex in the many questions it raises and the themes it explores, this novel is Ms. Walker's most intricate to date. Episodic in structure, it is a woven piece comprising non-chronological sections that are stitched together, 'making a quilt-like pattern' that links the past with the fabric of the present.

Ms. Walker said that she wanted to structure this book in a similar fashion to *Cane*, Jean Toomer's brilliant collage of poetry and prose, published in 1923:

> When I wrote *Meridian*, I realized that the chronological sequence is not the one that permits me the kind of freedom I need in order to create.... I wanted to do something like a crazy quilt, or like *Cane*... something that works on the mind in different patterns.[36]

The heroine Meridian Hill is the embodiment of black American spiritual continuity. In revolving episodes, this narrative tells the story of Meridian Hill, a young black girl growing up in the segregated South. A high-school drop-out and teenage mother, she moves away to attend university and joins the Civil Rights Movement. Meridian is transformed by this struggle, and continues to practise non-violence long after the 'movement' is over. In her search for effective change she comes to understand the spiritual legacy of her ancestors. Through this, Meridian's closest friends are moved and transformed as well. And it is Meridian's lover, Truman Held, who finally takes over the struggle from her.

Much of this creative book is loosely based on Ms. Walker's own life and Meridian's commitment to non-violence seems to mirror Walker's own. The novel attempts to confront the highly charged questions and dilemmas that are enmeshed in the fabric of every black American's life: racism, sexism, motherhood, intra-racial and inter-racial relationships, the effect of history on the present, the lessons to be learned from Native Americans, and black America's quest for 'wholeness'.

Although the novel consists of many episodes, veering back and forth in time, its heroine is a steadfast centre. Her name, Meridian, has many connotations – in fact, Walker quotes all the dictionary definitions of 'meridian' before the story starts. Among these connotations are: the South; noon-time; the highest points of power; the prime of life; and a distinctive character.

The novel begins with Truman Held, going South in search of Meridian. His first sight of her, and ours, registers her self-confidence, autonomy and moral power:

> 'I grieve in a different way', he said.
> 'I know,' Meridian panted.
> 'What do you know?'
> 'I know you grieve by running away. By pretending you were never there.'
> 'When things are finished it is best to leave.'
> 'Yes.'
> 'But that's not possible.'[37]

Barbara Christian has identified a source for Walker's title in Jean Toomer's poem 'The Blue Meridian', which envisages 'a new America,/to be spiritualized, by each new American.'[38] Walker's heroine carries this meaning too.

The concept of black people's collective culture is seen by Ms. Walker to be exemplified in the forms of music. Music, in some manner, threads its way through each chapter of the book, except for one, and Meridian discovers that the stoic spirit of the African-American's struggle is mirrored by it. Meridian then questions how it would be if black people rejected this spiritual legacy for a more violent means of change:

> But what none of them seemed to understand was that she felt herself to be, not holding on to something from the past, but *held* by something in the past... by the spirit of young girls singing in a country choir, their hair shining with brushings and grease, their voices the voices of angels. When she was transformed in church it was always by the purity of the singers' souls, which she could actually *Hear*, the purity that lifted their songs like a flight of doves above her music-drunken head. If they committed murder – and to her revolutionary murder was murder – *what would the music be like?*[39]

By challenging society's definition of motherhood, by exposing the often tangled relationships between black men and women, as well as the painful perplexities of inter-racial relationships, and by placing the sixties in a historical perspective, Alice Walker confronted sensitive issues. Michael G. Cooke, in an essay, said of *Meridian* that 'the genius of the novel lies in its ability to set up a restorative reaction without sentimentality or evasion.'[40]

Ms. Walker raises many complex questions in *Meridian*, but there is one theme that remains resolutely unquestionable for her: the necessity for black people to continue to engage in the rituals that have given them their spiritual legacy, which has been the sustaining substance of their survival:

> For it is the song of the people, transformed by the experience of each generation, that holds them together, and if any part of it is lost the people suffer and are without soul.[41]

● ● ●

> She ugly. He say. But she ain't no stranger to hard work. And she clean. And God done fixed her. You can do everything just like you want to and she ain't gonna make you feed it or clothe it.[42]

If one did not know the source of this passage, one would be inclined to think it was from a slave narrative or some book concerning slavery. But it is not. It's taken from Alice Walker's third novel, *The Color Purple* (1982), set in the South from 1909 to 1931. And, these words are not spoken by some white male racist, but come from the lips of a black man talking about a black woman.

The Color Purple gained Ms. Walker the Pulitzer Price and widespread national attention. One of the most controversial novels of African-American literature since Richard Wright's *Native Son*, its mention can still engender debate. Although certain facets of it may be problematic for some, *The Color Purple* must be recognized for its most moving story and the brilliant way in which it is told.

Walker chose the epistolary form. Celie's story unfolds in her letters to God, then her sister, then to God and the entire universe. But it is not just the form that exemplifies Ms. Walker's genius, it is that the most silenced and abused voice in American literature, that of a poor, black, ugly, uneducated, beaten-down woman *speaks*, with no authorial interference whatsoever. Everything is seen through Celie's eyes and depicted in her *own* language. We are startled from the very first page:

Dear God,
I am fourteen years old. ~~I am~~ I have always been a good girl. Maybe you can give me a sign letting me know what is happening to me ...

He never had a kine word to say to me. Just say You gonna do what your mammy wouldn't ... He push his thing inside my pussy. When that hurt, I cry. He start to choke me, saying You better shut up and git used to it.[43]

The reader remains riveted as Celie tells of her life through her letters to God. Raped and impregnated twice by a man she believes is her father, who gives away her children, she is then given to a man who uses and abuses her to such a degree that she cannot bear to speak his name. Eventually Celie blossoms into a love of self, fostered by the beautiful singer, Shug Avery. We witness a most moving transformation:

I'm pore, I'm black, I may be ugly and can't cook ... But I'm here.[44]

Celie belatedly receives letters from her sister Nettie, who managed to escape from her oppressive environment and become a missionary in Africa. These letters have been hidden from Celie by Mr.—, until Shug discovers their hiding place. This interruption of Celie's voice is something of a history lesson. Alice Walker intends to show the reader that black Americans have long historical links with their African cousins. She also points out, through these letters, that sexism is as prevalent in Africa as it is in America.

In this novel, Alice Walker develops the themes that dominated her previous works, but extends her canvas by depicting a lesbian relationship. Tackling this taboo subject, Alice Walker shows the relationship to be one of restoration and freedom, and emphasizes the importance of female friendship in the black community. Shug is the first person to love Celie, and through her, Celie comes to love herself. Indeed, with Shug's guidance, she discovers the loveliness of her own body, and the beauty of lovemaking:

Us kiss and kiss till we can't hardly kiss no more. Then us touch each other.
I don't know nothing bout it, I say to Shug.
I don't know much, she say.
Then I feel something real soft and wet on my breast, feel like one of my little lost babies mouth.
Way after while, I get like a little lost baby too.[45]

These gentle, intimate lesbian scenes are reduced, in the film version of *The Color Purple*, to a mere kiss between friends.

Another theme that was central to *Meridian*, that of humanity's close affinity with the land, reappears here. And the concept of God and Christianity in black life is given close scrutiny:

> Tell me what your God look like, Celie ... Okay, I say. He big and old and tall and graybearded and white ...
> Course that's the one in the white folks' white bible ...
> How come the bible just like everything else they make ... and all the colored folks doing is gitting cursed?
>
> Here's the thing ... The thing I believe. God is inside you and inside everybody else. You come to the world with God. But only them that search for it inside find it ... I believe God is everything ... I think it pisses God off if you walk by the color purple in a field somewhere and don't notice it.[46]

Shug's helpful and probing conversations, along with the love she lavishes upon Celie, begin to transform her. This change in Celie triggers a chain reaction, for the male characters in the novel are altered as well. Initially, they are all horrible, sexist creatures, or just plain dumb; but in the end they become compassionate and understanding individuals.

And it is the depiction of black men in this work that has caused such an uproar. Many black male, and some female, critics were disturbed by these seemingly stereotypic characterizations. For it does appear that Ms. Walker, so intent upon showing the oppression of some black Southern women, forgot to render her male characters with any complexity or depth. They are, for the most part, relentlessly brutal, and we never know why. They just stand as cardboard figures, mouthing obscenities and wielding vicious power. Darryl Pinckney, in *The New York Review of Books*, has said that:

> The black men are seen at a distance – that is, entirely from the point of view of the woman – as naifs incapable of reflection, tyrants filled with impotent rage, or as totemic do-gooders.[47]

When *The Color Purple* was made into a film by Steven Spielberg, controversy once again abounded. Hollywood took its usual licence with literary efforts and made this story into some kind of fairy tale. One could think that Mr. Spielberg missed the whole point of the novel when he said in a television interview that *The Color Purple* 'centres around twelve characters and a mailbox.'[48]

Leaving aside the disturbing and enduring arguments engendered by *The Color Purple*, there is little denying that Alice Walker has given us a wonderful story told by a 'voice' often silenced in American literature. And by letting that voice speak, in her own language, Ms. Walker has enriched our knowledge of black American women and paid homage to the lasting beauty and magic of the black oral tradition. Ms. Walker has made considerable claims for this novel:

> For Celie's speech pattern in *The Color Purple*, Celie's words reveal not only an intelligence that transforms illiterate speech into something that is, at times, very beautiful – as well as effective in conveying her sense of her world – her speech also reveals what has been done to her by a racist and sexist system, and her intelligent blossoming as a human being despite her oppression demonstrates why her oppressors persist even today in trying to keep her down. For if and when Celie rises to her rightful, earned place in society, across the planet, the world will be a different place, I can tell you.[49]

• • •

Womanist is to feminist as purple is to lavender.[50]

Alice Walker's *In Search of Our Mothers' Gardens: Womanist Prose* (1983), a compilation of various essays written over a period of sixteen years, was published in the year after *The Color Purple*. In it, Ms. Walker considers a wide range of topics: her search for, and discovery of, Zora Neale Hurston's proud and prodigious writing, 'The Black Writer and the Southern Experience', the Civil Rights Movement, 'The Divided Life of Jean Toomer', 'Nuclear Madness', intra-racism, acknowledgement of the vast numbers of black Southern women, including Phillis Wheatley, who sustained creative efforts in the face of great hardship, as well as many other topics.

Many of these essays are intelligent, innovative and compelling. Alice Walker discusses just about every subject and situation that could possibly be relevant to female African-American experiences. Yet, many of these essays express the considerations of not only black women but of women everywhere.

In Search of Our Mothers' Gardens is a rich and invaluable volume. Alice Walker often treads on volatile territory to ask difficult questions and to search for possible answers. And it is through this fearless probing that Ms.

Walker has given us her prolific gifts, and has begun to clarify many of her own queries:

> Guided by my heritage of a love of beauty and a respect for strength –
> in search of my mother's garden, I have found my own.[51]

● ● ●

> Pretty women wonder where my secret lies.
> I'm not cute or built to suit a fashion model's size
> But when I start to tell them
> They think I'm telling lies.
> I say,
> It's in the reach of my arms,
> The span of my hips,
> The stride of my step,
> The curl of my lips.
> I'm a woman
> Phenomenally
> Phenomenal woman,
> That's me.

(Maya Angelou, 'Phenomenal Woman'[52])

Maya Angelou is indeed phenomenal. Poet, singer, dancer, composer, actress, director, editor and autobiographer, her 'reach' embraces both writing and the performing arts.

As a black autobiographer, Ms. Angelou stands beside the escaped slave Frederick Douglass. Like him, she can win the minds of her audience and speak not only for herself, but for her race. She admits to taking on this representative role in the first volume of her autobiography:

> When I wrote *I Know Why The Caged Bird Sings*, I wasn't thinking so much about my own life or identity. I was thinking about a particular time in which I lived and the influences of that time on a number of people. I kept thinking what about that time? What were the people around young Maya doing? I used the central figure – myself – as a focus to show how one person can make it through those times.[53]

The five volumes of Maya Angelou's life-story span almost half a century, from the late 1920s to the early 1970s. They resonate with the love, wit, energy and spirit of an indomitable woman. Maya was initially reluctant to

write about her life, but her editor, Robert Loomis ensnared her by saying:
'To write an autobiography as literature, is the most difficult thing anyone
could do.'[54] That was all the challenge Maya needed.

Yet, to take up such a challenge and succeed, the black woman needs all
her ancestral powers of survival. Ms. Angelou comments:

> The fact that the adult American Negro female emerges a formidable
> character is often met with amazement, distaste and even belligerence.
> It is seldom accepted as an inevitable outcome of the struggle won by
> survivors and deserves respect if not enthusiastic acceptance.[55]

● ● ●

> There is a deep brooding
> in Arkansas.
> Old crimes like moss pend
> from poplar trees.
> The sullen earth
> is much too red for comfort.[56]

Maya Angelou was born Marguerite Johnson in St. Louis, Missouri, in
1928. When she and her brother Bailey were aged three and four, their
parents divorced and the children were sent to Stamps, Arkansas, to live
with their grandmother. Maya has stated that Stamps could just as well be
called 'Chitlin' Switch, Georgia; Hang 'Em High, Alabama; or Don't Let
The Sun Set On You Here, Nigger, Mississippi.'[57] Though racism ran a
ravine through the town, separating white from black, Stamps, Arkansas,
was to be the bedrock of Maya's strength, and her experience there sustained
her through the most difficult times of her life.

Here, in this small Southern community, Maya learned what it was like to
grow up a black girl in a world where her boundaries were set by whites.

Maya/Marguerite's story unfolds on Easter Day, when she realizes that
the dress her grandmother made her was not the beautiful creation she had
envisioned but just 'a plain ugly cut-down from a white woman's once-was-
purple throwaway.'[58] This demeaning realization made Maya ache for a
newness, a difference:

> Wouldn't they be surprised when one day I woke out of my black ugly
> dream, and my real hair, which was long and blond would take the
> place of the kinky mass that Momma wouldn't let me straighten? My
> light-blue eyes were going to hypnotize them.... Because I was really

white and because a cruel fairy stepmother... had turned me into a too-big Negro girl, with nappy hair, broad feet and a space between my teeth that would hold a number-two pencil.[59]

For a decade, Marguerite is raised by God-fearing Annie 'Momma' Henderson, the only black in Stamps to have a business. Mrs. Henderson owned a country store, and was a shrewd businesswoman. With a profound sense of moral duty and belief in hard work, she reared Maya with a strict hand. But as Maya has observed, 'I don't think she ever knew that a deep-brooding love hung over everything she touched.'[60]

Through the many instances of her grandmother's bravery and commonsense, Maya learned that not only could blacks overcome, they could also endure. This is best exemplified in a scene where Mrs. Henderson is mocked by 'powhitetrash' children. When one of them stands on her head without underwear, 'Momma' continues to sing hymns. This stoicism enables her to rise above such disrespect and provides a lasting lesson for Maya:

> She stood another whole song through. . . . Her face was a brown moon that shone on me. She was beautiful. Something had happened out there, which I couldn't completely understand, but I could see she was happy. . . . And she went behind the candy counter and hummed, 'Glory, glory, hallelujah, when I lay my burden down.'[61]

From this simple and extraordinary woman, Maya learned courage, control and 'grace under pressure'.

Ms. Angelou also enjoyed a close relationship with her beloved brother Bailey, Jr. They shared a love of literature, of Shakespeare, but primarily of black writers. This early exposure to African-American literature – Langston Hughes, James Weldon Johnson, Paul Laurence Dunbar and W. E. B. Du Bois – helped to strengthen Maya's knowledge of the creative gifts of her people.

And the church, with its moments of spirited singing and abandoned shouting, egged on by a masterful preacher, studded her Sundays.

This nurturing world was to crumble when Maya was eight years old. She went to visit her mother in St. Louis and the unimaginable happened. Maya Angelou was raped by her mother's boyfriend. The mere fact that Maya, having been abandoned by her mother, returned to her only to be raped by a man her mother saw fit to have a relationship with, must have devastated this eight-year-old child beyond comprehension. This horror was compounded by the 'silencing' of the event and the killing of the rapist by her uncles. Maya's last, small semblance of selfhood collapsed. She sealed herself up:

The only thing I could do was to stop talking.... If I talked to anyone... That person might die too.... I had to stop talking.[62]

Maya remained silent for five years. We wonder what painful and confused ragings must have gone on in her young head. But Maya's resolve, turned inward in those years, allows us to understand the woman she was to become. When that tenacity and strength of purpose were eventually turned outward, they enabled her to confront and overcome the many obstacles that life was to offer her.

The individual who was able to bring Maya out of her silenced world was Mrs. Flowers, the gentle, caring 'black aristocrat' of Stamps. She read literature and recited poetry with such grace and beauty that Maya herself was moved to do the same. Ms. Angelou stated that Mrs. Flowers 'made me proud to be a Negro, just by being herself.'[63]

Moving from the small world of Stamps to the big-city life of San Francisco, Maya began her determined struggle to make a place for herself in the world.

In this moving and brilliantly written first volume, we learn what people and forces came to mould Maya Angelou. And it is Maya, the author, who goes through and to her life as the child Marguerite, and recounts it with extraordinary skill and insight.

There are few autobiographies that read with such depth and articulation. We must stop and remind ourselves that yes, this is a life, not a fiction. And it is Maya's life of strength, love, and determination that we can use as a mirror to judge our own.

•   •   •

Let me hip you to the streets,
Jim,
Ain't nothing happening.
Maybe some tomorrows gone up in smoke,
raggedy preachers, telling a joke
to lonely, son-less old ladies' maids ...

That's the streets man,
Nothing happening.[64]

In Maya Angelou's second autobiographical instalment, *Gather Together in My Name* (1974), we find Ms. Angelou, now a mother, hitting the streets for various menial jobs, mostly waitressing. Young, and filled with romantic notions, Maya just barely escapes the life that these streets often offer to black Americans.

Although this book does not convey the depth of character and situation that her previous work did, it moves with humour and ease. One critic said that her writing here 'has a relaxed, airy style . . . because of all the breathing spaces in the prose.'[65]

In Maya's desperate but determined search for money and meaning in her life, we witness a young girl's entrapment in a world of sexism:

> My romance with R.L. was danced out in the rehearsal hall. . . . I gave no arguments to his monthly requests for lovemaking. After all, he was my teacher and my transportation to Broadway.[66]

Maya's affair with her dance teacher, as a means to stardom, as well as with a pimp and a dope-addict, show her to be incredibly naive and hopelessly in 'love with love'. Duped and used by most of these men, Maya had little guidance to do otherwise. The only hard-hitting and prophetic advice her mother had to give her was 'Be the best of anything you get into. If you want to be a whore, it's your life. Be a damn good one.'[67]

Careening from one bad involvement to another, Maya manages to survive. And, ironically, she owes her survival to the care and concern of a dope-addict who startled Ms. Angelou into reality by shooting-up in front of her. Without him, Maya might still be silenced, and we would have lost yet another beautiful black voice.

● ● ●

> Hearin' Stevie Wonder
> Cookin' beans and rice
> Goin' to the opera
> Checkin' out Leontyne Price
>
> . . . .
>
> Living our lives with flash and style
> Ain't we colorful folks?
>
> Now ain't we bad?
> Now ain't we black?
> Now ain't we fine?[68]

Maya Angelou's third volume, *Singin' and Swingin' and Gettin' Merry Like Christmas* (1976), is a spirited account of the years when she finally comes into her own. But as Maya comes closer, in her writing, to the woman she is now, we begin to feel a distancing from the issues and experiences that comprise her life. Yet, she makes up for this with the lively accounts of her life in show business. The vivid portrayal of the many people who made up the touring company of *Porgy and Bess* and the communal feeling that Maya enjoyed with them, are well worth the reading. Ms. Angelou comes to realize some of the many talents she possesses and the book is filled with joy and humour. A good time is had by all, but we feel that Ms. Angelou is keeping her interior thoughts to herself.

● ● ●

> supermarket roastin like the
> noon-day sun
> national guard nervous with his shining gun
> goose the motor quicker
> here's my nigga picka
> shoot him in the belly
> shoot him while he run.[69]

The Heart of a Woman (1981), Maya's fourth book of autobiography, traces her development as a writer and a committed Civil Rights worker. Clear focus, psychological depth and incisive writing make this work her strongest since *I Know Why The Caged Bird Sings*.

Inspired by the writer and activist John O. Killens, Maya Angelou joins the Harlem Writers' Guild. Aided by prominent authors such as James Baldwin and Paule Marshall, Ms. Angelou soon learned that 'If I wanted to write, I had to be willing to develop a kind of concentration found mostly in people awaiting execution.'[70]

And the concentration paid off, for her vignette of the great jazz singer, Billie Holiday, is memorable:

> All the jazz and rhythm-and-blues stations had oily-voiced commentators extolling the virtues of the great artist whose like would not be seen or heard again. Jazz buffs with glorious vocabularies wrote long and often boring tributes to the pulchritudinous Lady Day, her pleasing and intricate harmonies. I would remember forever the advice of a lonely sick woman with a waterfront mouth, who sang pretty songs to a twelve-year-old boy.[71]

Ms. Angelou's Civil Rights work brought her in contact with many leaders of the Movement: Martin Luther King, Bayard Rustin and Malcolm X. Her writing captures the excitement of the times – the visits of Castro and

Khruschev to Harlem, and Harlem's mass protest at the United Nations Building against the assassination of Patrice Lumumba.

We feel, in this volume, the emergence of a new, self-confident Maya Angelou. Organizing Civil Rights campaigns, travelling to Egypt with an African freedom fighter, then leaving him because of the restricted role she was expected to assume, Ms. Angelou continues to carve out her own path. It is now apparent that Ms. Angelou is indeed her own woman.

●   ●   ●

Taste one fruit
its juice free falling from
a mother tree

Know me

Africa.[72]

All God's Children Need Travelling Shoes (1986), is Maya Angelou's fifth and latest autobiographical volume. It concerns itself with the problematic idea that African-Americans can claim Africa as their homeland. Proud and liberated Ghana, with President Nkrumah at its head, does not yet know its African-American cousins. The white world's stereotypic image of black Americans still predominates in this country. Ms. Angelou is left to consider her position there:

> And now, less than one hundred years after slavery was abolished, some descendants of those early slaves taken from Africa, returned, weighted with a heavy hope, to a continent which they couldn't remember, to a home which had shamefully little memory of them.[73]

Struggling to find her place in this 'homeland', Ms. Angelou's writing conveys the questions that plague her, and which she is never able fully to answer: 'Was the odor of slavery so obvious that people were offended and lashed out at us automatically?'[74] Furious at their reception, one black American 'Revolutionist Returnee' assessed the situation thus: 'Damn these Africans ... are treating me like Charlie [the white man] did down on the plantation.'[75]

Throughout this volume, Maya Angelou can never really come to terms with this painful cultural divide, and never really manages to confront its deeper issues. Perhaps the situation was too overwhelming and still too close to address in a more probing manner:

> If the heart of Africa still remained elusive, my search for it had brought me closer to understanding myself and other human beings.[76]

Ms. Angelou comes to understand that she is indeed an American, and that, for better or for worse, that land is her home:

> Many of us had only begun to realize in Africa that the Stars and Stripes was our flag and our only flag, and that knowledge was almost too painful to bear....
>
> I shuddered to think that while we wanted that flag dragged into the mud and sullied beyond repair, we also wanted it pristine.... Watching it wave in the breeze of a distance made us nearly choke with emotion. It lifted us up with its promise and broke our hearts with its denial.[77]

● ● ●

Maya Angelou's five volumes of poetry, *Just Give Me a Cool Drink of Water 'Fore I Diiie* (1971), *Oh Pray My Wings Are Gonna Fit Me Well* (1975), *And Still I Rise* (1978), *Shaker, Why Don't You Sing* (1983) and *Now Sheba Sings the Song* (1987), illustrated by Tom Feelings, comprise the cornucopia of people, places and events that are a part of Ms. Angelou's life. From Arkansas to Harlem, from Africa to Hollywood, Maya's verses speak of the lives of black folk. Discrimination, exploitation, welfare, drug-addiction, sorrow, joy and survival are all depicted in her poetry.

Her poetic style ranges from the language and cadences of black street talk, to jazz rhythms and more formal structures. Her previously quoted poem, 'Letter to an Aspiring Junkie' speaks with the syncopated sounds of black city-dwellers, whereas 'My Arkansas' is more formal. The musicality of 'Ain't We Bad' literally rises off the page and makes one snap one's fingers. Ms. Angelou places herself in the persona of an old black domestic as she ponders the ironies of a black woman's life:

> Sixty years in these folks' world
> The child I works for calls me girl
> I say 'Yes ma'am' for working's sake,
> Too proud to bend

Too poor to break,
I laugh until my stomach ache
When I think about myself.[78]

Maya Angelou was the first black female director in Hollywood. She was screenwriter and composer for the film *Georgia, Georgia,* and author of the television series on African traditions in American life. Ms. Angelou has also directed numerous plays, among them *Moon on a Rainbow Shawl* by Errol John. Recipient of many honorary degrees, she now holds the Reynolds Chair at Wake Forest University in Winston-Salem, North Carolina.

With immense power and creativity, the 'silenced' voice of a little black girl is now heard throughout the world. We listen, as Maya's resonant words speak for her, and for black women everywhere:

You may write me down in history
With your bitter, twisted lies,
You may trod me in the very dirt
But still, like dust, I'll rise.

. . . .

Out of the huts of history's shame
I rise
Up from a past that's rooted in pain
I rise

. . . .

Bringing the gifts that my ancestors gave,
I am the dream and the hope of the slave.
I rise
I rise
I rise.[79]

9: 'The Unblinking Eye'

When and where did you first
Confront loneliness?
When and where did you resist
The urge to die? . . .

. . . .

Was anyone present? . . .
Did you survive? . . .
Were preventive measures always
Used? . . .

. . . .

Document.[1]

From the late 1960s, African-American women began to enter the economic mainstream of America. No longer just nurses, teachers, domestic workers, cooks, factory hands, dancers and singers, some became doctors, lawyers, professors, politicians and corporate workers. Educated, worldly, equipped with sass and strength, they took new directions. For the first time, some of these women had economic choices. In literature, the 'sister' stereotypes were being discarded, as African-American women writers uncovered the distinct yet common threads of black women's lives.

Yet some of these women found themselves caught in the trap of welfare, drugs, little or no education, undernourishment, bad-housing and teenage pregnancy. Left within a system dedicated to keeping them down, they were defiled and denied by society at large. But they were visible to the concerned and compassionate 'gaze' of the black woman writer.

As different as these women's circumstances might be, all had to contend with the age-old duo – sexism and racism. From the sophisticated city woman to the radical feminist, from the lesbian to the housewife, all were searching for a meaningful place in their communities. Many questioned the prescribed roles for black women, as well as the sacrifices of cultural identity needed to 'get ovah' in a white man's world.

From authors as diverse as their subject matter comes a literature that addresses all of these issues, and more. Using realism as their basic mode of expression, these women's stories range over a wide geographical expanse.

● ● ●

The group of women around the table long ago. They taught me my first lessons in the narrative art. They trained my ear. They set a standard of excellence. This is why the best of my work must be attributed to them; it stands as a testimony to the rich legacy of language and culture they so freely passed on to me in the wordshop of the kitchen.[2]

In her autobiographical essay, 'From the Poets in the Kitchen', Paule Marshall pays tribute to those women who, ignored or despised by the *literati*, handed on to a new generation of writers the culture of her mother tongue.

Paule Marshall (1929 –), born of Barbadian Parents who emigrated to Brooklyn, New York, has a creative and insightful voice. Through her writing, she has brought into focus the culture of the Caribbean peoples, in America or within their own island communities. Ms. Marshall found that the way of doing this lay through language. She explains:

I'm fascinated by language, because black people both here [the U.S.] and in the West Indies have used language as a way of retaining their humanity. That's why it holds such meaning for me. They've also made such great poetry out of it. They've taken the English language which has been imposed upon them and recreated it in their own image.[3]

It is with an unerring eye and ear that Paule Marshall presents characters who, through their language and actions, speak metaphorically for a larger group. One critic has observed that:

Marshall's great talent as a writer is her insightful portrayal of individual characters as they articulate the complex of a community's actions and desires.[4]

Paule Marshall's first novel, *Brown Girl, Brownstones*, was published in 1959. But like Gwendolyn Brook's novella, *Maud Martha*, it was ahead of its time. The book received very good reviews but failed to sell. Most of us came to Ms. Marshall's work when it was re-issued in the early 1980s. Barbara Christian comments on what has so often happened – and continues to happen – to the works of America's best black women writers:

> Marshall's subject matter, the development of a brown girl into a woman within the rituals and mores of a black cultural context, had yet to be seen as important. . . . It was being used as a book for juveniles, just as Toni Morrison's *The Bluest Eye* would be, despite their complex language and psychology.[5]

In *Brown Girl, Brownstones*, we are placed in a black Caribbean neighbourhood in Brooklyn, New York, in 1939. Much of the story mirrors Ms. Marshall's own upbringing. Thousands of Barbadians, from 1900 to 1940, went to America to escape poverty and lack of opportunity in that British colony. They worked incessantly to become a part of the American Dream and to 'buy house'. This desire, however, tended to push them further away from their own history and culture and closer to the values of American capitalism. The subtle self-hatred that this kind of behaviour engendered can be seen, when the Association of Barbadian Homeowners and Businessmen meet: '"We ain white yet. We's small-timers! . . . But we got our eye on the big-time. . . ."'[6]

The novel revolves around the Boyce household, with Selina Boyce as the keen-eyed daughter of Silla and Deighton Boyce, first generation immigrants to America. Marshall etches out these and other characters with remarkable skill. We feel the power of the strong-willed Silla, the proud, confused yearnings of Deighton, and the evolving clear-sighted bravery of the young Selina.

Silla is the most forceful character in this work; head-strong, and armed with the powerful cadences of her oral tradition, she knows that to make it 'in this white-man world you got to take yah mouth and make a gun.'[7]

Sitting around her kitchen-table, she admonishes, praises, advises and gives instructions to family and friends alike. From issues concerning God to the causes of World War Two and the allegiance of Barbadians to England, Selina's words slash the air:

> 'You think 'cause they does call Barbados "Little England" that you is somebody? What the King know 'bout you – or care?'[8]

And her perceptiveness takes in the political exploitation of her people:

'The rum shop and the church join together to keep we pacify an in ignorance.'[9]

Silla's realization of the injustices done to her people that drives her, but in her relentless determination for money and property she destroys her family. She frightens her daughter Ina into submissive meekness, and secretly sells her husband's land in Barbados to buy a brownstone. When he learns this, his fragile pride crumbles and he eventually commits suicide. Paule Marshall closely examines the intricate questions of assimilation, materialism and how black people can endure without loss. She poses all of these questions in the character of Silla. Mary Helen Washington observes that:

> Silla's life is a paradigm of the Barbadian community. She is the touchstone, for she proclaims aloud the chaotic trouble deep in the core of the community. Her endurance, her rage, her devotion to the dollar and property, her determination to survive in 'this man country' are theirs. Her lights and shadows are theirs.[10]

Selina grows up in the midst of this, absorbing culture and confusion. As Silla stands for the history of the abused and ignored black woman, Selina stands as its new hope. She is the bearer of the culture, yet the one who questions the means by which one survives while keeping that culture alive. And she, unlike her mother, has choices. Selina is aware that no matter what choices she makes, she will embody her culture, as well as having her own self-hood. This then is a novel of hope:

> *Brown Girl, Brownstones* is . . .one of the most optimistic texts in Afro-American literature, for it assigns even to an oppressed people the power of conscious political choice: they are not victims.[11]

Ms. Marshall's next publication was a collection of novellas entitled *Soul, Clap Hands and Sing* (1961). This collection continues her theme of personal identity within the framework of cultural history. The titles, 'Barbados', 'Brooklyn', 'British Guiana' and 'Brazil' (the first two now published in *Merle: a Novella and Other Stories*), signal a wider geographical scope. By placing most of the novellas in the Caribbean, Ms. Marshall makes her characters directly confront their African ancestry. These stories all deal with old men, who have to face the consequences of the denial of their culture and their people. The most effective of these is 'Barbados', which tells the story of a Barbadian who has spent most of his life in America working assiduously so that he can go home and live like his white colonial oppressors. From an early age his perceptions have been conditioned:

But because of their whiteness and wealth he had not dared to hate them. Instead, his rancor, like a boomerang had rebounded, glancing past him to strike all the dark ones like himself. . . .[12]

This collection is a turning point for Ms. Marshall: using the Caribbean as the focus for her stories, she consciously explores political themes. She continues her examination of personal identity and social analysis in her three short stories, 'Reena' (1962), 'To Da-duh in Memoriam' (1964) and 'Some Get Wasted' (1968). (The first two now published in *Merle: a Novella and Other Stories*.)

'Reena' could be a continuation of *Brown Girl, Brownstones*, as it explores what Selina might have become in middle-age. The story takes place at a wake for Reena's aunt Vi, who had worked as a live-in domestic, to make money to 'buy house', but did not live to achieve her goal. Because of this, Reena contemplates her own choices: the disappointment of left-wing politics, the restrictions of middle-class marriage, and the problems of an inter-racial relationship. As she surveys her own life, Reena realizes that the history of the black woman is still a part of her:

> 'They condemn us . . . without taking history into account. We are still, most of us, the black woman who had to be almost frighteningly strong in order for all of us to survive. . . . And we are still, so many of us, living that history.'[13]

'To Da-duh in Memoriam' is one of Ms. Marshall's most moving short stories. It concerns a nine-year-old girl's trip from America back to Barbados to visit her grandmother. The child represents modernity, cold and technologically superior, and Da-duh embodies the history and culture of black people. The tension of the tale is between these two polarities, as one character tries to show the other how superior their home is. The competition between them heightens, as Da-duh shows her grand-daughter the magnificence of her island: abundant fruit, colourful flowers and the majesty of the island's trees. The young child counters this with Manhattan's magnificence: electric lights, radios, and skyscrapers. The Empire State Building completely outdoes the tall, trembling palms and when the first airplanes fly over Da-duh's village, she dies.

The narrator tries to exorcize her guilt towards Da-duh by acknowledging her grandmother's traditions, and by doing so, incorporates them into her own life.

> She died and I lived, but always to this day even, within the shadow of her death. For a brief period after I was grown I went to live alone, like one doing penance in a loft above a noisy factory . . . and there painted

seas of sugar cane and huge swirling, Van Gogh suns... while the thunderous thread of the machines downstairs jarred the floor beneath my easel, mocking my efforts.[14]

These short stories foreshadow Paule Marshall's next novel, *The Chosen Place, the Timeless People* (1969), which takes on the politics and policies of the Caribbean, England and America. The heroine, Merle Kibona is an amalgamation of black Caribbean culture and Western ideologies. She is the middle-aged, wordly-wise black woman who grapples with her cultural identity and its viability in a modern technological world. Ms. Marshall explains:

> What I'm trying to do in [this] work, is to take the black woman as character to another level, to give her an added dimension. There is the quest for self, but at the same time ... to suggest that [her] search is linked to this larger quest which has to do with the liberation of us as a people..... She [Merle] has been shaped by forces in the West Indies and by England and so she, in effect, *embodies* the history of the hemisphere.[15]

As the embodiment of both cultures, Merle intersects with the poor black people of Bournehills, as well as with whites and blacks who embrace the capitalist system: her English, female lover, who tries to manipulate her with money, the well-meaning white American Saul, who comes to realize that his company's technological advances for Merle's village are yet another means of oppression, and the many black officials in Bournehills who ape the actions of a colonial regime.

Merle is torn between these two worlds and undergoes an arduous journey, geographically and psychologically, to come to grips with who she is and how to become an effective member of her community.

Marshall uses the ritual of carnival to bring these tensions to the fore, emphasizing the importance of the past in conjunction with the present. Hortense J. Spillers comments:

> the totality of the Carnival in Bournehills allows us to understand more precisely why this work is entitled *The Chosen Place, the Timeless People*. The agents in that regard do not belong simply to themselves, in their discrete time and place. Their renewal is altogether essential to a redemptive historical scheme that must play itself out.[16]

This ritual of bringing the past to the present is done each year by acting out and discussing the famous slave revolt of the region, led by Ned Cuffee. The celebration ensures that the people of Bournehills acknowledge their ancestors and their history. And it is this factor, so grievously missing from most of modern life, that Ms. Marshall emphasizes in the novel:

> You have to try and learn from all that's gone before – and again from
> both the good and the bad.... Use your history as a guide.... Because
> many times what one needs to know for the present ... has been spelled
> out in past events. That it's all there if only they would look.[17]

In Ms. Marshall's third novel, *Praisesong for the Widow* (1983), she
continues the theme of the black woman's search for identity in a world
bereft of ancestral connection.

This is a moving and beautifully written work about an African-
American, middle-class woman, who has sacrificed all the joys of black
culture to become a part of the American Dream. Avey Johnson and some of
her friends have full-blown familiarity. We know these Aveys; smartly
suited, carefully coiffeured, yet somehow lacking in luminosity and depth.
They are pleasant women, seeking fulfilment in beautiful houses,
sumptuous meals and the accumulation of things.

Avey Johnson's story unfolds on a pleasure cruise to the Caribbean. But it
is also another journey for Avey – a painful, yet illuminating encounter with
herself and her past. Plagued by recurrent dreams, she argues with her long-
dead great-aunt Cuney, who urges her to follow her back in time. This link
with African-American history and slavery finally overcomes Avey, and she
leaves her cruise in Grenada.

Her guide to the past is Lebert Joseph, who 'saw how far she had come
since leaving the ship and the distance she had yet to go.'[18] Avey travels with
him to Carriacou, and on this journey loses all her material possessions. She
is also sea-sick, and this purging stands for the break with her bourgeois life.
But Paule Marshall uses this scene on the ship, not only for loss, but also for
the gain of historical connections:

> She was alone in the deckhouse ... yet she had the impression as her
> mind flickered on briefly of other bodies lying crowded in with her in
> that hot, airless dark. A multitude it felt like lay packed around her in
> the filth and stench of themselves, just as she was. Their moans, rising
> and falling with each rise and plunge of the schooner, enlarged upon
> the one filling her own head. Their suffering – the depth of it, the
> weight of it, in the cramped space – made hers of no consequence.[19]

In *Praisesong for the Widow*, Ms. Marshall fuses the physical with the
psychic, as Avey Johnson goes back in time, to re-evaluate her old life and
emerge anew.

Paule Marshall uses traditional narrative form in all of her work. In a
period of literary fragmentation and experiment, this 'wholeness' comes out
of a desire to give coherence to the history of a disrupted people. Susan

Willis discusses this:

> Clearly, the desire for totality and the urgent need to invent a narrative capable of producing closure exist only for people who realize they no longer have totality in their lives but remember that such a state once existed. I think this summarizes Paule Marshall's position as a writer and as an immigrant.[20]

It is not only in the structure of Ms. Marshall's works that we, as black people, experience 'closure', but also through the values that inform them.

● ● ●

> a changed changer
> i continue to continue
> where i have been
> most of my lives is
> where i'm going[21]

All the authors discussed in this chapter give close scrutiny to the intricacies of black women's lives. I have suggested that in doing so, most have chosen realism, drawing on the tradition of the naturalistic novel with its objectivity about actual conditions. But Paule Marshall reminds us of an older and broader tradition – the narrative art handed down from Africa – that is still vigorous in these women's works.

Gloria Naylor (1950 –), whose first novel, *The Women of Brewster Place*, won the American Book Award in 1983, shows both these traditions to be very much alive. Composed of seven stories, this novel interconnects the varied lives of urban black women who live on the imaginary street of Brewster Place. This book is very much like Pat Barker's *Union Street* (1982), which tells the intertwined stories of poor urban whites in the North of England.
Here are Naylor's women:

> Nutmeg arms leaned over windowsills, gnarled ebony legs carried groceries up double flights of steps, and saffron hands strung out wet laundry on back-yard lines.... They were hard-edged, soft-centred, brutally demanding, and easily pleased, these women of Brewster Place.[22]

The intermingled lives of bright, desperate, determined, resilient black women fill these pages. And each has her story. There is the young, spirited

Kiswana Browne, who questions her mother's middle-class values. Mrs. Browne clearly shows that there might be cosmetic differences between blacks, but it is the commonalities that hold them together:

> Then, know this... I am alive because of the blood of proud people who never scraped or begged or apologized for what they were.... And I learned through the blood of these people that black isn't beautiful and black isn't ugly – black is![23]

We also meet Luciela Louise Turner, a young, unwed mother trying to make a home in the midst of poverty and strife. When tragedy strikes, Ms. Naylor uses the incantatory style of the black preacher to bring a long line of female loss and suffering to the fore:

> Ciel moaned. Mattie rocked. Propelled by the sound, Mattie rocked her out of that bed, out of that room, into a blue vastness just underneath the sun and above time.... She rocked her on and on, past Dachau, where soul-gutted Jewish mothers swept their children's entrails off laboratory floors. They flew past the spilled brains of Senegalese infants whose mothers had dashed them on the wooden sides of slave ships. And she rocked on.[24]

Of the many stories told here, the most devastating is entitled 'The Two'. This is an unflinching 'gaze' into the confined world of a lesbian couple. Not only is this a statement about homophobia. Ms. Naylor also questions whether a monogamous relationship can fulfil the needs of both women. And in a community that mirrors the frustrated and hopeless state of many black urban young men, this lesbian relationship provides an easy scapegoat:

> Bound by the last building on Brewster and a brick wall, they reigned in that unlit alley like dwarfed warrior-kings.... Baptized with the steam from a million non-reflective mirrors, these men wouldn't be called upon to... point a finger to move a nation, or stick a pole into the moon – and they knew it. They only had that three-hundred-foot alley to serve them as a stateroom.... So Lorraine found herself on her knees, surrounded by the most dangerous species in existence – human males with an erection to validate in a world that was only six-feet wide.[25]

In her next novel, *Linden Hills* (1985), Gloria Naylor uses the imaginary landscape of a black-owned, black-inhabited middle-class neighbourhood. In this work, Naylor has attempted to depict a modern equivalent of Dante's *Inferno*. The swirling, serpentine story is told through the eyes of two young black men, living on the outskirts of this sought-after suburban enclave. Work takes them inside the homes of its residents and they come to question the wrecked lives of these 'better-off' black folks. Realizing the sacrifices their people have made to 'get a piece of the pie', they are determined to find a more fulfilling existence. Greed, manipulation, madness and suicide proliferate as black men try to become 'white', and women try to piece together who they are, or if, in fact, they do exist.

> There was the profile of her nose and lips. It was impossible to determine the shape of her eyes, even from the side, but this was enough. No doubt remained – she was there.[26]

Many characters inhabit *Linden Hills*, all contributing to one of the most distressing accounts of black middle-class existence in African-American literature. One critic assessed the novel:

> *Linden Hills* is an uncomfortable and dangerous book which pricks the conscience. . . . Naylor has risked much by writing such a disturbing tale . . . she could lose a black audience that feels unjustly challenged and a white audience that thinks the novel's hard questions are not meant for them. . . . But because Naylor knows who she is, where she has been, and where she wants to go, she dares to tell her tale and dares the reader to reckon with it.[27]

Gloria Naylor's most recent novel, *Mama Day* (1988), departs further from the world of realism, to incorporate magic and myth.

The story is set on an all-black island called Willow Springs, on the south-eastern coast of the United States. There, since 1823, blacks have had the freedom to shape their own destinies. The timespan takes us from the eighteenth century to 1990, but most of the novel takes place in the present. Told by the three voices of Cocoa, George and 'Willow Springs', the story concerns Cocoa's departure from the island to live in New York City. There she meets and marries a northern black man, George, and they return to Willow Springs for a vacation. A tragedy occurs, and the ancient inheritance of magic and herbal medicine displaces modern technology. Ms. Naylor captures the sounds of city and rural life without missing a beat. She wittily depicts the black northern woman's existence:

> 'You mean, you want to bring back segregation?' I looked at him like he was a fool – where had it gone? I just wanted to bring the clarity . . . back – it would save me a whole lot of subway tokens. What I was left to deal with were the ads labelled *Equal Opportunity Employer*, or

nothing – ... And if I wanted to limit myself to the sure bets, then it was an equal opportunity to be what, or earn what? That's where the headwork came in.[28]

And humorous folk wisdom abounds:

Just as a woman on the TV gets up to ask why it is that all the visitations from outer space have been friendly.... The man from Oregon had just bent over to respond, but he did not answer that woman's need. Her husband beats her, Miranda thinks, having seen the slight twitch around her mouth and that's what she wants explained.[29]

In this funny and evocative book, Ms. Naylor deftly combines the African past with a contemporary setting. By doing this, she gives credence and validity to black history and notes its necessity in the modern world.

Asked by a critic as to her views on this wide-reaching narrative, she saw its themes quite simply: 'It's a celebration of two things I've always believed in – love and magic.'[30]

With the emergence of many new and exciting voices, we now have a more diverse representation of African-American women's lives. Rosa Guy's *A Measure of Time* (1983) explores the determination of a black woman to shed poverty, often by means outside the law, in order to attain wealth and status as a Harlem millionairess. And that same dogged determination to survive is finely depicted in the humorous and movingly written *Mama* (1987), by Terry McMillan. Marita Golden's *A Woman's Place* (1986) deftly describes the choices that three contemporary black women make and their problematic outcomes. *Sarah Phillips* (1984), by Andrea Lee, gives a disturbing glimpse into a black woman's alienation from her culture and history.

Most of these themes and many more are explored by the political essayist, poet, professor and playwright, June Jordan (1936 –). With a searing, perceptive, radical black voice, Ms. Jordan emerges as a clear-eyed, passionate arguer and changer of her world. And that world primarily encompasses black people, whether in America or elsewhere.

Author of five volumes of poetry, many of them collected in *Things I Do in the Dark* (1977) and *Passion* (1980), June Jordan has also written children's books and two plays. She is also the first black woman to have two books of political essays published in the United States: *Civil Wars* (1981) and *On Call* (1985).

Her work is wide-reaching and the forms she employs are diverse, but the unifying theme in all her writing is her dedication to black Americans and her concern for their survival. Never a mainstream writer, June Jordan has not, until very recently, been given serious attention by the majority of critics or publishers. In the introduction to *On Call*, she discusses this exclusion:

> I have encountered new and considerable resistance to the publication of my work. In this way, I have been whitelisted by editors who have... said to me: 'We love your writing but too many of us have problems with your position on Nicaragua.'[31]

She notes the dearth of black political journalists on any major American newspaper, and that black women journalists hardly exist:

> In a sense, this book must compensate for the absence of a cheaper and more immediate print outlet for my two cents. If political writing by a Black woman did not strike so many editors as presumptuous or simply bizarre then, perhaps this book would not be needed.... But if you will count the number of Black women with regular and national forums for their political ideas, and the ideas of their constituency, you will comprehend the politics of our exclusion: I cannot come up with the name of *one* Black woman in that position.[32]

In her first political volume, *Civil Wars*, June Jordan approaches most of her essays from a personal and often autobiographical position. Many of these essays focus on children, such as 'White English/Black English', which argues for the validity of African-American speech. 'The Voice of the Children' discusses the work produced by inner-city children in innovative poetry workshops, and 'Testimony', a vocal, cinematic collage of the filmcrew and actors of the movie *Cool World*, questions the white script and direction of this film about black children in a black community. In 'Black Studies: Bringing Back The Person', Ms. Jordan emphasizes the need for such courses:

> We choose a real, a living enlargement of our only life. We choose community: Black America, in white. Here we began like objects chosen by the blind. And it is here that we see fit to continue – as subjects of human community. We will bring back the person, alive and sacrosanct. We mean to rescue the person from the amorality of time and science.[33]

This volume, which is a strong and significant contribution to American letters, confronts the problems of black American life, from a child's 'silence' to a people's survival.

On Call continues to examine and address black life in white America as well as black life throughout the world: 'South Africa: Bringing It All Back Home', 'Report from the Bahamas', 'Black Folks on Nicaragua: "Leave Those Folks Alone"' and 'Nicaragua: Why I had to go there', give credence to Ms. Jordan's expanded political world view. And history is treated with evocative beauty and rage, as Ms. Jordan considers the life and work of Phillis Wheatley:

> A poet is somebody free. A poet is someone at home.
>
> How should there be Black poets in America? It was not natural. And she was the first. It was 1761 – so far back before the revolution that produced these United States, so far back before the concept of freedom disturbed the insolent crimes of this continent . . . when seven year old Phillis stood, as she must . . . at last after the long, annihilating horrors of the Middle Passage. Phillis standing on the auctioneer's rude platform: Phillis For Sale.
>
> Was it a nice day? Does it matter?[34]

This is an extremely important work, a clear-sighted cry for some sense and direction in a world twisted on its axis.

● ● ●

> What will we do
> when there is nobody left
> to kill?[35]

Many of the issues that June Jordan addresses in her essays are complemented by her poems: violence, 'black annihilation', rape, black history, world-wide oppression of people of colour, understanding her relationship with her parents, the concern for her son and for all black children and people. Ms. Jordan feels a close affinity with the works of Walt Whitman, and believes that his poetry has not been given its rightful place in the American canon. She explains why this is so in her preface to *Passion*:

> It is the voice of the poet who assumes that he speaks to an equal and that he need not fear that equality; on the contrary, the intimate distance between the poet and the reader is a distance that assumes there is everything important, between them, to be shared.[36]

And Ms. Jordan's poetry is not oblique, obscure or evasive – it is to the people and to the point. With jarring realism, she poses this question for America:

Tell me something
what you think would happen if
everytime they kill a black boy
then we kill a cop
everytime they kill a black man
then we kill a cop

you think the accident rate would lower
subsequently?[37]

With an equally alarming confrontational stance, June Jordan makes her
statement about self-determination:

I am the history of rape
I am the history of the rejection of who I am
I am the history of the terrorized incarceration of
my self
I am the history of battery assault and limitless
armies against whatever I want to do with my mind
and my body and my soul

. . . .

but I can tell you that from now on my resistance
my simple and daily and nightly self-
determination
may very well cost you your life.[38]

And it is with that sense of history that Ms. Jordan has written a poem for
her mother, herself and for black women everywhere. An incantation, this
poem is propelled by the names given to black women from slavery to today.
This personal and collective 'voice' sings with urgency and fire. Its lines
scorch tracks across the mind:

MOMMA MOMMA MOMMA
momma momma
mammy
nanny
granny
woman
mistress
sista
luv

blackgirl
slavegirl

gal,

. . . .

Black Momma
Black bitch
Black pussy
piecea tail
nice piecea ass

. . . .

Teach me to survive my
momma
teach me how to hold a new life
momma
help me
turn the face of history
to your face[39]

• • •

How much of this truth can I bear to see
and still live
unblinded?
How much of this pain
can I use?[40]

Audre Lorde (1934 –) writes with an unblinking vision of the world and her existence in it. Too often, it has been a painful world, as a black feminist and lesbian. But Ms. Lorde has taken that pain, alienation, anger and frustration, deep inside herself, to bring a new reading to its definitions – through poetry. She sees her creativity coming from an empowering, old and feminine source:

These places of possibility within ourselves are dark because they are ancient and hidden. They have survived and grown strong through that darkness. Within these deep places, each one of us holds an incredible reserve of creativity and power, of unexamined and unrecorded emotion and feeling. The woman's place of power within each of us is neither white nor surface; it is dark, it is ancient, and it is deep.[41]

Many of Ms. Lorde's ideas come as fresh and radical ways in which to see and interpret our lives. In *Sister Outsider* (1984), a compilation of speeches, interviews and essays, she challenges many old prejudices and assumptions under headings such as 'Sexism: An American Disease in Blackface', 'Eye to Eye: Black Women, Hatred, and Anger', 'The Transformation of Silence into Language and Action', 'Poetry Is Not A Luxury'. There is also a sympathetic interview with the lesbian poet Adrienne Rich, which highlights their similarities as lesbians, but illuminates the problems of racism, and her most exciting and thought-provoking essay, 'Uses of The Erotic: The Erotic as Power'. In this ground-breaking work, Ms. Lorde recovers the erotic from its usual sexual or pornographic sense and equates it with the powerful creative urge that women have, but are rarely able to recognize or use:

> The erotic is a resource within each of us that lies in a deeply female and spiritual plane, firmly rooted in the power of our unexpressed or unrecognized feeling. In order to perpetuate itself, every oppression must corrupt or distort those various sources of power within the culture of the oppressed that can provide energy for change. For women, this has meant a suppression of the erotic as a considered source of power and information in our lives.[42]

In most of the essays in *Sister Outsider*, Ms. Lorde's attention is focused on women, but her poetry covers a wide range of themes – black pride and survival in an urban and global setting, as well as black feminist and lesbian issues.

In her *Chosen Poems: Old and New* (1982) and the volume *Our Dead Behind Us* (1986), Audre Lorde acknowledges the thread of violence and destruction done to blacks in America and the world over. Witness her global connections in 'Equinox', a poem fusing the assassinations of Kennedy and Malcom X with the responses to oppression throughout the hemisphere:

> As I read his words the dark mangled children
> came streaming out of the atlas
> Hanoi Angola Guinea-Bissau Mozambique Pnom-Phen
> merged into Bedford-Stuyvesant and Hazelhurst Mississippi
> haunting my New York tenement that terribly bright
>   summer
> while Detroit and Watts and San Francisco were burning[43]

She addresses a particular issue in a more personal way in 'Evening News', a poem concerned with the popular uprising against Apartheid in South Africa:

> I am kneading my bread Winnie Mandela
> while children who sing in the streets of Soweto
> are jailed for inciting to riot
>
> . . . .
>
> Winnie Mandela I am feeling your face
> with pain of my crippled fingers
> our children are escaping their births
> in the streets of Soweto and Brooklyn[44]

And the tie becomes closer still, as a lesbian relationship is connected with the atrocities done to African mothers and their children:

> The edge of our bed was a wide grid
> where your fifteen-year-old daughter was hanging
> gut-sprung on police wheels[45]

In her poetry, Audre Lorde often uses images of the media as a signal for the way violence is reproduced on television and radio, in newspapers and magazines, without addressing the significance of specific events. In 'Afterimages', Ms. Lorde juxtaposes two Southern 'media stories' to bring out the full complexity of their relationship. One story is that of Emmett Till, a young black boy who was murdered in Mississippi by white men for whistling at a white woman. The other is of a Mississippi flood, years later, that has demolished the home of a white Southern woman. The technical meaning of 'after images' is what stays on the retina, as a camera flash does when the thing itself is no longer in sight. But Audre Lorde gives it a more profound meaning in that events and images have one definition at first sight, then suggest other meanings beyond that:

> However the image enters
> its force remains within
> my eyes
>
> . . . .
>
> A white woman stands bereft and empty
> a black boy hacked into a murderous lesson
> recalled in me forever[46]

Audre Lorde's perception is rare, in that most Americans see no connection between these two events, and have only a prurient interest in the sensational murder of Emmett Till:

His broken body is the afterimage of my 21st year
when I walked through a northern summer
my eyes averted
from each corner's photographies
newspapers protest posters magazines

. . . .

the veiled warning, the secret relish
of a black child's mutilated body
fingered by street-corner eyes
bruise upon livid bruise
and wherever I looked that summer
I learned to be at home with children's blood[47]

Yet the compassion as well as veiled contempt that Ms. Lorde holds for the Southern white woman in 'Afterimages', begins to touch upon the problematic relationship between black and white women in America. She writes elsewhere, with aching honesty:

A Black woman and a white woman
charter our courses close
in a sea of calculated distance
warned away by reefs of hidden anger
histories rallied against us
the friendly face of cheap alliance

. . . .

A Black woman and a white woman
in the open fact of our loving
with not only our enemies' hands
raised against us
means a gradual sacrifice
of all that is simple[48]

Audre Lorde's poetic vision has also been informed by her experience with cancer, which she discusses in *The Cancer Journals* (1980). In this painful and honest account of her battle with, and final triumph over, the disease, which included a mastectomy, Lorde rejects the illusory media images of women. By confronting her own fear and anger and in finally accepting difference, Audre Lorde inspires and gives courage to thousands of women in similar circumstances.

In *Zami* (1983), her 'biomythography', which is a 'Carriacou name for women who work together as friends and lovers', Lorde examines the difficult relationship between mothers and daughters. This work, like the poetry and essays, does not seek to simplify the issues, but pursues the harder question of an honest and more complex truth. By acknowledging the hitherto silenced lives of black lesbians, she asks, 'what are the words you do not have?'[49] Just as Toni Morrison has written the books she wanted to read, Audre Lorde has invented the poems she did not have.

There are others now who are inventing and recreating the lives of black lesbians in literature; Ann Allen Shockley's *Loving Her* (1987) and *The Black and White of It* (1987), Becky Birtha's *Lover's Choice* (1987), and, in poetry, Cheryl Clarke and the late Pat Parker, among others.

With an unaverted eye, black women writers are now exploring the lives of African-American women, giving them the dimensionality that they have always had in life:

> when I was eight I listened to stories of love
> and etiquette while my mother's sisters
> sat on grandma's horsehair sofa
> naked under their starched dresses
> words flew from their fingers
> in a dance as old as the moon
> but I dreamed of other places
> of dark bodies bending
> to a language too dreamlike
> and concise to decode.[50]

10: 'for colored girls'

as we demand to be heard / we want you to hear us.
we come to you the way leroi jenkins comes or
cecil taylor / or b. b. king. we come to you alone/
in the theater / in the story / & the poem. like with
billie holiday or betty carter / we shd give you a
moment that cannot be re-created / a specificity
that cannot be confused, our language shd
let you know who's talkin, what we're talkin abt
& how we cant stop sayin this to you. some urgency
accompanies the text. something important is going on.
we are speakin. reachin for yr person / we cannot
hold it / we dont wanna sell it / we give you ourselves /
if you listen. [1]

With the diversity of black women's lives now acknowledged in literature, African-American women writers search for new ways to express old and new situations and silences. Using blues and jazz, black urban speech, contemporary music, history, science fiction, recipes, dreams, magic and the mundane, these women are speaking out, and in their own way. Mary Helen Washington sees it this way:

Black women are searching for a specific language, specific symbols, specific images with which to record their lives, and, even though they can claim a rightful place in the Afro-American Tradition and in the feminist tradition of women writers, it is also clear that, for purposes of liberation, black women writers will first insist on their own name, their own space. [2]

One of the forms frequently used in black literature is the blues. Langston Hughes was the first poet to recognize its power, and in the late 1970s

African-American women writers also pursued its literary possibilities. By using this form as a basis for written expression, these writers have merged the old with the new and captured the essence of black tradition and culture. By doing so, they honour not only the beauty and resilience of black life but also the women who are the substance of their songs.

• • •

> You never get nothing by being an angel child,
> You'd better change your way and get real wild.
> I wanta tell you something, I won't tell you no lie,
> Wild women are the only kind that ever get by,
> Wild women don't worry,
> Wild women don't have the blues.[3]

The blues, black America's spirited and often ironical statement of hard times, hopes and triumph, was first performed – and frequently written – by black women in the 1920s. These blues singers gave the music world-wide recognition, and their profession gave them freedom and independence from back-breaking field-work or domestic servitude. Daphne D. Harrison has said that 'the blues [was] a driving force with which the women could act on personal and artistic agendas simultaneously. In short, the blues is life which is art.'[4]

In fancy feathers and fine apparel, the blues queens sang of their lives, without saccharine or sentimental lyrics, which was the white musical mode of the day. These women told it like it was, usually with a note of optimism or defiance:

> I'm alone every night and the lights are sinking low
> I've never had so much trouble in my life before.
> My good man, he done quit me and there's talking all over town,
> And I know my baby, you can't keep a good woman down...
>
> Now I'm blue, yes I'm blue, but I won't be blue always,
> Because the sun is going to shine in my back door someday.[5]

Ma Rainey, Bessie Smith, Clara Smith, Trixie Smith, Ida Cox, Sarah Martin, Chippie Hill, Sippie Wallace, Alberta Hunter, Edith Wilson, Lorie Austin, and many more, rocked the rafters with these life-songs, claiming their existence, as well as their culture.

The blues has been the underlying ingredient of most popular music today. But its importance lies not only in sound, but also in its relationship to the history of a people; Amiri Baraka explains:

The term *blues* relates directly to the Negro, and his [her] *personal* involvement in America. *Blues* means a Negro experience, it is the one music the Negro made that could not be transferred into a more general significance than the one the Negro gave it initially.[6]

The contemporary black poetry that is based on the blues is a welding together of white western literary forms with black oral and musical expression: repetition, call and response, double entendre, and word definition reversals. Lucille Clifton (1936 –), in much of her poetry, uses the blues device to speak to a black collective audience:

Come home from the movies,
Black girls and boys...
Come home from the show,
don't be the show...
show our fathers how to walk like men,
they already know how to dance.[7]

The poet, teacher, critic and novelist Sherley Anne Williams (1944 –) not only uses the blues form in much of her poetry but also makes a blues singer the subject of one of her poems, and connects herself with that subject. In *'Some One Sweet Angel Child'* (1982), Ms. Williams, as a black woman poet/singer, inherits the 'blues-line' of her foremothers:

Bessie on my wall: Bessie singing
                            just behind the beat
                            that sweet sweet
                            voice throwing
                            its light on me

fifteen: I looked in her face
                    and seed the woman
                    I'd become...
                    no matter what words
                    come to my mind the
                    song'd be her'n jes as
                    well as it be mine.[8]

From recollections, pictures, dreams and fragments, Ms. Williams sings a stunning and evocative blues song to Bessie Smith. And by merging Ms. Smith's life with her own, she acknowledges the creative legacy of black women, which she herself continues to carry on. For Williams, the blues was of and for the black community, and the poetry should be likewise:

> The devices and structures of the classic blues form are transformed, thus allowing the poetry to function in much the same way as blues forms once functioned within black communities across the country.[9]

Ms. Williams's first publication, *Give Birth to Brightness* (1972), is a discussion of black oral tradition and its influence on 'Neo-Black Literature', as well as a particular vision that has evolved from black-centred writing. She sees

> black existence and life from the inside as life experiences which have significance in and of themselves rather than as a culturally deprived heritage which takes its significance and meaning from the fact that it has been a source of irritation and embarrassment for white America.[10]

Although writers from the Harlem Renaissance held the same views, the difference between the two schools of thought is that this poetry speaks directly 'to black people about themselves'.[11]

Ms. Williams has also written another volume of poetry, *The Peacock Poems* (1975). And, in her most recent work, the novel *Dessa Rose* (1986), she reaches back into history to give us the imagined story of an escaped woman slave who is befriended by a white southern woman. Williams's basis for the work came from two different incidents; one about a pregnant black woman who helped organize a slave revolt, the other about a white woman who gave sanctuary to escaped slaves. Sherley Williams has written a most moving narrative about the imaginary meeting between these two historically separate people.

As the blues singer uses the sliding of a note, the swoop of a word to denote a different meaning from what is actually being sung, Ms. Williams applies similar devices of deception in her novels. By using circumvention, an un-educated slave, Dessa Rose, outwits a white writer:

> Oh, you a teacher man.... Was a teacher man on the coffle.... He teached hisself to read from the Bible, then he preach.... He be alright till he want to teach other niggas to read.... And when his massa find out what he be doing, he be sold south....

As the white man tries to discern if this particular slave was one of the recent escapees, Dessa laughingly answers:

'Onliest freedom he be knowing is what he call righteous freedom, that
what the Lawd be giving him or what the massa be giving him and he
was the first one the patterrollers killed.'[12]

Alexis De Veaux (1948 –) journalist, playwright and innovative short
story writer, also employs blues and jazz forms in her writing. One of her
most outstanding works has been a biography of Billie Holiday, entitled
Don't Explain (1980). Called a song of Billie Holiday, it is a prose poem, a
blues rendition of the great jazz singer's life. Billie's story unfolds in the
rhythmic phrases that echo the strains of her music:

Closer to the audience she could connect
her life with theirs.
That was her style.
Up close where lies are not told.
Eyelids blink together in one rhythm one song.
My face reflects yours reflects the universe
here.[13]

Another writer who has used the blues to stunning effect is J. J. Phillips
(1944 –) in her novel *Mojo Hand* (1966). A black contemporary Orphic tale,
the story is often told through blues lyrics. Its theme is the restorative and
releasing properties of the blues for Eunice, a young, middle-class black
woman who, through this music, learns of her culture and becomes her own
person. Eunice is lured by Blacksnake Brown's musical call, and leaves her
Californian home:

I'm going to Louisiana and get me a mojo hand
I'm going to Louisiana and get me a mojo hand
I'm going to show all you womens just how to fix
    your man.[14]

Mojo Hand constantly flows in and out of rhyme, using not only blues
lyrics, but also rhyming patterns within the dialogue of characters:

'You seed that Ford what come by here today? Well, that be Miss Sally
Mae coming 'round to check on him. I believe she done already got
wind of you, so stay out of that big mama's way.'[15]

The most impassioned and brilliantly depicted usage of the blues form,
and of its contextual essence, can be read in the first novel of Gayl Jones
(1949 –), *Corregidora* (1975). Ms. Jones is an exceptional storyteller, and the
book's movement flows with no authorial intrusions. The art of storytelling
is of major importance in Jones's work, for she 'hears' her writing, rather
than 'sees' it. She explained this to Robert Stepto:

I liked writing dialogue in stories, because I was 'hearing' people talk.... In storytelling you can do that.... When you tell a story, you automatically talk about traditions, but they're never separate from the people, the human implications. You're talking about language, you're talking about politics and morality and economics and culture, and you never have to come out and say you're talking about these things – you don't have to isolate them and therefore freeze them – but you're still talking about them.[16]

All these factors come into play as Gayl Jones weaves the 'blues-feel' history of a particular family of black women. This is a searing account of four generations of women told by the youngest, who must remember the abuses done to them and continue to tell the tale.

In this gothic story, a Portuguese slave owner in Brazil keeps some of his slave women for his own use and amusement. Ursa, the blues-singing youngest 'Corregidora' woman, tells her lover of her family's history:

He fucked his own whores and fathered his own breed. They did the fucking and had to bring him the money they made. My grandmama was his daughter, but he was fucking her too. She said when they did away with slavery down there they buried all the slavery papers so it would be like they never had it.[17]

As we soon learn, the slave owner not only raped his slave, but fathered on his daughter another Corregidora woman, who becomes the mother of Ursa. She escapes with *her* daughter to America, where the history of these generations must be kept alive:

My great-grandmother told my grandmama the past she lived through that my grandmama didn't live through and my grandmama told my mama what they both lived through and my mama told me what they all lived through and we were supposed to pass it down like that from generation to generation so we'd never forget. Even though they burned everything to play like it didn't never happen.[18]

Ursa, unlike the 'Corregidora' women before her, is unable to 'produce generations', as she was thrown down the stairs by her husband and had to have a hysterectomy.

This novel spans twenty years, the time it takes for Ursa to outgrow the guilt she feels at not being able to carry on the 'Corregidora' tradition and also the misanthropy her mother has instilled in her. Her awakening enables her to understand that the feelings that the 'Corregidora' women have had for men were a way of deflecting their own anger and pain. Realizing this, she also realizes that black men are not inherently bad, but are the products of their history and society, as are black women.

This complex psychological narrative probes the effect of systematic abuse, which has resulted in sexism, obsession and violence. Yet, it shows that intensely painful experiences may offer illumination and hope. In a startling section of the novel, Ursa comes to understand her past in its historical and sexual dimensions. The paradoxes of human nature are rendered brilliantly in the following passage, and echo one of the complex themes of the blues:

> It had to be sexual, I was thinking, it had to be something sexual that Great Gram did to Corregidora. I knew it had to be sexual. 'What is it a woman can do to a man that make him hate her so bad he want to kill her one minute and keep thinking about her and can't get her out of his mind the next?' In a split second I knew what it was, and I think he might have known too. A moment of pleasure and excruciating pain at the same time, a moment of broken skin but not sexlessness, a moment just before sexlessness, a moment that stops before it breaks the skin: 'I could kill you.'[19]

In her next novel, *Eva's Man* (1976), Gayl Jones continues the themes of violence, oppression and sexism, but takes them a step further. Eva does not accept the tensions between men and women, and does what Ursa 'Corregidora' only contemplates; she commits an act of sexual violence. This chilling tale is told by Eva, in prison, with flashbacks. We at once realize, by her distorted confusion of time and space, as well as her repetitions, that the narrator of this story is insane. Yet her perceptions are really quite believable, as we come to see that her ravings are but exaggerations of the oppression and violence that black women have often had to endure. Eva, who is kept in a room by her jealous lover and is not even allowed to comb her hair, turns into a Medusa figure. She has become a sex-object and is driven to madness by her lover's possessiveness.

It is not only this situation, but many more, that eventually drive her over the edge: the young boy who used dirty popsicle sticks to probe her sexually when she was a young girl, her cousin who takes her to bars to proposition her, her husband who doesn't allow a telephone in the house and Davis, the man who imprisons her in a room. Eva surmises what, some men, black and white, think of black women:

> He kept thinking I was that kind of woman. Always. They would, wouldn't they. Always. No matter what I. Just because the places I went, the way I talked or how I wore my hair. Any woman's talk. You know. So he came and sat down. I wasn't going to nobody else. But he thought I would. After he left me or I left him. He thought I was. The way he was looking at me. James wouldn't let me have no telephone. When he was sitting on that bed, the way he was looking at me. He came in the house. I was sitting there in the dark. I scared him. He

didn't have to be scared. He could have said anything to me anytime. Every man could look at me the way he was looking. They all would. Even when I. He thought I was his.[20]

Although Eva seems to succumb to the patriarchal system by phoning the police and placing herself in the hands of psychiatrists, she refuses to talk to them. All of her thoughts are directed to the reader, thereby rendering the authorities powerless.

The structure of this excellent novel progressively tightens and, near the finale, Eva's focus becomes smaller and smaller until she reaches the core of her problem: sexual abuse and emotional silence.

Gayl Jones has also written a series of short stories, *White Rat* (1977), which continues these themes. She is no polemicist and does not write from an overtly political standpoint, but explores the complex inner problems that a particular political structure can create.

Although that political structure has been oppressive, it has brought forth one of the most enduring statements of black culture: the blues. It is the aforementioned authors, together with many others, who have continued to claim that song and keep it alive. As Sherley Anne Williams wrote:

These the old blues
 and I sing em, sing em, sing em. Just like
any woman do.
My life ain't done yet
 Naw... My song ain't through.[21]

• • •

As black women writers venture into new forms, unexpected aspects of the culture are also being addressed. For Verta-Mae Smart-Grosvenor (1938–), it is black cooking that receives praise and examination. Her *Vibration Cooking* (1972) set new standards for African-American cookbooks. Not only was food a major ingredient but history, travel and black life were all combined to give a resonant portrayal of her people.

In her essay 'A Kitchen Crisis', we get a sense of this original and witty writer:

Eating Is A Very Personal Thing. Some people will sit down and eat with anybody.... You can't eat with everybody. You got to have the right vibrations.... PROTECT YOUR KITCHEN.[22]

Verta-Mae immediately sets the guidelines for what is necessary to enjoy a proper meal. And she also gives us a history of black cooking in America:

It was no accident that in the old old south where they had slaves they was eating fried chicken coated with batter and biscuits so light they could have flown across the Mason-Dixon line if they had wanted to. There was pound-cake that had to be beat at eight hundred strokes. Who do you think was doing this beating? It sure wasn't Missy. Missy was beating the upstairs house nigger for not bringing her mint julep quick enough.[23]

Lover of good food, protector of her kitchen, Verta-Mae knows that African-Americans have received little acknowledgement for some of the best food America has produced. She says:

When they do mention our food they act like it is some obscure thing that niggers down south made up and don't nobody else in the world eat it. Food ain't nothing but food. Everybody eats.[24]

The joys of eating, the love of friends and the history of one black family are beautifully rendered in *Spoonbread and Strawberry Wine: Recipes And Reminiscences Of A Family* (1978) by Norma Jean and Carole Darden, who illustrated their book with snapshots from the family album. Verta-Mae should worry no more. Folks is taking care of their culture and their cooking.

The new, as well as the old, are given voice in the works of the science-fiction writer Octavia E. Butler, author of *Pattermaster* (1976), *Mind of My Mind* (1977) and *Survivor* (1978). All these books are concerned with new societies where equality reigns and the hierarchies of race and religion are abolished. *Kindred* (1979), takes a contemporary black woman back in time to the days of slavery. Ms. Butler makes a metaphorical statement in this novel about the need for cultural and historical knowledge in order to survive in a modern world. The heroine, Dana, listens to the wise words of her ancestors, and learns the lessons of survival:

Sometimes old people and children lounged there, or house servants or even field hands stealing a few moments of leisure. I liked to listen to them talk sometimes and fight my way through their accents to find out more about how they survived lives of slavery. Without knowing it, they prepared me to survive.[25]

A subtle and penetrating new voice is in our midst. Rita Dove (1953 –) is a poet with a superb eye for the unexpected and unexplored in black life. But the landscape to which Ms. Dove brings her craft and clear-sightedness is 'as wide as the world is wide'. Merging history with the personal, Rita Dove's economical poetic style shows the makings of great artistry.

From the 1960s onward, many black poets have loosened their structure and directed their orally-based work to a large black audience. Ms. Dove, it seems, has turned that tide, and given us a new structure, a new vision, very much as Gwendolyn Brooks did years ago. Arnold Rampersad has said that Rita Dove is 'perhaps the most disciplined and technically accomplished black poet to arrive since Gwendolyn Brooks began her remarkable career in the nineteen forties.'[26]

Author of three volumes of poetry, *The Yellow House on the Corner* (1980), *Museum* (1983) and *Thomas and Beulah* (1986), Ms. Dove encompasses in these works European and Western history, as seen through a black woman's eyes, as well as addressing the seemingly small and insignificant events of African-American life. In these poems, each word is weighted, and carries deep meaning and nuance. As she said to an interviewer:

> Language is everything ... it is the sounds of the language, the way of telling something, that makes a poem for me. There's nothing new under the sun, but it's the way you *see* it. For me, as a poet, language becomes an integral part of that perception. The *way* one sees it.[27]

And it is her vision, her way of seeing the underside of things, an alternate view, that colours and gives depth to her work. Her poems are taut and sharply focused, as if she were taking a photographic close-up of a moment or event. This is most brilliantly exemplified in her poem 'Parsley' from *Museum*, which is based on the story of the Dominican dictator Trujillo. In 1957 he 'ordered 20,000 black Haitians killed because they couldn't roll their Rs. And he chose the Spanish word for "parsley" [perejil] in order to test this.'[28]

> There is a parrot imitating spring
> in the palace, its feathers parsley green.
> Out of the swamp the cane appears
>
> To haunt us, and we cut it down. El General
> searches for a word; he is all the world
> there is. Like a parrot imitating spring,
>
> we lie down screaming as rain punches through
> and we come up green. We cannot speak an R ...[29]

In this poem of quietly contained rage, Rita Dove's excellent use of the rolling Rs in *parsley, parrot, spring, feathers, General*, appears not only to give us a resonant, reverberating sound, but is also an encoded commentary on the subject of the poem.

This understatement of 'history' makes the poem all the more poignant. Ms. Dove approaches most of her historical subjects with stories of real lives rather than fictional events. In *The Yellow House on the Corner*, one of the five sections is devoted to the history of slavery and freedom. Here, and in *Museum*, she gives us poems about known and unknown victims of this 'peculiar institution': they include the writer Solomon Northrop, a free black who was abducted into slavery, David Walker, the revolutionary, and Benjamin Banneker the scientist. History intrigues Ms. Dove for what has been unsaid rather than for what is already evident. She explains:

> I found historical events fascinating for looking underneath – not for what we always see or what's always said about a historical event, but for the things that can't be related in a dry, historical sense.[30]

In this way, Rita Dove's perceptions of history are very much like Toni Morrison's in her novel *Beloved*.

Dove's poetry is often that of the observer; her distance gives clarity to what she sees and experiences. Her originality as a poet often lies in the form of her narrative, which is told with lucid objectivity. She feels that this distancing has come from her time in Europe where she found 'that there was another way of looking at things'. Dove notes that while she was there,

> I was treated differently than people treat me here [in the U.S.A.] because I'm Black ... I became an object. I was a Black American and therefore became a representative for all of that. . . . So there was that sense of being there and not being there. . . . Then because you are there, you can see things a little clearer sometimes.[31]

With objectivity and economy, Rita Dove gives us emotions that are stripped of sentimentality, thereby investing her subjects with more depth and potency. An example of this can be seen in the first two lines of her poem 'Promises':

> Each hurt swallowed
> is a stone...[32]

We can feel these words, they become tactile, something we can hold. Ms. Dove's poetry abounds with such realizable images.

The poem 'Promises' is from her volume *Thomas and Beulah*, which concerns the lives of a black couple growing up in the Midwest from 1900 to 1960. One half of the book is from Thomas's view, the other from Beulah's. This 'double-vision' is not unusual for Dove, for she often questions perceptions and 'truth'. She captures the lives of this couple with a clear-sighted distance, yet, at the same time, evokes a tender and warm familiarity. 'Promises' is about the marriage of Thomas and Beulah's daughter. The uncertainty of this event is captured with brilliant economy:

> Beneath the airborne bouquet
> a meadow of virgins
> urged her to be light on the water.

A deep breath, then the plunge
through the sunbeams and kisses,
rice drumming
the both of them blind.[33]

A disciplined writer, Dove shuns sentimentality and keeps a cool eye when it comes to racial or political stances. Wary of the trap many black writers find themselves in, she continues to keep all options open. Hers is an innovative voice that speaks with sonority, not stridence. Quiet and compelling, her song seeks the centre and takes hold. In her poem 'Upon Meeting Don L. Lee, in a Dream', it becomes quite apparent that the strictures of 'black arts poetry' will not restrain her. Dove rejects the 'scream' and goes for the eye, heart and mind:

I lie down, chuckling as the grass curls around me.
He can only stand, fists clenched, and weep
Tears of iodine, while the singers float away
Rustling on brown paper wings.[34]

● ● ●

The voice of my work is bop.[35]

These words were spoken, not by the acclaimed jazz singer Betty Carter, nor by the innovative jazz saxophonist Charlie Parker, or by any musician, but by the short story writer, editor, script-writer and novelist, Toni Cade Bambara (1939 –).

Bambara, among other writers, has taken on this intricate, urban black music and incorporated its style and form into their written work. Langston Hughes again, was the first to do this, best exemplified in his poetic collage 'Montage of A Dream Deferred', but it is black women who are now 'riffing' their way to us on the page, and giving us some powerful and unforgettable messages.

Toni Cade Bambara explains how this particular musical form has moulded her writing:

The musicians of the forties and fifties ... determined my voice and pace and pitch.... I grew up in New York City, be-bop haven – and it's still music that keeps that place afloat. I learned more from Bud Powell, Dizzy, Y'Bird, Miss Sassy Vaughan about what can be communicated, can be taught through structure, tone, metronomic sense, and just sheer holy boldness than from any teacher or language art, or from any book, for that matter.[36]

In her first volume of short stories, *Gorilla, My Love* (1972), Bambara's use of black urban idiom, coupled with the rhythms and cadences of jazz, gives us one of the most exciting collections of black literature to date. And, this woman is funny. The basic theme of communal love and concern underlies all of the stories in this volume and it is with a concern of her own that she gives 'A Sort of Preface' to the collection:

> It does no good to write autobiographical fiction cause the minute the book hits the stand here comes your mama screamin how could you and sighin death where is thy sting. . . .
> So I deal in straight-up fiction myself, cause I value my family and friends, and mostly cause I lie a lot anyway.[37]

The stories, for the most part, give a real sense of urban environment, as they take place in the street, at the movies, in a park or a restaurant, or at a community centre.

The title story exemplifies her style, technique and wit. It is narrated by Hazel, a young girl who has been consistently disappointed by the unkept promises made by adults:

> grown ups messing over kids just cause they little and can't take 'em to court.[38]

Like most of the heroines of these stories, Hazel is a feisty, strong-willed and lovable character. Whereas adults in her family represent the careless way children are sometimes treated, the white-owned movie-house represents the same disregard on another level. Advertising a film about a gorilla, they change the movie without alerting the customers. Hazel angrily responds to this:

> So I kick the door open wider and just walk right by him and sit down and tell the man about himself and that I want my money back. . . . And he still trying to shuffle me out the door even though I'm sittin which shows him for the fool he is. . . . So he ain't gettin up off the money. So I was forced to leave, takin the matches from under his ashtray, and set a fire under the candy stand, which closed the raggedy ole Washington down for a week. . . . Cause if you say Gorilla, My Love, you suppose to mean it.[39]

Much of the work in the collection focuses on adolescents adjusting to the perceptions of their world and keeping their sense of individuality, as they openly question the extent to which adults in the black community have lost that individuality in a capitalist society.

Toni Cade Bambara's second volume of short stories, *The Sea Birds Are Still Alive* (1977), departs from the small black community to encompass a wider geographical perspective. These stories take in blacks from across the country, as well as the women of Asia in the title story. And they contain a much more overt political message. Bambara is focusing here on the need for oppressed peoples to find a common language and spirituality to enable them to survive. In 'The Organizer's Wife' and 'The Sea Birds Are Still Alive', Bambara's political ideas come clearly to the fore. In 'The Organizer's Wife', she connects the triangular route of the slave trade with the contemporary oppressors that divide the black community. The heroine, visiting her activist husband in jail, comes to realize she must change and be a part of, not an appendix to, the struggle:

> She was turning the bend now, forgetting to not look, and the mural the co-op had painted in eye-stinging colors stopped her. FACE UP TO WHAT'S KILLING YOU, it demanded. Below the statement a huge triangle that from a distance was just a triangle, but on approaching, as one muttered 'how deadly can a triangle be?' turned into bodies on bodies. At the top, fat, fanged beasts in smart clothes, like the ones beneath it laughing, drinking, eating, bombing, raping, shooting, lounging on the backs of, feeding off the backs of, the folks at the base, crushed almost flat but struggling to get up and getting up, topple the structure.[40]

Bambara's first volume was effervescent and full of hope, but *The Sea Birds Are Still Alive* does not hold such joy, for it poses harder questions to answer. Susan Willis has discussed the differences between the two collections:

> These stories [*The Sea Birds Are Still Alive*] develop the integral relationship between the revolutionary leader and the community. Significantly, the family, which functioned in *Gorilla, My Love* as the displaced representation of the black community, is abandoned – often thrown into question – while the notion of a collectivity expands into the community at large: the revolutionary band, the neighborhood, or small town.[41]

Toni Cade Bambara's novel, *The Salt Eaters* (1980), continues much of the thematic material explored in *The Sea Birds Are Still Alive*. Her writing style here is a complete departure from the clear and concise prose of her former works. *The Salt Eaters* is a difficult novel. Comprised of many, many voices, from the present as well as the past, that intersect and interrupt one another, this is a work of high complexity.

The narrative revolves around Velma Henry, once a resilient community organizer, who has attempted suicide. All of the action takes place in less than two hours, but the layering of the many elements and voices gives this novel the sense of a much longer time-span.

We find Velma in the Southwest Community Infirmary, sitting on a white stool opposite the 'fabled healer of the district', Minnie Ransom. Minnie is trying to bring the shattered pieces of Velma's life back together again, and these two women represent the symbolic basis of the novel: the coming together of the past and the present.

But to say that is to simplify the range of ideas that Toni Cade Bambara encompasses. Gloria Hull gives a listing of subjects and themes included in this work:

> ancient and modern history, world literature, anthropology, mythology, music, astronomy, physics, biology, mathematics, medicine, political theory, chemistry, philosophy, and engineering. Allusions to everything from space-age technology through Persian folklore to black blues....[42]

Her basic theme, however, is evident. It is that, in the 1970s, blacks have dispersed within their communities and set up various political camps. This division only aids their oppression, and Bambara pointedly argues for a cohesive community. She also sees the importance of African-Americans allying themselves with Third World peoples. This powerful coalition could dismantle oppression worldwide. Like other black thinkers of her generation, Bambara is committed to a new internationalism that focuses on common goals rather than differences. Nevertheless, she is incensed with the new black bourgeois man, who expects the women to do all the work in the community:

> Once again the women took up their pens. They listened to Hampden while calculating: money to be raised, mailing lists to be culled, halls to be booked, flyers to be printed up, hours away from school, home, work, sleep to be snatched. Not that he spoke of these things.[43]

Bambara also addresses incisively the ignorance and complacency of many blacks in relation to ecological destruction is a subject that Bambara addresses with incisiveness:

> 'All this doomsday mushroom-cloud end-of-planet numbah is past my brain. Just give me the good ole-fashioned honky-nigger shit. I think all this ecology stuff is a diversion.'
> 'They're connected. Whose community do you think they slip radioactive waste through...? Who do you think they hire for the dangerous dirty work at those plants? What parts of the world do they test-blast in?... The crops dying, the sheep dying, the horses, water, cancer, Ruby, cancer. And the plant on the Harlem River and – Ruby, don't get stupid on me.'[44]

In Toni Cade Bambara's essay, 'What It Is I Think I'm Doing Anyhow', she explains the reasons for writing this comprehensive work:

> There is a split between the spiritual, psychic, and political forces in my community.... It is a wasteful and dangerous split. The novel grew out of my attempt to fuse the seemingly separate frames of reference of the camps; it grew out of an interest in identifying bridges; it grew out of a compulsion to understand how the energies of this period will manifest themselves in the next decade.[45]

The Salt Eaters is an exciting, though somewhat problematic attempt at addressing these issues. Because the reader is frequently overwhelmed by the multitude of voices, forever tripping on one another, the novel never quite seems to centre itself. Yet there are many thoughts and moments that can be grasped, and Bambara expertly questions the role of black people in contemporary society.

No matter how disturbing the situation, Bambara remains positive, in her life and in her art:

> As for my own writing, I prefer the upbeat. It pleases me to blow three or four choruses of just sheer energetic fun and optimism, even in the teeth of rats, racists, repressive cops, bomb lovers, irresponsibles, murderers. I am convinced, I guess, that everything will be alright.[46]

●　　●　　●

> talk abt yrself
> yr blkwomanself/neo-african
> in the midst of a land caught up in
> worshippin' twentieth century minstrels ...
>
> talk like you an oracle
> bearing witness to changing times ...
>
> talk Shange, talk ...[47]

One of the most powerful, prolific and provocative 'talkers' about black female contemporary existence in America is the poet, playwright, actress, dancer, educator and novelist, Ntozake Shange (1948 –). With an unswerving eye and a jazz musician's ear, Shange depicts the struggles that African-American women still face today. Her style of writing is driven, sharp and innovative. Shange's voice is recognizable and distinctive. She is concerned that if black writers are not careful, they will have some kind of 'collective' voice, without idiosyncratic or recognizable distinctions. She discusses this when she appeals to black writers to have their own 'voice', just as black musicians do:

> That's the division of a realm bordered by bebop & one sunk in syllable / where only the language defines reality. we have poets who speak to you of elephants & avenues / we have others who address themselves to worlds having no existence beyond the word. that's fine. we live in all those places. but, if we don't know the voice of a writer / the way we know 'oh… that's trane' / then something is very wrong. we are unfortunately / selling ourselves down the river again. & we awready know abt that. if we go down river again / just cuz we don't know or care to recognize our particularities / wont nobody come / cuz dont nobody care / if you don't know yr poets as well as yr tenor horns.[48]

Shange first came into public prominence with the production of her choreo-poem, *for colored girls who have considered suicide/when the rainbow is enuf* (1976). A startling new dramatic approach to black life, this 'play' is comprised of seven female characters (ladies in brown, yellow, orange, red, purple, blue and green). Through poetry, dance and song, they tell of their trials and triumphs in a world bent on their eradication and silence:

> ever since I realized there waz someone callt
> a colored girl and evil woman a bitch or a nag
> i been tryin not to be that & leave bitterness
> in somebody else's cup /…
> so this is a requiem for myself/cuz i have died in a
> real way /… cuz i don't know
> anymore / how to avoid my own face wet wit my
> tears / cuz i had convinced myself colored girls had no
> right to sorrow /…
> i cdnt stand it
> i cdnt stand bein sorry & colored at the same time
> its so redundant in the modern world[49]

The play received rave reviews as well as scathing ones. Many black men were outraged at their portrayal as non-caring, violent oppressors. Although the male characters receive little psychological probing, the words of the women characters were received by a large section of the black female audience with resounding 'Amens'. One of the first black feminist plays to speak honestly about the terrible rupture in male/female relationships and the denial of black women's voices in American society, it was a moving, expressive and highly creative work.

Shange's honest appraisal of black life can be seen in all of her works. She explains the need to touch the deeper, less expressed emotions that we all carry around – in deliberate defiance of western notions of decorum:

> Our society allows people to be absolutely neurotic and totally out of touch with their feelings and everyone else's feelings, and yet be very respectable. This, to me, is a travesty. So I write to get at the part of people's emotional lives that they don't have control over, the part that can and will respond.[50]

Ntozake Shange grew up in the Midwest, in St. Louis, Missouri. Her upbringing was rich in the knowledge of her own culture, and her home a gathering place for many black artists and educators, among them Dizzy Gillespie, Chuck Berry, Charlie Parker, Miles Davis, Josephine Baker and W. E. B. Du Bois. This black middle-class section of St. Louis enabled Shange to meet blacks from all over the world, so that she knew 'I wasn't on this planet by myself. I had some connection with other people.'[51]

In a poem from *A Daughter's Geography* (1983), Shange poignantly expresses this black world-view, with the realization that the history and greatness of her people are being lost:

> it hasnt always been this way
> ellington was not a street
> robeson no mere memory
> du bois walked up my father's stairs...
>
> our house was filled with all kinda folks...
> nkrumah was no foreigner...
>
> it hasnt always been this way
> ellington was not a street[52]

And she concludes this section of the volume, in 'Take the A train', when she acknowledges her link with the history of black people:

> i could sleep with a man
> but i'll lay with the souls of black folks...[53]

In this collection Shange expands her world to show black oppression throughout the hemisphere. She, along with many other African-American writers, now sees the global connections of violation and abuse, and 'speaks on it':

> i have a daughter / mozambique
> i have a son / angola
> our twins
> salvador & johannesburg / cannot speak
> the same language
> but we fight the same old men /[54]

The themes in this volume range from female violation and rape, international oppression, to love poems. Many of the titles, as well as the poetic forms employed, use jazz as a signifier, together with other aspects of black culture: 'Mood Indigo', 'Improvisation', and 'From Okra to Greens' (which comprises a whole section of the volume).

In Shange's first collection of poetry, *Nappy Edges* (1978), many of the poems are women-centred, and resonate with shattering honesty. Skilfully written, memorable and moving, these poems grip you, shake you and jolt you out of complacency:

> you cd just take what
> he's got for you
> i mean what's available
> cd add up in the long run...
> whatever good there is to
> get / get it & feel good...
> snatch it & feel good
> grab it & feel good
> steal it & feel good
> borrow it & feel good...
> you cd
>   oh yeah
>   & feel good.[55]

We groove in the rhythms and fine feelings of this poem, but soon Shange snaps us up with startling specificity:

> every 3 minutes a woman is beaten
> every five minutes a
> woman is raped / every ten minutes
> a lil girl is molested...
>
> every three minutes
> every five minutes
> every ten minutes
> every day[56]

Yet, it is music, be-bop, jazz that inform much of Shange's writing, and she is well aware of this connection. She pays homage to this great black artistic expression in 'i live in music':

> i live in music
> is this where you live
> i live here in music
> i live on C# street...
> sound
> falls round me like rain on other folks
> saxophones wet my face...
>
> i live in music[57]

Shange's ties to black culture are not only evident in the musical idiom and the content of her work. They are also expressed in the way she re-invents English spelling and punctuation, and its placement on the page. She explains this to Claudia Tate:

> It bothers me... to look at poems where all the first letters are capitalized. That's why I use the lower-case alphabet. Also, I like the idea that letters dance.... I need some visual stimulation, so that reading becomes not just a passive act and more than an intellectual activity, but demands rigorous participation.... Basically, the spellings reflect language as I hear it. I write this way because I hear the words.[58]

It is words, wedded to music and dance, that Shange employs in her experimental theatre works, *Spell#7* (1979) and *Boogie Woogie Landscapes* (1979). The first involves nine characters, friends who gather in a bar to discuss their lives. All are black actors and actresses, who expose the restrictions and racism of America's theatres. If not willing to play stereotypic characters, then they are left without work. One of the women sums up their situation:

> & at least yr not playin a whore /
> if some other woman comes in here & tells
> me she's playin a whore / i think i might kill
> her[59]

Boogie-Woogie Landscapes is the more experimental of the two, as Shange mixes surrealism and expressionism in a portrait of 'night-life companions': who sing, dance and share emotional moments as black women in America.

A play basically concerned with women's rights, one character makes a powerful statement on its behalf:

> it really is not so good to be born a girl when we have to be infibulated, excised, clitorectomized & STILL be afraid to walk the streets or stay home at night... monsters and rapists. They are known all over the world & are proliferating at a rapid rate...[60]

A Photograph: Lovers in Motion (1979) comprises the third of the trilogy of *Spell #7*. It comes closest to traditional theatrical form, using five characters who intertwine within each other's lives. The story concerns a black male photographer: he is pursued by the other characters who want some kind of sexual and/or emotional commitment from him, as he tries to become a worthy artist representative of his black culture.

Ntozake Shange has also written two novels, *Sassafrass, Cypress and Indigo* (1982) and *Betsey Brown* (1985). *Sassafrass, Cypress and Indigo* is about three sisters, who choose alternative ways of resisting the standards set by society. Cypress is involved only with women and her life revolves around a female-centred existence. The other, Sassafrass, is a weaver and writer, and chooses to live with a junkie jazz musician. The novel gives us their varying perceptions of life, and the choices available to black women in modern society. Her latest novel, *Betsey Brown,* is a beautifully and tenderly written story of a girl growing up in the midst of the Civil Rights Movement. We watch Betsey, in this warm and nurturing middle-class household, grow to understand a world in turmoil. Set in 1957, in St. Louis, we can assume that this narrative is somewhat autobiographical, as Shange experienced upheaval when bussing and integration laws came into existence during her childhood.

Shange captures the impatience of adolescent passions, as well as the stress of these times on a black family and community. Rarely has a novel about African-American middle-class life been rendered so eloquently and lovingly.

Ntozake Shange has written and produced many more plays, including an adaptation of Brecht entitled *Mother Courage and Her Children.* An excellent actress and reader, Shange now performs her poetry to jazz music, giving it yet another exciting dimension.

Through her expressive, explosive and evocative work, Shange has placed her finger on the pulse of black women's lives in contemporary urban society. The language snaps with sassiness, the content cries with sensitivity and the music merges it all together in the new and urgent song of the black woman writer. No one can express this better, or with more immediacy, than the poet herself:

there is somethin
sacred abt bein invited to bring
yrself to someone's song if you
come w / me next time music
will ask us both to come into
ourselves 'n be our own children
who forget what we were told
rememberin only to be what we are...[61]

●　　●　　●

As I write these words, new voices of black women are emerging, to change the scene, to change your mind, to make change. We are here, have been here and will continue to be here, because:

Our song is strong and we will be heard.

Notes

Chapter One – Out of Slavery

1. Lucy Terry, 'Bar's Fight', from *The American Museum or Repository of Ancient and Modern Fugitive Pieces, etc. Prose and Poetical*, vol. I, no. vi (June 1787). See also George Sheldon, *A History of Deerfield, Massachusetts* (Deerfield 1895), and Erlene Stetson ed., *Black Sister* (Bloomington: Indiana University Press, 1981), p. 12.

2. Alexander Falconbridge, 'Account of The Slave Trade on the Coast of Africa' (London 1788), in Phillip S. Foner, *History of Black Americans* (Westport, CT/London: Greenwood Press, 1975), p. 121.

3. John Josselyn, *An Account of Two Voyages to New England Made During the Years 1638, 1663* (1865), p. 26. See also Herbert G. Gutman, *The Black Family in Slavery and Freedom* (Oxford: Basil Blackwell, 1976), p. 352, and Lerone Bennett, Jr., *Before the Mayflower* (Harmondsworth/New York: Penguin, 1985), pp. 42–3.

4. June Jordan, 'The Difficult Miracle of Black Poetry in America or Something Like a Sonnet for Phillis Wheatley', in *On Call: Political Essays* (London: Pluto Press, 1986), p. 87.

5. M. A. Richmond, *Bid the Vassal Soar* (Washington, DC: Howard University Press, 1974) p. 21. See also notes, pp. 67–8.

6. Alice Walker, *In Search of Our Mothers' Gardens* (London: The Women's Press, 1984), p. 236.

7. Phillis Wheatley, 'To the University of Cambridge in New England', in *The Poems of Phillis Wheatley*, ed. Julian D. Mason (Chapel Hill: University of North Carolina Press, 1966), p. 5.

8. Phillis Wheatley, 'On Being Brought from Africa to America', ibid., p. 7.

9. Phillis Wheatley, 'To The Right Honourable William, Earl of Dartmouth', ibid., p. 33.

10. J. Saunders Redding, *To Make a Poet Black* (Chapel Hill: University of North Carolina Press, 1939), pp. 8–11. See also Richmond, *Bid the Vassal Soar*, p. 62.

11. M. A. Richmond, *Bid the Vassal Soar*, p. 47.

12. ibid., p. 52.

13. Abraham Chapman, ed., *Steal Away: Slaves Tell Their Own Stories* (London: Ernest Benn Ltd., 1973), p. xiii.

14. S. Harley and R. Terborg-Penn, *The Afro-American Woman: Struggles and Images* (Port Washington, NY: National University Publications, 1978), p. 20.

15. Sojourner Truth, Elizabeth Cady Stanton, Susan B. Anthony and Matilda Joslyn Gage eds., *History of Woman Suffrage* (Rochester, NY: 1881), vol. I, p. 116. See also Erlene Stetson ed., *Black Sister* (Bloomington: Indiana University Press, 1981), pp. 24–5, and B. J. Loewenberg and R. Bogin eds., *Black Women in Nineteenth-Century American Life* (Pennsylvania/London: Pennsylvania State University Press, 1976), p. 235.

16. Sarah Bradford, *Harriet Tubman, The Moses of her People* (New York: 1886; Corinth Books, 1961). See also B. J. Loewenberg and R. Bogin eds., *Black Women in Nineteenth-Century American Life*.

17. Dorothy Sterling, ed., *We Are Your Sisters: Black Women in the Nineteenth Century* (London/New York: W. W. Norton, 1984), pp. 157–8.

18. Jean Yellin was to make this discovery in 1981, although as early as 1947 Marion Sterling argued for its validity. See discussion in '"Hear My Voice, Ye Careless Daughters": Narratives of Slave and Free Women before Emancipation', in Hazel Carby, *Reconstructing Womanhood: The Emergence of the Afro-American Woman Novelist* (New York/Oxford: Oxford University Press, 1987), p. 45. See also notes, Chapter 3, Number 8.

19. Harriet 'Linda Brent' Jacobs, *Incidents in the Life of a Slave Girl: Written by Herself* ed. L. Maria Child, (New York: Harcourt Brace Jovanovich, 1973), pp. xiii-xiv. (Original publication, Boston: for the author, 1861.)

20. See Houston A. Baker, 'Figurations for a New American Literary History', in *Blues, Ideology, and Afro-American Literature* (Chicago: University of Chicago Press, 1984), pp. 50–6.

21. Harriet 'Linda Brent' Jacobs, *Incidents in the Life of a Slave Girl: Written by Herself*, p. 49.

22. ibid., p. 35. See also Baker's discussion in *Blues, Ideology and Afro-American Literature*, p. 51.

23. Hazel Carby, *Reconstructing Womanhood*, p. 61.

24. T. W. Talley, *Negro Folk Rhymes, Wise and Otherwise* (New York: MacMillan, 1922), p. 277.

25. Sara Martin, 'Mean-Tight Mama', in T. W. Talley, *Negro Folk Rhymes, Wise and Otherwise*, p. 99. See also D. D. Harrison, 'Black Women in the Blues Tradition', in Harley and Terborg-Penn eds., *The Afro-American Woman: Struggles and Images*, p. 82.

26. J. B. T. Marsh, *The Story of the Jubilee Singers; With Their Songs* (Boston, 1880), p. 132.

27. William Francis Allen, Charles Pickard Ware and Lucy McKim Garrison, compilers, *Slave Songs of the United States* (New York, 1867, Oak Publications; 1965), p. 148.

28. 'The Gospel Train', in Johnson and Okum eds., *Negro Workaday Songs* (Chapel Hill: University of North Carolina Press, 1926), p. 114.

29. Lawrence Gellert, 'Negro Songs of Protest: North and South Carolina and Georgia', in Nancy Cunard ed., *Negro: An Anthology* (New York: Frederick Ungar, 1970), p. 229.

30. Harriet E. Wilson, *circa* 1852, from *Our Nig; or, Sketches from the Life of a Free Black*, introduction by Henry Louis Gates Jr. (Boston: by the author, 1859; reprinted New York: Random House, 1983; London: Allison & Busby, 1984), p. xi.

31. ibid., p. xii.

32. ibid., see introduction by Henry Louis Gates.

33. ibid., p. xxviii.

34. ibid., p. i.

35. Hazel Carby, *Reconstructing Womanhood*, p. 43.

36. Frances E. W. Harper, 'An Appeal To My Countrywomen', in *Poems* (Philadelphia: George S. Ferguson, 1895). See also Stetson ed., *Black Sister*, pp. 31–2.

37. Frances E. W. Harper, 'Simon's Countrymen', in *Idylls of the Bible* (Philadelphia: George S. Ferguson, 1901).

38. Hazel Carby, *Reconstructing Womanhood*, p. 89.

39. Frances E. W. Harper, *Iola Leroy, or Shadows Uplifted* (Philadelphia: Garrigues Brothers, 1892; reprinted Boston: Beacon Press, 1987), p. 64.

40. ibid., p. 38.

41. ibid., pp. 166–7.

42. ibid., p. 188.

43. Hazel Carby, *Reconstructing Womanhood*, p. 128.

44. ibid.

45. Pauline E. Hopkins, *Contending Forces: A Romance Illustrative of Negro Life North and South* (Boston: Colored Co-operative Publishing Co., 1900), p. 87.

46. Sojourner Truth, in Loewenberg and Bogin eds., *Black Women in Nineteenth-Century American Life*, p. 236.

Chapter Two – Words to a White World

1. Angelina W. Grimké, 'Reason and Synopsis' from *Rachel: A Play in Three Acts* (Boston: Cornhill, 1920; reprinted College Park, MD: McGrath, 1969). Cited by Gloria T. Hull, *Color, Sex and Poetry: Three Women Writers of the Harlem Renaissance* (Bloomington: Indiana University Press, 1987), p. 118.

2. W. E. B. Du Bois, *The Souls of Black Folks* (New York: Dodd, Mead, 1961), pp. 78–9.

3. Nathan Huggins, *Harlem Renaissance* (Oxford/New York: Oxford University Press, 1971), p. 61.

4. Gloria T. Hull, *Color, Sex and Poetry*, p. 40.

5. ibid., p. 80.

6. Nathan Huggins, *Harlem Renaissance*, p. 63.

7. Alice Dunbar Nelson, 'Violets' (also called 'Sonnet' and 'Sonnet to April'), published in *The Crisis* 18 (August 1919). See also Stetson ed., *Black Sister*, p. 65, and Gloria T. Hull ed., *Give Us Each Day: The Diary of Alice Dunbar Nelson* (New York/London: Norton, 1984), p. 146.

8. Alice Dunbar Nelson, 'St. Rocque', in *The Goodness of St. Rocque and Other Stories* (New York: Dodd, Mead, 1899), p. 1.

9. Alice Dunbar Nelson, 'The Praline Woman', ibid., p. 177.

10. Alice Dunbar Nelson, 'From A Woman's Point of View', published in the *Pittsburgh Courier*, 23 January 1926.

11. Gloria T. Hull ed., *Give Us Each Day*, p. 260.

12. ibid., p. 409. Johnson's quote from Cecil Gray, *A Survey of Contemporary Music*, p. 246.

13. *Rachel*, programme for the Washington DC premiere production, sponsored by the N.A.A.C.P., 3 and 4 March 1916. Cited by Gloria T. Hull, *Color, Sex and Poetry*, p. 117.

14. Robert Kerlin ed., *Negro Poets and their Poems* (Washington DC: Associated Publishers, 1923), p. 153.

15. Angelina Grimké, 'At April', in *Opportunity* 3 (March 1925). See also Stetson ed., *Black Sister*, p. 61.

16. Angelina Grimké, 'A Mona Lisa', in Countee Cullen ed., *Caroling Dusk: An Anthology of Verse by Negro Poets* (New York: Harper, 1927), p. 42. See also *Black Sister*, p. 60.

17. Gloria T. Hull, *Color, Sex and Poetry*, p. 152.

18. ibid., p. 152.

19. Anne Spencer's biographical sketch in Cullen ed., *Caroling Dusk* (1955 edition), p. 155.

20. James Weldon Johnson ed., *The Book of American Negro Poetry* (New York: Harcourt, Brace and World, 1922; revised 1959), p. 213.

21. Anne Spencer, 'Lady, Lady', in Alain Locke ed., *The New Negro: An Interpretation* (New York: Albert and Charles Boni, 1925), p. 148. See also *Black Sister*, p. 72.

22. Georgia Douglas Johnson, *Bronze, a book of verse* (Boston: B. J. Brimmer, 1922), p. 3.

23. ibid., p. 7.

24. 'Black Woman', ibid., p. 43.

25. 'The Octoroon', ibid., p. 36.

26. Georgia Douglas Johnson, *The Heart of a Woman and Other Poems* (Boston: Cornhill, 1918) p. 1.

27. Georgia Douglas Johnson, 'Cosmopolite', in *Bronze*, p. 59.

28. Arthur Davis and Michael Peplow eds., *The New Negro Renaissance: An Anthology* (New York: Holt, Rinehart and Winston, 1975), p. 168.

29. Alain Locke, *The New Negro*, p. 14. See also Huggins, *Harlem Renaissance*, p. 59.

30. Huggins, *Harlem Renaissance*, p. 59.

31. Jessie Fauset, 'Noblesse Oblige', in *Caroling Dusk*, p. 67.

32. Nathan Huggins, *Harlem Renaissance*, p. 146.

33. Jessie Fauset, 'The Negro in Art, How Shall He Be Portrayed?', in *The Crisis* (March–November 1926). See also Davis and Peplow, *The New Negro Renaissance*, p. 479.

34. Jessie Fauset, *Plum Bun* (London: Pandora Press, 1985), introduction by Deborah McDowell, p. x.

35. Nathan Huggins, *Harlem Renaissance*, p. 148.

36. Jessie Fauset, *Plum Bun*, p. 78.

37. Nella Larsen, *Quicksand and Passing* (New Jersey: Rutgers University Press, 1986, p. 96; London: Serpent's Tail, 1989), p. 96.

38. ibid., p. 95.

39. ibid., p. 103.

40. ibid., introduction by McDowell, p. xxii.

41. Alice Dunbar Nelson, 'As in a Looking Glass', column in the *Washington Eagle*, 3 May 1929. See also Hull, *Color, Sex and Poetry*, p. 87.

42. Nella Larsen, *Passing*, p. 190.

43. ibid., p. 194.

44. ibid., p. 239.

45. ibid., p. 239.

46. Gwendolyn Bennett, 'To A Dark Girl', in *Opportunity* 5 (1927). See also *Caroling Dusk*, p. 157, *Black Sister*, p. 76, and Johnson ed., *The Book Of American Negro Poetry*, p. 243.

Chapter Three – A Jump at de Sun

1. Giles Oakley, *The Devil's Music: A History of the Blues* (New York: Harcourt Brace Jovanovich, 1978), p. 15.

2. Zora Neale Hurston to Mrs. Mason, 25 November 1930. Alain Locke Papers, Moorland-Spingarn Research Centre, Howard University Library. See also Alice Walker ed., *I Love Myself When I Am Laughing . . .: A Zora Neale Hurston Reader* (New York: The Feminist Press, 1979), introduction by Mary Helen Washington, pp. 7–24.

3. Robert E. Hemenway, *Zora Neale Hurston: A Literary Biography* (Urbana: University of Illinois Press, 1978; London: Camden Press, 1986), p. 9.

4. Zora Neale Hurston, *Dust Tracks on a Road* (Philadelphia: J. B. Lippincott, 1942; reprinted 1971, appendix added 1984; London: Virago, 1986), p. 177.

5. *Zora Neale Hurston*, 'Folklore', typescript, Florida Federal Writers' Project, c.1938; cited by Hemenway, *Zora Neale Hurston*, p. 159.

6. It has now been established by Professor Cheryl Wall that Zora Neale Hurston was born on 7 January 1891 rather than 1 January 1901. See Hull, *Color, Sex and Poetry* , p. 218 (note).

7. Zora Neale Hurston, *Dust Tracks on a Road*, p. 21.

8. Zora Neale Hurston, *Their Eyes Were Watching God* (Philadelphia: J. B. Lippincott, 1937; reprinted Urbana: University of Illinois Press, 1978; London: Virago, 1986), pp. 9–10.

9. Zora Neale Hurston, *Dust Tracks on a Road*, p. 116.

10. ibid., p. 156.

11. Zora Neale Hurston, 'Spunk', *Opportunity* 3 (June 1925), pp. 171–3. Reprinted in Locke ed., *The New Negro*, pp. 105–11, and in *Spunk: The Selected Stories of Zora Neale Hurston* (Berkeley: Turtle Island, 1985; London: Camden Press, 1987), pp. 1–8.

12. Langston Hughes, *The Big Sea* (New York: Alfred A. Knopf, 1940; reprinted London: Pluto Press, 1986), p. 235.

13. See Nathan Huggins, *Harlem Renaissance*, p. 131.

14. Zora Neale Hurston, 'Characteristics of Negro Expression', in Nancy Cunard ed., *Negro: An Anthology* (London: Wishart, 1934; reprinted New York: Frederick Ungar, 1970), pp. 24–31. Also in Hurston, *The Sanctified Church* (Berkeley: Turtle Island, 1983), p. 28.

15. Zora Neale Hurston, 'Spirituals and Neo-Spirituals', in *Negro* (1970 edition), pp. 223–4. See also *The Sanctified Church*.

16. Zora Neale Hurston, 'Characteristics of Negro Expression', in *Negro* (1970 ed.), p. 25.

17. ibid., p. 25.

18. ibid., p. 26.

19. ibid., p. 27.

20. Zora Neale Hurston, *Mules and Men* (Philadelphia: J. B. Lippincott, 1935; reprinted, with an introduction by Darwin Turner, New York: Harper and Row, 1970; New York: Negro University Press, 1969), pp. 17–18.

21. ibid., p. 4.

22. ibid., pp. 91–2.

23. Zora Neale Hurston, *Jonah's Gourd Vine* (Philadelphia: J.B. Lippincott, 1934; reprinted 1971; London: Virago, 1987), pp. 59–60.

24. Zora Neale Hurston, *Their Eyes Were Watching God*, p. 29.

25. ibid., p. 48.

26. ibid., p. 48.

27. ibid., p. 24.

28. ibid., p. 161.

29. ibid., p. 286.

30. ibid., p. 9.

31. Zora Neale Hurston, *Tell My Horse* (Philadelphia: J. B. Lippincott, 1938), p. 16. See also Alice Walker ed., *I Love Myself When I Am Laughing . . .*, p. 125.

32. Zora Neale Hurston, *Tell My Horse*, p. 137.

33. ibid., p. 137.

34. Zora Neale Hurston, *Moses, Man of the Mountain* (Philadelphia: J. B. Lippincott, 1939; reprinted Urbana: University of Illinois Press, 1984) pp. xxi-xxii (author's introduction).

35. ibid., pp. 156–7.

36. ibid., pp. 103–4.

37. Alice Walker, 'A Cautionary Tale and a Partisan View', in *In Search of Our Mothers' Gardens* (London: The Women's Press, 1984), p. 91.

38. See Hemenway, *Zora Neale Hurston*, p. 288.

39. Cited by Hemenway, p. 287.

40. The full unedited chapters can now be found as an appendix in the 1984 Harper and Row and 1986 Virago editions.

41. Dellita L. Martin's introduction to the Virago edition of *Dust Tracks on a Road*, p. xiii. (This is her version of Alice Walker's comment on the autobiography, 'it rings false', on p. 91 of *In Search of Our Mothers' Gardens*.)

42. Zora Neale Hurston, *Dust Tracks on a Road*, p. 41.

43. ibid., p. 41.

44. ibid., p. 249.

45. ibid., p. 284.

46. Zora Neale Hurston, 'How It Feels To Be Colored Me', *World Tomorrow* 11 (May 1928), pp. 215–16; also in Alice Walker ed., *I Love Myself When I Am Laughing*..., p. 153.

47. Zora Neale Hurston, *Dust Tracks on a Road*, pp. 285–6.

48. Hemenway, p. 348; see also p. 353, note 45.

Chapter Four – Urban Realities

1. Nia Damili, 'Birth of a Poet', in *Black American Literature Forum*, vol. 20, no. 3, (Fall 1986).

2. Ann Petry, *The Street* (Boston: Houghton Mifflin, 1946; reprinted London: Virago, 1986), pp. 56–7.

3. ibid., p. 232.

4. James W. Ivy, 'Ann Petry Talks About Her First Novel', in *Crisis*, Feb. 1946, pp. 48–9.

5. Ann Petry, *The Street*, p. 36.

6. ibid., p. 149.

7. ibid., p. 150.

8. ibid., p. 221.

9. Louise Meriwether, *Daddy Was A Number Runner* (Englewood Cliffs, NJ: Prentice Hall, 1970; reprinted New York: Feminist Press, 1986; London: Methuen, 1987), foreword by James Baldwin, pp. 6–7.

10. ibid., p. 5.

11. ibid., p. 45.

12. ibid., pp. 42–3.

13. ibid., p. 203.

14. Dorothy West, *The Living Is Easy* (Boston: Houghton Mifflin, 1948; reprinted New York: Feminist Press, 1982; London: Virago, 1987), p. 105.

15. Alice Childress, 'A Candle in a Gale Wind', in Mari Evans ed., *Black Women Writers: Arguments and Interviews* (New York: Anchor Press/Doubleday, 1984; London: Pluto Press, 1985), p. 112.

16. Alice Childress, *Like One of the Family: Conversations from a Domestic's Life* (Brooklyn, New York: Independence Publishers, 1956; Boston: Beacon Press, 1986), p. 26.

17. ibid., p. 27.

18. ibid., p. 3.

19. Alice Childress, *Florence, A One Act Drama,* in *Masses and Mainstream,* 3 (October 1950), pp. 34–47.

20. ibid.

21. Lorraine Hansberry, *To Be Young, Gifted and Black: Lorraine Hansberry in Her Own Words,* adapted by Robert Nemiroff (Englewood Cliffs, NJ: Prentice Hall, 1969; New York: New American Library, 1970), p. 98.

22. ibid., frontispiece.

23. ibid., p. 96.

24. Lorraine Hansberry, *A Raisin in the Sun: a Drama in Three Acts* (London: Methuen, 1960), pp. 97–100.

25. Lorraine Hansberry, *To Be Young, Gifted and Black,* p. 109.

26. Adrienne Rich, *Blood, Bread and Poetry* (New York: Norton, 1986; London: Virago, 1987), p. 13.

27. Lorraine Hansberry, *To Be Young, Gifted and Black,* p. 39.

28. Margaret Walker, 'For My People', in *For My People* (New Haven: Yale University Press, 1942; reprinted 1968), pp. 13–14. See also Langston Hughes, Arna Bontemps eds., *The Poetry of the Negro: 1746–1970* (New York: Doubleday, 1970), pp. 314–16.

29. Margaret Walker, 'Lineage', in *For My People,* p. 25. See also *Black Sister,* p. 94.

30. Margaret Walker and Nikki Giovanni, *A Poetic Equation: Conversations Between Nikki Giovanni and Margaret Walker* (Washington DC: Howard University Press, 1974), p. 91.

31. Margaret Walker, 'Memory', in *For My People,* p. 56.

Chapter Five – Birth in a Narrow Room

1. Gwendolyn Brooks, 'The Egg Boiler', in *The Bean Eaters* (1960); *Blacks* (Chicago: The David Company, 1987), p. 382.

2. Gwendolyn Brooks, 'Kitchenette building', in *A Street In Bronzeville* (1945); *Blacks*, p. 20.

3. Gwendolyn Brooks, 'The mother', ibid., p. 21.

4. Gwendolyn Brooks, 'of De Witt Williams on his way to Lincoln Cemetery', *Blacks*, p. 39.

5. ibid, p. 39.

6. Gwendolyn Brooks, 'The ballad of chocolate Mabbie', ibid., p. 30.

7. Gwendolyn Brooks, 'Hattie Scott: at the hairdressers', ibid., p. 53.

8. Gwendolyn Brooks, 'The Sundays of Satin-Legs Smith', ibid., pp. 42–4.

9. W. E. B. Du Bois, *The Souls of Black Folks*, p. 3.

10. Gwendolyn Brooks, 'The Womanhood, Section XII: beauty shopper', from *Annie Allen*, in *Blacks*, p. 134.

11. Gwendolyn Brooks, 'Notes from The Childhood and The Girlhood: The birth in a narrow room', ibid., p. 83.

12. Gwendolyn Brooks, 'The Anniad', ibid., pp. 99–100.

13. Gwendolyn Brooks, 'The Womanhood: the children of the poor', ibid., p. 118.

14. ibid.

15. Gwendolyn Brooks, 'Men of careful turns, haters of forks in the road', ibid., p. 140.

16. Gwendolyn Brooks, *Report From Part One* (Detroit: Broadside Press, 1972), pp. 190–1.

17. Mary Helen Washington, '"Taming all that anger down": rage and silence in Gwendolyn Brooks' *Maud Martha*', in Henry Louis Gates, Jr. ed., *Black Literature and Literary Theory* (London/New York: Methuen, 1984), p. 249.

18. Barbara Christian, *Black Feminist Criticism* (New York/Oxford: Pergamon Press, 1985), p. 129.

19. Gwendolyn Brooks, *Maud Martha* (1953), in *Blacks*, pp. 143–4.

20. ibid., pp. 229–30.

21. See Christian, 'Nuance and the Novella: A Study of Gwendolyn Brooks' *Maud Martha*', in *Black Feminist Criticism*, pp. 127–41.

22. Gwendolyn Brooks, *Maud Martha*, pp. 146–7.

23. ibid., p. 164.

24. Gwendolyn Brooks, 'A Bronzeville Mother Loiters in Mississippi. Meanwhile, A Mississippi Mother Burns Bacon', in *The Bean Eaters*, in *Blacks*, p. 333.

25. ibid., p. 339.

26. Charles Israel, 'Gwendolyn Brooks', in *Dictionary of Literary Biography Volume Five* (Detroit: Gale Research Company), p. 101.

27. Gwendolyn Brooks, 'We Real Cool', in *The Bean Eaters*, in *Blacks*, p. 331.

28. Gwendolyn Brooks, *Report From Part One*, pp. 155–6.

29. Gwendolyn Brooks, 'The Ballad of Rudolph Reed', in *The Bean Eaters*, in *Blacks*, pp. 376–8.

30. Gwendolyn Brooks, *Report From Part One*, p. 165.

31. Claudia Tate, *Black Women Writers at Work* (New York: Continuum, 1983; Harpenden: Oldcastle Books, 1985), p. 40.

32. Gwendolyn Brooks, *In The Mecca: Poems* (1968), in *Blacks*, p. 404.

33. ibid., p. 406.

34. ibid., p. 416.

35. ibid., p. 433.

36. ibid., pp. 423–4.

37. ibid., p. 441.

38. ibid., p. 442.

39. ibid., pp. 444–5.

40. Brooks, 'The Second Sermon On The Warpland', ibid. pp. 453–6.

41. Claudia Tate, *Black Women Writers at Work*, p. 45.

42. Gwendolyn Brooks, 'Riot' (1969), in *Blacks*, p. 471.

43. Nellie McKay, 'Gwendolyn Brooks' *Report From Part One* An Act of Willful Self-Creation', in Victor Kramer ed., *The Harlem Renaissance Revisited* (New York: AMS Press, 1988).

44. Gwendolyn Brooks, letter to the author, January 1988.

45. Gwendolyn Brooks, *Report From Part One*, p. 204.

46. Gwendolyn Brooks, 'The Boy Died in my Alley', in *Beckonings* (Detroit: Broadside Press, 1975), p. 5.

47. Charles Israel, 'Gwendolyn Brooks', *Dictionary of Literary Biography*: *Volume Five*, p. 105.

48. Claudia Tate, *Black Women Writers at Work*, p. 48.

49. Gwendolyn Brooks, '"Boys. Black"', in *Beckonings*, p. 16.

Chapter Six – Black Talk, Black Judgement

1. Nikki Giovanni, 'The True Import of Present Dialogue, Black vs. Negro', in *Black feeling, Black talk, Black judgement* (New York: William Morrow, 1970), p. 19.

2. Gwendolyn Brooks, *Jump Bad: A New Chicago Anthology* (Detroit: Broadside Press, 1971), p. 12.

3. Carolyn Rodgers, 'U Name This One', in *How I Got Ovah* (New York: Doubleday, 1969); see also Stetson ed., *Black Sister*, p. 183.

4. William H. Grier and Price M. Cobbs, *Black Rage* (New York: Basic Books, 1968), p. 125.

5. Grace Sims Holt, '"Inversion" in black communication', in Thomas Kochman ed., *Rappin' and stylin' out* (Urbana: University of Illinois Press, 1972), p. 154.

6. Jewel Latimore, 'Folk Fable', cited by Carolyn Rodgers, 'Black Poetry – where it's at', in Kochman ed., *Rappin' and stylin' out*, p. 340.

7. Carolyn Rodgers, 'Black Poetry – where it's at', in *Rappin' and stylin' out*, p. 345.

8. ibid., pp. 336–7.

9. Mari Evans, 'Viva Noir', in *I Am A Black Woman* (New York: William Morrow, 1970), pp. 70–2; see also Stephen Henderson ed., *Understanding the New Black Poetry* (New York: William Morrow, 1972), p. 247.

10. Cited by Angela Davis, *If They Come in the Morning* (London: Orbach and Chambers, 1971), p. 117.

11. Nikki Giovanni, 'The Weather as a Cultural Determiner', in *Gemini* (New York: Viking Press, 1973), p. 96.

12. Nikki Giovanni, 'Poem (No Name No. 2)', in *Black feeling, Black talk, Black judgement* (New York: William Morrow, 1968), p. 18.

13. Nikki Giovanni, 'A Short Essay of Affirmation Explaining Why (With Apologies to the Federal Bureau of Investigation)', in *Black feeling, Black talk, Black judgement*, p. 21.

14. Nikki Giovanni, 'Poem (No Name No. 3)', ibid., pp. 24–5.

15. Nikki Giovanni, 'Love Poem (For Real)', ibid., pp. 33–4.

16. Nikki Giovanni, 'Seduction', ibid., p. 38.

17. Nikki Giovanni, 'Nikki Rosa', ibid., pp. 58–9.

18. Nikki Giovanni, 'For Saundra', ibid., pp. 88–9.

19. Nikki Giovanni, 'Revolutionary Dreams', in *Recreation* (Detroit: Broadside Press, 1970), p. 26.

20. Suzanne Juhasz, *Naked and Fiery Forms* (New York: Octagon Books, 1978), p. 168.

21. Nikki Giovanni, 'Categories', in *My House* (New York: William Morrow, 1972), p. 30.

22. Nikki Giovanni, *Those Who Ride the Nightwinds* (New York: William Morrow, 1983), p. 51.

23. Nikki Giovanni, 'It's a Case of...', in *Gemini*, p. 84.

24. Nikki Giovanni, 'Gemini', in *Gemini*, p. 144 (New York: Viking Press, 1971; 1973 edn.).

25. Nikki Giovanni and Margaret Walker, *A Poetic Equation: Conversations Between Nikki Giovanni and Margaret Walker* (Washington, DC: Howard University Press, 1974), p. 33.

26. Sonia Sanchez, 'Memorial', in *Homecoming* (Detroit: Broadside Press, 1970). See also *Black Sister*, pp. 242–5.

27. Sonia Sanchez, 'For Unborn Malcolms', in *Homecoming*.

28. Sonia Sanchez, 'to Blk/record/buyers', in *Homecoming*. See also Henderson ed., *Understanding the New Black Poetry*, p. 272.

29. Sonia Sanchez, 'Summer Words For a Sister Addict', in *Homecoming*. See also *Black Sister*, p. 246.

30. Sonia Sanchez, 'Memorial', in *Homecoming*. See also *Black Sister*, pp. 244–5.

31. Jacqueline Jones, *Labor of Love, Labor of Sorrow* (New York: Vintage Books/Random House, 1986), p. 312.

32. Eldridge Cleaver, *Soul on Ice* (London: Jonathan Cape, 1969), p. 209.

33. ibid., p. 14.

34. Artie Seale, in *The Black Panther: Black Community News* (San Francisco, CA, vol. IV, no. 22 (2 May 1970), p. 7.

35. Jacqueline Jones, *Labor of Love, Labor of Sorrow*, p. 283.

36. ibid., p. 312.

37. Fareedah Allah (Ruby C. Saunders), 'HUSH HONEY', in *Black Sister*, pp. 164–7.

38. Carolyn Rodgers, 'The Last M. F.', in Henderson ed., *Understanding the New Black Poetry*, pp. 346–7.

39. Angela Davis, *Angela Davis: An Autobiography* (New York: Random House, 1974; London: The Women's Press, 1990), p. 161.

40. Paula Giddings, *When and Where I Enter* (New York: William Morrow/Bantam, 1985), p. 318.

41. Nikki Giovanni and James Baldwin, *A Dialogue: James Baldwin and Nikki Giovanni* (Philadelphia: Lippincott, 1973; London: Michael Joseph, 1975), p. 31 in 1973 edn.

42. Bell Hooks, *Ain't I A Woman: Black Women and Feminism* (Boston: South End Press, 1982; London: Pluto Press, 1985), p. 181.

43. Carolyn Rodgers, 'Poem For Some Black Women', in *How I Got Ovah*. See also *Black Sister*, pp. 176–8.

44. Sherley Anne Williams, 'Driving Wheel', in *The Peacock Poems* (Middletown, CT: Wesleyan University Press, 1977). See also *Black Sister*, pp. 260–4.

Chapter Seven – A Deeper Reckoning

1. Toni Morrison, 'What The Black Woman Thinks About Women's Lib', *New York Times Magazine* (22 August 1971), p. 63.

2. In Sandi Russell, 'It's OK to say OK', *Women's Review* (London: no. 5 March 1986, p. 23. Reprinted in Nellie McKay, ed., *Critical Essays on Toni Morrison* (Boston: G. K. Hall, 1988), pp. 43–7.

3. Barbara Christian, *Black Feminist Criticism* (New York/Oxford: Pergamon Press, 1985), p. 178.

4. Toni Morrison, Talk at A.F.E.A. Conference on American Women Writers, University of Toulouse, France, April 1985.

5. Gene Redmond, Interview with Toni Morrison in *River Styx* (Missouri Arts Council, no. 19, 1986), p. 14.

6. Toni Morrison, Talk at A.F.E.A. Conference, Toulouse, 1985.

7. Sandi Russell, 'It's OK to say OK', in McKay ed., *Critical Essays on Toni Morrison*, p. 45.

8. Claudia Tate, *Black Women Writers at Work* (New York: Continuum, 1983; Harpenden: Oldcastle Books, 1985), p. 126.

9. Toni Morrison, 'Rootedness: The Ancestor as Foundation', in Mari Evans ed., *Black Women Writers: Arguments and Interviews* (London: Pluto Press, 1985), p. 341.

10. ibid., pp. 344–5.

11. Toni Morrison, *The Bluest Eye*, (London: Chatto and Windus, 1979), p. 34.

12. ibid., p. 1.

13. ibid., p. 2.

14. ibid., p. 28.

15. Charles Ruas ed., *Conversations with American Writers* (New York: Alfred A. Knopf, 1985), p. 220.

16. Toni Morrison, *The Bluest Eye*, p. 3.

17. ibid., p. 126.

18. ibid., pp. 95–6.

19. Sandi Russell, 'It's OK to say OK', in McKay ed., p. 44.

20. Toni Morrison, Talk at A.F.E.A. Conference, Toulouse, 1985.

21. Toni Morrison, *Sula* (London: Chatto and Windus, 1980), p. 4.

22. ibid., p. 5.

23. Barbara Christian, *Black Women Novelists* (Westport, CT/London: Greenwood Press, 1984), p. 153.

24. Robert Stepto, '"Intimate Things in Place": A Conversation with Toni Morrison', in Michael Harper and Robert Stepto eds., *Chant of Saints: A Gathering of Afro-American Literature, Art and Scholarship* (Champaign/London: University of Illinois Press, 1979), p. 155.

25. Barbara Christian, *Black Women Novelists*, p. 155.

26. Toni Morrison, *Sula*, p. 14.

27. ibid., p. 66.

28. Sandi Russell, 'It's OK to say OK', in McKay ed., p. 46.

29. Toni Morrison, Talk at A.F.E.A. Conference, Toulouse, 1985.

30. Toni Morrison, *Sula*, pp. 89–90.

31. ibid., p. 41.

32. ibid., p. 71.

33. ibid., pp. 51–2.

34. ibid., p. 52.

35. Toni Morison, Talk at A.F.E.A. Conference, Toulouse, 1985.

36. Toni Morrison, *Sula*, p. 121.

37. ibid., p. 18.

38. ibid., p. 122.

39. ibid., p. 113.

40. Claudia Tate, *Black Women Writers at Work*, p. 130.

41. Sandi Russell, 'It's OK to say OK', in McKay ed., p. 46.

42. Toni Morrison, *Sula*, p. 174.

43. Gloria Naylor and Toni Morrison, 'A Conversation', *Southern Review*, vol. 21, no. 3 (Summer 1985), p. 578.

44. Sandi Russell, 'It's OK to say OK', in McKay ed., p. 45.

45. Toni Morrison, *Song of Solomon* (London: Chatto and Windus, 1978), p. 6.

46. Toni Morrison, 'Rootedness', in Mari Evans ed. *Black Women Writers*, p. 342.

47. Claudia Tate ed., *Black Women Writers at Work*, p. 124.

48. Toni Morrison, Talk at A.F.E.A. Conference, Toulouse, 1985.

49. Toni Morrison, *Song of Solomon*, p. 53.

50. See Toni Morrison 'Rootedness', in Mari Evans ed., *Black Women Writers*, pp. 339–45.

51. Toni Morrison, *Song of Solomon*, p. 13.

52. ibid., p. 55.

53. Sandi Russell, 'It's OK to say OK', in McKay ed., p. 44.

54. Joseph T. Skerrett Jr., 'Recitation to the GRIOT: Storytelling and Learning in Toni Morrison's *Song of Solomon*', in M. Pryse and H. J. Spillers eds., *Conjuring: Black Women, Fiction and Literary Tradition* (Bloomington: Indiana University Press, 1985), p. 195.

55. Toni Morrison, *Song of Solomon*, pp. 29–30.

56. See Susan Willis, 'Eruptions of funk: historicizing Toni Morrison', in *Specifying: Black Women Writing the American Experience* (Madison: University of Wisconsin Press, 1987), pp. 83–109. See also H. L. Gates Jr. ed., *Black Literature and Literary Theory* (London: Methuen, 1984), chapter 12.

57. Toni Morrison, *Song of Solomon*, pp. 310–11.

58. ibid., p. 337.

59. Cited by Susan Blake, 'Toni Morrison', in *Dictionary of Literary Biography, Volume Thirty-three* (Detroit: Gale Research Company), p. 194.

60. Toni Morrison, *Tar Baby* (London: Chatto and Windus, 1981), p. 308.

61. Thomas Le Clair, '"The Language Must Not Sweat"', *New Republic*, no. 184 (21 March 1981), pp. 25–9.

62. Toni Morrison, *Tar Baby*, p. 224.

63. Marilyn E. Mobley, 'Narrative Dilemma: Jadine as Cultural Orphan in Toni Morrison's *Tar Baby*', *Southern Review*, vol. 23, no. 4 (Autumn 1987), p. 768.

64. Toni Morrison, *Tar Baby*, p. 72.

65. ibid., pp. 216–17.

66. ibid., p. 4.

67. ibid., pp. 266–7.

68. ibid., pp. 308–9.

69. ibid., p. 276.

70. Nellie McKay, 'An Interview with Toni Morrison', in *Contemporary Literature*, vol. XXIV, no. 4 (Winter 1983), pp. 421–2.

71. Toni Morrison, *Beloved* (London: Chatto and Windus, 1987), p. 165.

72. Mervyn Rothstein, 'Toni Morrison in her New Novel, Defends Women', *New York Times*, 26 August 1987.

73. ibid.

74. Toni Morrison, *Beloved*, p. 149.

75. ibid., p. 5.

76. ibid., pp. 4–5.

77. ibid., p. 142.

78. ibid., p. 6.

79. ibid., p. 17.

80. ibid., p. 11.

81. ibid., p. 220.

82. ibid., p. 79.

83. ibid., p. 66.

84. ibid., p. 61.

85. ibid., p. 203.

86. Toni Morrison, interview with Melvyn Bragg, *The South Bank Show*, London Weekend Television, 11 October 1987.

87. Toni Morrison, *Beloved*, p. 181.

88. ibid., p. 180.

89. ibid., p. 45.

90. ibid., p. 216.

91. Judith Thurman, 'A House Divided', *New Yorker* (2 November 1987), p. 175.

92. *New York Times Book Review*, 24 January 1988.

93. Toni Morrison, *Beloved*, p. 275.

94. *The South Bank Show*, London Weekend Television, 1987.

95. Toni Morrison, *Beloved*, pp. 88–9.

Chapter Eight – The Silenced Speak

1. Alice Walker, 'Remember', in *Horses Make a Landscape Look More Beautiful* (London: The Women's Press, 1985), pp. 1–2.

2. Emmett J. Scott, *Negro Migration During the War* (New York: Oxford University Press, 1969; originally published 1920), pp. 48, 24. See also Jacqueline Jones, *Labor of Love, Labor of Sorrow*, p. 160.

3. Alice Walker, 'In Search of Our Mothers' Gardens', in *In Search of Our Mothers' Gardens* (London: The Women's Press, 1984), pp. 232–3.

4. Alice Walker, 'The Black Writer and the Southern Experience', ibid., p. 17.

5. Alice Walker, Interview in John O'Brien ed., *Interviews With Black Writers* (New York: Liveright, 1973), p. 193.

6. Alice Walker, *In Search of Our Mothers' Gardens*, p. 241.

7. ibid.

8. Alice Walker, 'Once', in *Once* (Orlando: Harcourt Brace Jovanovich, 1968; London: The Women's Press, 1986).

9. Alice Walker, in O'Brien ed., *Interviews With Black Writers*, p. 190.

10. ibid., p. 189.

11. ibid., p. 209.

12. Barbara Christian, 'Alice Walker', *Dictionary of Literary Biography: Volume Thirty-three* (Detroit: Gale Research Company), p. 260.

13. Alice Walker, 'Be Nobody's Darling', in *Revolutionary Petunias* (New York: Harvest, 1973; London: The Women's Press, 1988), pp. 31–2.

14. Alice Walker, in O'Brien ed., *Interviews With Black Writers*, p. 208.

15. ibid.

16. Alice Walker, 'Revolutionary Petunias', in *Revolutionary Petunias*, p. 29.

17. Alice Walker, 'Women', ibid., p. 5.

18. Alice Walker, 'Did This Happen to Your Mother? Did Your Sister Throw Up a Lot?', in *Good Night, Willie Lee, I'll See You in the Morning* (New York: Harvest, 1984; London: The Women's Press, 1987), pp. 2–3.

19. Alice Walker, 'On Stripping Back from Myself', ibid., p. 23.

20. Alice Walker, 'forgiveness', ibid., p. 51.

21. Alice Walker, 'The Diamonds On Liz's Bosom', in *Horses Make a Landscape Look More Beautiful*, p. 11.

22. Alice Walker, 'We Alone', ibid., p. 12.

23. Alice Walker, 'Each One, Pull One', ibid., p. 52.

24. Alice Walker, 'These Days', ibid., p. 79.

25. Alice Walker, *In Search of Our Mothers' Gardens*, p. 240.

26. Alice Walker, in O'Brien ed., *Interviews With Black Writers*, p. 198.

27. Houston Baker, Jr. and Charlotte Pierce Baker, 'Patches: Quilts and Community in Alice Walker's "Everyday Use"', *Southern Review*, vol. 21, no. 3 (July 1985), p. 706.

28. Barbara Christian, 'The Black Woman as Wayward', in *Black Feminist Criticism*, p. 87.

29. Alice Walker, 'Everyday Use', in *In Love and Trouble* (London: The Women's Press, 1984; New York: Harvest, 1973), p. 57.

30. Barbara Christian, 'The Black Woman as Wayward', in *Black Feminist Criticism*, p. 87.

31. ibid., pp. 81–99.

32. Alice Walker, 'Advancing Luna – and Ida B. Wells', in *You Can't Keep A Good Woman Down* (London: The Women's Press, 1983), p. 93.

33. Barbara Christian, 'Novels for Everyday Use: The Novels of Alice Walker', in *Black Women Novelists* (Westport, CT/London: Greenwood Press, 1980), p. 180.

34. Alice Walker, *The Third Life of Grange Copeland* (London: The Women's Press, 1985), p. 207.

35. Barbara Christian, *Black Women Novelists*, p. 204.

36. Claudia Tate ed., *Black Women Writers at Work*, p. 176.

37. Alice Walker, *Meridian* (London: The Women's Press, 1982), pp. 13–14.

38. Jean Toomer, 'The Blue Meridian', in Darwin T. Turner ed., *The Wayward and the Seeking: A Collection of Writings by Jean Toomer* (Washington, DC: Howard University Press, 1982), p. 214.

39. Alice Walker, *Meridian*, pp. 14–15.

40. Michael G. Cook, *Afro-American Literature in the Twentieth Century: The Achievement of Intimacy* (New Haven, CT: Yale University Press, 1984), p. 161.

41. Alice Walker, *Meridian*, pp. 205–6.

42. Alice Walker, *The Color Purple* (London: The Women's Press, 1983), pp. 9–10.

43. ibid., p. 1.

44. ibid., p. 176.

45. ibid., p. 97.

46. ibid., pp. 165–7.

47. Darryl Pinckney, 'Black Victims, Black Villains', *New York Review of Books*, vol. XXXIV, no. 1 (29 January 1987), p. 17.

48. David Blum, 'Why Hollywood Loves to Hate Sensational Spielberg', in *Cosmopolitan*, (London, July 1986), p. 137.

49. Alice Walker, 'Finding Celie's Voice', in *Ms.* (December 1985), p. 72.

50. Alice Walker, *In Search of Our Mothers' Gardens*, p. xii.

51. ibid., p. 243.

52. Maya Angelou, 'Phenomenal Woman', in *And Still I Rise* (London: Virago Press, 1986), p. 8. (Originally published New York: Random House, 1978).

53. Claudia Tate ed., *Black Women Writers at Work*, p. 6.

54. ibid.

55. Maya Angelou, *I Know Why the Caged Bird Sings* (London: Virago Press, 1984), p. 265 (Originally published New York: Random House, 1970).

56. Maya Angelou, 'My Arkansas', in *And Still I Rise*, p. 21.

57. Maya Angelou, *I Know Why the Caged Bird Sings*, p. 47.

58. ibid., p. 4.

59. ibid., pp. 4–5.

60. ibid., p. 55.

61. ibid., p. 32.

62. ibid., p. 85.

63. ibid., p. 92.

64. Maya Angelou, 'Letter to an Aspiring Junkie', in *Just Give Me A Cool Drink of Water 'Fore I Diiie* (London: Virago Press, 1988), p. 27. (Originally published New York: Random House, 1971).

65. Jill Neville, 'Southern Sequel', *Times Literary Supplement* (14 June 1985), p. 674.

66. Maya Angelou, *Gather Together in My Name* (London: Virago Press, 1985), p. 131.

67. ibid., p. 30.

68. Maya Angelou, 'Ain't That Bad', in *And Still I Rise*, pp. 43–4.

69. Maya Angelou, 'Riot: 60's', in *Just Give Me A Cool Drink of Water 'Fore I Diiie*, p. 35.

70. Maya Angelou, *The Heart of a Woman* (New York: Random House, 1981; London, Virago Press, 1986), p. 41.

71. ibid., p. 17.

72. Maya Angelou, 'For Us Who Dare Not Dare', in *Just Give Me A Cool Drink of Water 'Fore I Diiie*, p. 81.

73. Maya Angelou, *All God's Children Need Travelling Shoes* (New York: Random House, 1986; London: Virago Press, 1987), p. 20.

74. ibid., p. 35.

75. ibid., p. 31.

76. ibid., p. 196.

77. ibid., p. 127.

78. Maya Angelou, 'When I Think About Myself', in *Just Give Me A Cool Drink of Water 'Fore I Diiie*, p. 25.

79. Maya Angelou, 'And Still I Rise', in *And Still I Rise*, p. 42.

Chapter Nine – The Unblinking Eye

1. Pinkie Gordon Lane, 'Sexual Privacy Of Women On Welfare', in *Black Sister*, pp. 230–1.

2. Paule Marshall, 'From the Poets in the Kitchen', in *Merle: a Novella and Other Stories* (London: Virago, 1985), pp. 11–12. Originally published in *New York Times Book Review* (1983).

3. Paule Marshall, Interview with Sandi Russell, Richmond, Virginia, November 1986.

4. Susan Willis, 'Describing Arcs of Desire', *Specifying*, p. 54.

5. Barbara Christian, *Black Feminist Criticism*, p. 107.

6. Paule Marshall, *Brown Girl, Brownstones* (New York: Feminist Press, 1981; London: Virago, 1982), p. 221. (Originally published New York: Random House, 1959).

7. ibid., p. 70.

8. ibid., pp. 69–70.

9. ibid., p. 70.

10. Mary Helen Washington, Afterword in *Brown Girl, Brownstones*, p. 315.

11. ibid., p.322.

12. Paule Marshall, 'Barbados', in *Merle*, p. 55.

13. Paule Marshall, 'Reena', in *Merle*, p. 86.

14. Paule Marshall, 'To Da-Duh in Memoriam', in *Merle*, p. 106.

15. Paule Marshall, Interview with Sandi Russell.

16. Hortense J. Spillers, 'Chosen Place, Timeless People: Some Figurations on the New World', in *Conjuring*, p. 166.

17. Paule Marshall, *The Chosen Place, the Timeless People* (New York: Random House/Vintage Books, 1984), p. 315. (Originally published Harcourt, Brace and World, 1969.)

18. Paule Marshall, *Praise Song for the Widow* (New York: E. P. Dutton, 1984; London: Virago, 1983), p. 172.

19. ibid., 209.

20. Susan Willis, *Specifying*, p. 67.

21. Lucille Clifton, 'I Am Not Done Yet', in *An Ordinary Woman* (New York: Random House, 1974), p. 59.

22. Gloria Naylor, *The Women of Brewster Place* (New York: Penguin, 1983; London: Methuen, 1983), pp. 4–5. (Originally published New York: Viking, 1982.)

23. ibid., p. 86.

24. ibid., p. 103.

25. ibid., pp. 169–70.

26. Gloria Naylor, *Linden Hills* (New York: Ticknor and Fields, 1985; London: Methuen, 1986), p. 268.

27. Catherine C. Ward, 'Gloria Naylor's *Linden Hills*: A Modern Inferno', *Contemporary Literature* vol. XXVIII, no. 1 (1987), p. 81.

28. Gloria Naylor, *Mama Day* (New York: Ticknor and Fields, 1988; London: Hutchinson, 1988), p. 19.

29. ibid., p. 40.

30. Gloria Naylor, interview with Kate Saunders in *The Independent*, 4 May 1988, London.

31. June Jordan, *On Call* (Boston: South End Press, 1985; London: Pluto Press, 1986) p. 3.

32. ibid., p. 1.

33. June Jordan, *Civil Wars* (Boston: Beacon Press, 1981), p. 47.

34. June Jordan, *On Call*, p. 88.

35. June Jordan, 'Poem for Nana', in *Passion* (Boston: Beacon Press, 1980), p. 1.

36. June Jordan, 'For the Sake of a People's Poetry: Walt Whitman and the Rest of Us', in *Passion*, p. xiii.

37. June Jordan, 'Poem about Police Violence', in *Passion*, p. 34.

38. June Jordan, 'Poem about My Rights', ibid., pp. 89–90.

39. June Jordan, 'Getting Down to Get Over', in Marge Piercy ed., *Early Ripening* (London/Boston: Pandora, 1987), pp. 107–14. (Originally published in *New Days: Poems of Exile and Return*, 1974.)

40. Audre Lorde, 'Need: A Choral of Black Women's Voices', in *Chosen Poems: Old and New* (New York: W. W. Norton, 1982), p. 115.

41. Audre Lorde, 'Poetry Is Not A Luxury', in *Sister Outsider* (Trumansburg, New York: The Crossing Press, 1984, pp. 36–7).

42. Audre Lorde, 'Uses of the Erotic: The Erotic as Power', ibid., p. 53.

43. Audre Lorde, 'Equinox', in *Chosen Poems*, p. 39.

44. Audre Lorde, 'Evening News', in *Chosen Poems*, p. 101.

45. Audre Lorde, 'Sisters in Arms', in *Our Dead Behind Us* (New York/London: W. W. Norton, 1986; London: Sheba Feminist Publishers, 1987), p. 3.

46. Audre Lorde, 'Afterimages', in *Chosen Poems*, p. 102.

47. ibid, pp. 103–4.

48. Audre Lorde, 'Outlines', in *Our Dead Behind Us*, p. 5–9.

49. Audre Lorde, 'The Transformation of Silence into Language and Action', in *Sister Outsider*, p. 41.

50. Coleen J. McElroy, 'Tapestries', in Marge Piercy ed., *Early Ripening*, p. 156.

Chapter Ten – *'for colored girls'*

1. Ntozake Shange, 'taking a solo/a poetic possibility/a poetic imperative', in *Nappy Edges* (London: Methuen, 1987), p. 11. (Originally published New York: St. Martin's Press 1978.)

2. Mary Helen Washington, introduction to *Any Woman's Blues* (London: Virago, 1981), p. xvi. (Originally published *Midnight Birds*, New York: Anchor Books, 1980).

3. Ida Cox, 'Wild Women Don't Have The Blues', Paramount, 1924.

4. Daphne D. Harrison, *Black Pearls* (New Brunswick/London: Rutgers University Press, 1988), p. 8.

5. Bertha 'Chippie' Hill, 'Trouble in Mind', Circle J1003A, c. 1946.

6. LeRoi Jones (Amiri Baraka), *Blues People* (New York: William Morrow, 1963), p. 94.

7. Lucille Clifton, 'Come home from the movies', in *An Ordinary Woman* (New York: Random House, 1974), p. 23.

8. Sherley Anne Williams, 'Someone Sweet Angel Child', in *Someone Sweet Angel Child* (New York: William Morrow, 1982). See also Harper, Stepto eds., *Chant of Saints* (Urbana/London: University of Illinois Press, 1979), p. 117.

9. Sherley Anne Williams, 'Blues Roots of Contemporary Afro-American Poetry', in *Chant of Saints*, p. 135.

10. Sherley Anne Williams, *Give Birth To Brightness* (New York: Dial Press, 1972).

11. Stephen Henderson, ed., *Understanding the New Black Poetry*.

12. Sherley Anne Williams, *Dessa Rose* (London: Futura, 1988; New York: William Morrow, 1981), p. 66.

13. Alexis De Veaux, *Don't Explain* (New York: Writers and Readers, 1988), p. 134. (Originally published New York: Harper and Row, 1980.)

14. J. J. Phillips, *Mojo Hand* (London: Serpent's Tail, 1987). (Originally published New York: Trident Press, 1966.)

15. ibid., p. 161.

16. Gayl Jones, interview with Robert Stepto in *Chant of Saints*, p. 353.

17. Gayl Jones, *Corregidora* (Boston: Beacon Press, 1986; London: Camden Press, 1986), p. 9. (Originally published New York: Random House, 1975.)

18. ibid., p. 9.

19. ibid., p. 184.

20. Gayl Jones, *Eva's Man* (Boston: Beacon Press, 1987), p. 171. (Originally published New York: Random House, 1977.)

21. Sherley Anne Williams, 'Any Woman's Blues', in *The Peacock Poems* (Middletown, CT: Wesleyan University Press, 1975).

22. Verta-Mae Smart Grosvenor, 'A Kitchen Crisis', in *Amistad 1: Writings on Black History and Culture* (New York: Random House, 1970), p. 294. See also Grosvenor, *Vibration Cooking* (New York: Random House, 1972).

23. ibid., p. 296.

24. ibid.

25. Octavia E. Butler, *Kindred* (London: The Women's Press, 1988), p. 94.

26. Arnold Rampersad, 'The Poems of Rita Dove', in *Callaloo*, vol. 9, no. 1, 1986, p. 53.

27. Stan Sanvel Rubin and Earl G. Ingersoll, 'A Conversation with Rita Dove', *Black American Literature Forum*, vol. 20, no. 3 (Fall 1986), p. 238.

28. ibid., p. 229.

29. Rita Dove, 'Parsley', in *Museum* (Pittsburgh: Carnegie-Mellon, 1986). See also *Black American Literature Forum*, vol. 20, no. 3, (Fall 1986) pp. 227–9.

30. Rita Dove, *Black American Literature Forum*, p. 230.

31. ibid., p. 233.

32. Rita Dove, 'Promises', in *Thomas and Beulah* (Pittsburgh: Carnegie-Mellon, 1986), p. xx. See also *Callaloo*, p. 43.

33. ibid.

34. Rita Dove, 'Upon Meeting Don L. Lee, in a Dream', in *The Yellow House on the Corner* (Pittsburgh: Carnegie-Mellon, 1980).

35. Toni Cade Bambara, interview with Claudia Tate in *Black Women Writers at Work*, p. 29.

36. ibid.

37. Toni Cade Bambara, 'A Sort of Preface', in *Gorilla, My Love* (London: The Women's Press, 1984), pp. ix-x. (Originally published New York: Random House, 1972.)

38. ibid., p. 17.

39. ibid.

40. Toni Cade Bambara, 'The Organizer's Wife', in *The Sea Birds Are Still Alive* (London: The Women's Press, 1984), p. 17. (Originally published New York: Random House, 1982.)

41. Susan Willis, 'Problematizing the Individual', in *Specifying*, p. 149.

42. Gloria Hull, 'What It Is I Think She's Doing Anyhow', in *Conjuring*, p. 226.

43. Toni Cade Bambara, *The Salt Eaters* (London: The Women's Press, 1982), p. 27. (Originally published New York: Random House, 1980.)

44. ibid., p. 242.

45. Toni Cade Bambara, 'What It Is I Think I'm Doing Anyhow', in Janet Sternburg ed., *The Writer on her Work* (New York/London: W. W. Norton, 1980), p. 174.

46. ibid., p. 168.

47. Kalamu ya Salaam, 'NTOZAKE SHANGE (to those who wish she would shut up)', in Ishmael Reed and Al Young eds., *Quilt* 1, (1981), pp. 127–8.

48. Ntozake Shange, 'taking a solo/poetic possibility/a poetic imperative', in *Nappy Edges*, (1981) p. 4.

49. Ntozake Shange, *for colored girls who have considered suicide/when the rainbow is enuf* (New York: Macmillan Bantam Books, 1980), pp. 44–6. (Originally published San Lorenzo, CA: Shameless Hussy Press, 1976; London: Methuen, 1978.)

50. Ntozake Shange, interview with Claudia Tate in *Black Women Writers at Work*, p. 156.

51. ibid., p. 157.

52. Ntozake Shange, 'Mood Indigo', in *A Daughter's Geography* (London: Methuen, 1985), p. 13. (Originally published New York: St. Martin's Press, 1983.)

53. Ntozake Shange, 'Take the A train', ibid., p. 18.

54. Ntozake Shange, 'Bocas: A Daughter's Geography', ibid., p. 21.

55. Ntozake Shange, 'get it & feel good', in *Nappy Edges*, pp. 50–2.

56. Ntozake Shange, 'with no immediate cause', ibid., pp. 114–17.

57. Ntozake Shange, 'i live in music', ibid., p. 126.

58. Ntozake Shange, interview with Claudia Tate in *Black Women Writers at Work*, p. 163.

59. Ntozake Shange, 'Spell#7', in *Three Pieces* (New York: St. Martin's Press, 1981), p. 23.

60. Ntozake Shange, 'Boogie-Woogie Landscapes', in *Three Pieces*, p. 135.

61. Ntozake Shange, 'an invitation to my friends', in *Nappy Edges*, p. 147.

Select Bibliography

Works by Individual Authors

Andrews, William, ed.

Six Women's Slave Narratives. Oxford: Oxford University Press, 1988.

Sisters of the Spirit: Three Black Women's Autobiographies of the Nineteenth Century. Bloomington: Indiana University Press, 1986.

Angelou, Maya

All God's Children Need Travelling Shoes. London: Virago, 1987.

And Still I Rise. London: Virago, 1986.

Gather Together in My Name. London: Virago, 1985.

I Know Why the Caged Bird Sings. London: Virago, 1984.

Just Give Me A Cool Drink of Water 'Fore I Diiie. London: Virago, 1988.

Now Sheba Sings The Song. London: Virago, 1987.

Singin' and Swingin' and Gettin' Merry Like Christmas. London: Virago, 1985.

The Heart of a Woman. London: Virago, 1986.

Bambara, Toni Cade

Gorilla, My Love. London: The Women's Press, 1984.

	The Salt Eaters. London: The Women's Press, 1982.
	The Sea Birds Are Still Alive. London: The Women's Press, 1984.
Barthelemy, Anthony, ed.	*Collected Black Women's Narratives*. Oxford: Oxford University Press, 1988.
Birtha, Becky	*Lovers' Choice*. London: The Women's Press, 1988.
Brooks, Gwendolyn	*Report From Part One*. Detroit: Broadside Press, 1972.
	Beckonings. Detroit: Broadside Press, 1975.
	Blacks. Chicago: The David Co., 1987; this includes:

    Annie Allen.

    The Bean Eaters.

    In The Mecca.

    Maud Martha.

    A Street In Bronzeville.

Butler, Octavia	*Kindred*. London: The Women's Press, 1988.
Childress, Alice	*Like One of the Family: Conversations from a Domestic's Life*. Boston: Beacon Press, 1986.
Clarke, Cheryl	*Narratives: poems in the tradition of blackwomen*. New York: Kitchen Table, 1982.
Clifton, Lucille	*An Ordinary Woman*. New York: Random House, 1974.
De Veaux, Alexis	*Don't Explain*. New York: Writers and Readers, 1988.
Dove, Rita	*Fifth Sunday*. Lexington: University of Kentucky, 1985.
	Museum. Pittsburgh: Carnegie-Mellon, 1986.
	The Yellow House on the Corner. Pittsburgh: Carnegie-Mellon, 1980.

Thomas and Beulah. Pittsburgh: Carnegie-Mellon, 1986.

Dunbar-Nelson, Alice

The Works of Alice Dunbar-Nelson. Oxford: Oxford University Press, 1988.

Give Us Each Day: The Diary of Alice Dunbar-Nelson. Gloria T. Hull ed. New York/London: W. W. Norton, 1984.

Fauset, Jessie

Comedy American Style. New York: Frederick A. Stokes, 1933.

Plum Bun. London/Boston: Pandora Press, 1985.

The Chinaberry Tree. New York: Frederick A. Stokes, 1931.

There Is Confusion. New York: Boni and Liveright, 1924.

Giovanni, Nikki

Black feeling, Black talk, Black judgement. New York: William Morrow, 1970.

Gemini. New York: Viking Press, 1973.

My House. New York: William Morrow, 1972.

Recreation. Detroit: Broadside Press, 1970.

Those Who Ride the Nightwinds. New York: William Morrow, 1973.

Golden, Marita

A Woman's Place. New York: Doubleday, 1986; London: Methuen, 1988.

Grimké, Charlotte Forten

The Journals of Charlotte Forten Grimké. Oxford: Oxford University Press, 1988.

Grosvenor, Verta-Mae

Vibration Cooking. New York: Random House, 1972.

Guy, Rosa

A Measure of Time. London: Virago, 1984.

Bird At My Window. London: Virago, 1989.

Hansberry, Lorraine	*To Be Young, Gifted and Black: Hansberry in Her Own Words*, adapted by Robert Nemiroff. New York: New American Library, 1970.
	Les Blancs: The Collected Last Plays of Lorraine Hansberry. New York: Random House, 1972.
	A Raisin in the Sun. London: Methuen, 1960.
	The Sign in Sidney Brustein's Window in *Three Negro Plays*. Harmondsworth: Penguin, 1969.
Harper, Frances	*Iola Leroy; or, Shadows Uplifted*. Oxford: Oxford University Press, 1988.
	Complete Poems of Frances E. W. Harper. Oxford: Oxford University Press, 1988.
Hopkins, Pauline	*Contending Forces*. Oxford: Oxford University Press, 1988.
	The Magazine Novels of Pauline Hopkins. Oxford: Oxford University Press, 1988.
Hurston, Zora Neale	*Dust Tracks on a Road*. London: Virago, 1986.
	I Love Myself When I am Laughing . . . : A Zora Neale Hurston Reader. Alice Walker ed. New York: The Feminist Press, 1979.
	Jonah's Gourd Vine. London: Virago, 1987.
	Mules and Men. Bloomington: Indiana University Press, 1978.
	Spunk: The Selected Stories of Zora Neale Hurston. London: Camden Press, 1987.
	Tell My Horse. Philadelphia: J. B. Lippincott, 1938.
	Their Eyes Were Watching God. London: Virago, 1986.

The Sanctified Church. Berkeley, CA: Turtle Island Press, 1983.

Jacobs, Harriet   *Incidents in the Life of a Slave Girl: Written by Herself*. Oxford: Oxford University Press, 1988.

Johnson, Georgia Douglas   *Bronze, a book of verse*. Boston: B. J. Brimmer, 1922.

The Heart of a Woman and Other Poems. Boston: Cornhill, 1918.

Jones, Gayl   *Corregidora*. London: Camden Press, 1989.

Eva's Man. Boston: Beacon Press, 1987.

White Rat. New York: Random House, 1977.

Jordan, June   *Civil Wars*. Boston: Beacon Press, 1981.

Lyrical Campaigns: Selected Poems. London: Virago, 1989.

Moving Towards Home: Political Essays. London: Virago, 1989.

On Call: Political Essays. London: Pluto Press, 1986.

Passion: new poems, 1977–1980. Boston: Beacon Press, 1980.

Keckley, Elizabeth   *Behind the Scenes*. Oxford: Oxford University Press, 1988.

Larsen, Nella   *Quicksand and Passing*. London: Serpent's Tail, 1989.

Lee, Andrea   *Sarah Phillips*. New York/ Harmondsworth: Penguin, 1985.

Loewenberg, B. J., Bogin, Ruth, eds.   *Black Women in Nineteenth-Century American Life*. University Park/London: Pennsylvania State University Press, 1976.

Lorde, Audre   *Chosen Poems: Old and New*. New York: W. W. Norton, 1982.

Our Dead Behind Us. London: Sheba Feminist Publishers, 1987.

Sister Outsider. Trumansburg, NY: The Crossing Press, 1984.

Zami: A New Spelling of My Name. London: Sheba Feminist Publishers, 1984.

Marshall, Paule *Brown Girl, Brownstones*. London: Virago, 1982.

Merle: A Novella and other stories. London: Virago, 1985.

Praise Song for the Widow. London: Virago, 1983.

The Chosen Place, The Timeless People. New York: Random House, 1984.

McMillan, Terry *Mama*. Boston: Houghton Mifflin, 1987; London: Jonathan Cape, 1987.

Meriwether, Louise *Daddy Was a Number Runner*. London: Methuen, 1987.

Morrison, Toni *The Bluest Eye*. London: Chatto and Windus, 1979.

Sula. London: Chatto and Windus, 1980.

Song of Solomon. London: Chatto and Windus, 1978.

Tar Baby. London: Chatto and Windus, 1981.

Beloved. London: Chatto and Windus, 1987.

Naylor, Gloria *Linden Hills*. London: Methuen, 1986.

Mama Day. New York: Ticknor and Fields, 1988; London: Hutchinson, 1988.

The Women of Brewster Place. London: Methuen, 1987.

Phillips, J. J. *Mojo Hand*. London: Serpent's Tail, 1987.

Petry, Ann *The Street*. London: Virago, 1986.

Rodgers, Carolyn *How I Got Ovah*. New York: Doubleday, 1969.

Sanchez, Sonia

Homecoming. Detroit: Broadside Press, 1970.

homegirls & handgrenades. New York: Thunder Mouth Press, 1984.

Generations: Selected Poetry: 1969–1985. London: Karnak House, 1986.

Shange, Ntozake

A Daughter's Geography. London: Methuen, 1985.

Betsey Brown. London: Methuen, 1985.

for colored girls who have considered suicide/when the rainbow is enuf. New York: Macmillan Bantam Books, 1980.

Nappy Edges. London: Methuen, 1987.

Ridin' the Moon in Texas: Word Paintings. New York: St. Martin's Press, 1987.

Three Pieces. New York: St. Martin's Press, 1981.

Shockley, Ann Allen

Loving Her. Tallahassee, FL: The Naiad Press, 1987.

The Black and White of It. Tallahassee, FL: The Naiad Press, 1987.

Say Jesus and Come to Me. Tallahassee, FL: The Naiad Press, 1987.

Stewart, Maria; Lee, Jarena; Foote, Julia A. J.; Broughton, Virginia W.

Spiritual Narratives. Oxford: Oxford University Press, 1988.

Walker, Alice

Good Night, Willie Lee, I'll See You in the Morning. London: The Women's Press 1988.

Horses Make a Landscape Look More Beautiful. London: The Women's Press, 1985.

In Love and Trouble. London: The Women's Press, 1984.

In Search of Our Mothers' Gardens: womanist prose. London: The Women's Press, 1984.

Living by the Word. Selected Writings, 1973–1987. London: The Women's Press, 1988.

Meridian. London: The Women's Press, 1982.

Once. London: The Women's Press, 1986.

The Color Purple. London: The Women's Press, 1983.

The Temple of My Familiar. London: The Women's Press, 1989.

The Third Life of Grange Copeland. London: The Women's Press, 1985.

Revolutionary Petunias. London: The Women's Press, 1989.

You Can't Keep a Good Woman Down. London: The Women's Press, 1982.

Walker, Margaret   *For My People*. New Haven: Yale University Press, 1968.

Jubilee. Boston: Houghton Mifflin, 1966.

Prophets for a New Day. Detroit: Broadside Press, 1970.

West, Dorothy   *The Living Is Easy*. London: Virago, 1987.

Wheatley, Phillis   *The Collected Works of Phillis Wheatley*. Oxford: Oxford University Press, 1988.

Williams, Sherley Anne   *The Peacock Poems*. Middletown, CT: Wesleyan University Press, 1977.

Someone Sweet Angel Child. New York: William Morrow, 1982.

Dessa Rose. London: Futura, 1988.

Give Birth to Brightness. New York: Dial Press, 1972.

Wilson, Harriet E.   *Our Nig, or Sketches from the Life of a Free Black*. London: Allison & Busby, 1984.

Further Reading

Anderson, Jervis

Harlem: The Great Black Way, 1900–1950. London: Orbis, 1982.

Baker, Houston A., Jr.

Blues, Ideology, and Afro-American Literature. Chicago/London: University of Chicago Press, 1984.

Modernism and the Harlem Renaissance. Chicago/London: University of Chicago Press, 1987.

Singers of Daybreak: Studies in Black American Literature. Washington, DC: Howard University Press, 1974.

Bambara, Toni, ed.

The Black Woman. New York: New American Library, 1970.

Bell, Bernard

The Afro-American Novel and Its Tradition. Amherst: University of Massachusetts Press, 1987.

Bennett, Lerone, Jr.

Before the Mayflower: A History of Black America. Harmondsworth: Penguin, 1984.

Berzon, Judith R.

Neither White nor Black: The Mulatto Character in American Fiction. New York: New York University Press, 1978.

Blassingame, John W.

The Slave Community: Plantation Life in the Antebellum South. Oxford: Oxford University Press, 1979.

Carby, Hazel

Reconstructing Womanhood: The Emergence of the Afro-American Woman Novelist. Oxford: Oxford University Press 1987.

Chamberlain, Mary, ed.

Writing Lives: Conversations Between Women Writers. London: Virago, 1988.

Chapman, Abraham

Steal Away: Slaves Tell Their Own Stories. London: Ernest Benn, 1973.

Christian, Barbara

Black Women Novelists. Westport, CT/London: Greenwood Press, 1984.

Black Feminist Criticism: Perspectives on Black Women Writers. New York/Oxford: Pergamon Press, 1985.

Cooke, Michael G.   *Afro-American Literature in the Twentieth Century: The Achievement of Intimacy*. New Haven, CT/London: Yale University Press, 1984.

Cruse, Harold   *The Crisis of the Negro Intellectual*. New York: William Morrow, 1967.

Davis, Angela   *Women, Race and Class*. London: The Women's Press, 1982.

Davis, A. and Peplow, M., eds.   *The New Negro Renaissance: An Anthology*. New York: Holt, Rinehart and Winston, 1975.

Du Bois, W. E. B.   *The Souls of Black Folks*. New York: Dodd, Mead, 1961.

Ellison, Ralph   *Shadow and Act*. New York: Vintage Books, 1972.

Evans, Mari   *Black Women Writers: Arguments and Interviews*. London: Pluto Press, 1985.

Foner, Philip S.   *History of Black Americans*. Westport, CT/London: Greenwood Press, 1975.

Fox-Genovese, E.   *Within the Plantation Household: Black and White Women of the Old South*. Chapel Hill: North Carolina University Press, 1988.

Gates, Henry Louis, ed.   *Black Literature and Literary Theory*. London: Methuen, 1984.

'Race', Writing and Difference. Chicago/London: University of Chicago Press, 1986.

The Signifying Monkey: A Theory of Afro-American Literary Criticism. Oxford: Oxford University Press, 1988.

Gayle, Addison, ed.   *Black Expression*. New York: Weybright and Talley, 1969.

Genovese, Eugene

Roll, Jordan, Roll: The World the Slaves Made. New York: Vintage, 1976.

Giddings, Paula

When and Where I Enter: The Impact of Black Women on Race and Sex in America. New York/Bantam: William Morrow, 1985.

Giovanni, N. and
Walker, M.

A Poetic Equation: Conversations Between Nikki Giovanni and Margaret Walker. Washington, DC: Howard University Press, 1974.

Grier, W. H. and
Cobbs, P. M.

Black Rage. New York: Basic Books, 1968.

Gutman, Herbert G.

The Black Family in Slavery and Freedom. New York: Random House, 1977.

Harley S. and
Terborg-Penn, R.

The Afro-American Woman: Struggles and Images. Port Washington, NY: National University Publications, 1978.

Harper, M.,
& Stepto, R., eds.

Chant of Saints: A Gathering of Afro-American Literature, Art, and Scholarship. Champaign/London: University of Illinois Press, 1979.

Hemenway, Robert

Zora Neale Hurston: A Literary Biography. London: Camden Press, 1986.

Henderson, Stephen

Understanding the New Black Poetry: Black Speech and Black Music as Poetic References. New York: William Morrow, 1972.

Hooks, Bell

Ain't I A Woman: Black Women and Feminism. London: Pluto Press, 1985.

Huggins, Nathan

Harlem Renaissance. Oxford: Oxford University Press, 1971.

Hull, Gloria T.

Color, Sex and Poetry: Three Women Writers of the Harlem Renaissance. Bloomington: Indiana University Press, 1987.

Hull, G. T., Scott, P. B.,
Smith, B., eds.

All The Women Are White, All The Blacks Are Men, But Some Of Us Are Brave. New York: Feminist Press, 1982.

Johnson, James Weldon, ed. — *The Book of American Negro Poetry*. New York: Harcourt, Brace and World, 1959.

Jones, Jacqueline — *Labor of Love, Labor of Sorrow: Black Women, Work and the Family, from Slavery to the Present*. New York: Vintage Books/Random House, 1986.

Jones, Le Roi — *Blues People: Negro Music in White America*. New York: William Morrow, 1963.

Kotchman, Thomas, ed. — *Rappin' and stylin' out: Communication in Urban Black America*. London: University of Illinois Press, 1972.

Kramer, Victor, ed. — *The Harlem Renaissance Revisited*. New York: AMS Press, 1988.

Lerner, Gerda, ed. — *Black Women's Writings in White America*. New York: Vintage, 1973.

Levine, Lawrence — *Black Culture and Black Consciousness: Afro-American Folk Thought from Slavery to Freedom*. Oxford: Oxford University Press, 1977.

Lewis, David Levering — *When Harlem Was in Vogue*. New York: Vintage, 1982.

Lock, Alain, ed. — *The New Negro*. New York: Albert and Charles Boni, 1925.

McKay, Nellie, ed. — *Critical Essays on Toni Morrison*. Boston: G. K. Hall, 1988.

Piercy, Marge — *Early Ripening: American Women's Poetry Now*. London/Boston: Pandora Press, 1987.

Pryse, M., & Spillers, H. J., eds. — *Conjuring: Black Women, Fiction and the Literary Tradition*. Bloomington: Indiana University Press, 1985.

Richmond, M. A. — *Bid the Vassal Soar: Interpretative Essays on Phillis Wheatley and George Moses Horton*. Washington, DC: Howard University Press, 1974.

Smitherman, Geneva

Talkin and Testifyin: The Language of Black America. Detroit: Wayne State University Press, 1986.

Sterling, Dorothy, ed.

We Are Your Sisters: Black Women in the Nineteenth Century. New York/London: W. W. Norton, 1984. Bloomington: Indiana University Press, 1981.

Stetson, Erlene, ed.

Black Sister: Poetry by Black American Women, 1746–1980. Bloomington: Indiana University Press, 1981.

Tate, Claudia, ed.

Black Women Writers at Work. New York: Continuum, 1983. Harpenden: Oldcastle Books, 1985.

Washington, Mary H., ed.

Any Woman's Blues. London: Virago, 1981.

Black-eyed Susans: Classic Stories by and about Black Women. New York: Anchor Books, 1975.

Invented Lives: Narratives of Black Women, 1860–1960. London: Virago, 1989.

White, Deborah Grey

Ar'n't I a Woman? Female Slaves in the Plantation South. New York/London: W. W. Norton, 1985.

Willis, Susan

Specifying: Black Women Writing: The American Experience. Madison: University of Wisconsin Press, 1987.

I have been unable to include all African-American women writers in this book. Here are some who could not be mentioned.

19th CENTURY

Josephine Delphine (Henderson) Heard
Henrietta Cordelia Ray
Eloise Bibb Thompson
Ellen Craft
Amanda Berry Smith
Nancy Prince
Sarah Parker Redmond
Fannie Barrier Williams
Lucy Craft Laney
Frances Jackson Coppin
Anna Julia Cooper
Zilpha Elaw
Julia A. J. Foote
Mrs. N. F. Mossell
Ann Plato
Emma Dunham Kelly-Hawkins
Virginia W. Broughton
Bethany Veney
Louisa Picquet
Susie King
Mary Prince
Mattie J. Jackson
Old Elizabeth
Lucy A. Delaney
Mary Seacole
Octavia V. Rogers Albert
Silvia Du Bois
Mary E. Tucker Lambert
Adah Issacs Menken
Ada
Clara Ann Thompson
Mrs. A. E. Johnson

20th CENTURY

Helene Johnson
Mary Church Terrell
Shirley Graham (Du Bois)
Eulalie Spence
May Miller
Marita Bonner
Rosalie Jonas
Lucy Ariel Williams
Carrie Williams Clifford

Bessie Calhoun Bird
Pauli Murray
Mae V. Cowdery
Margaret Goss Burroughs
Gloria C. Oden
Naomi Long Madgett
Margaret Danner
Kattie M. Cumbo
Sarah Webster Fabio
Alice S. Cobb
Jane Cortez
Della Burt
Linda Piper
Carole C. Gregory
Jo Ann Hall-Evans
Barbara Mahone
Irma McClaurin
Patricia Parker
Patricia Jones
Thadious M. Davis
Melba Joyce Boyd
Angela Jackson
Ellease Southerland
Adrienne Kennedy
Toi Dericotte
Brenda Marie Osbey
Effie Lee Newsome
Sarah Wright
Barbara Masekela
Hattie Gossett
Regina Williams
Thylias Moss
Donna Kate Rushin
Hilary Kay
Lorraine Bethel
Stephanie Byrd
Mildred Taylor
Kristin Hunter
Nikkey Finney
Jamaica Kincaid
Michelle Cliff
Thulani Davis
Joyce Carol Thomas
Delores Kendrick
Paulette Childress White
Jill Witherspoon Boyer
Beah Richards
Kathleen Collins
P. J. Gibson

Aishah Rahmen
Elaine Jackson
Adrienne Kennedy
Saundra Sharp
J. California Cooper
Frenchy Hodges
Gale Jackson
Violet Dias Lannoy
Wanda Coleman
Harryette Mallen
Marilyn Richardson
Ai
Elizabeth Alexander
Beth Brown
Shelly L. Hall
Sharon Stockard Martin

and many more

      to come...

Index of Authors

READERS' NOTES

READERS' NOTES

READERS' NOTES

READERS' NOTES

READERS' NOTES

READERS' NOTES